THE EVERYTHING

MEDITERRANEAN DIET BOOK

Dear Reader,

Now that you've made the decision to make changes in your eating pattern, I hope you will find that this book gives you simple tips and enjoyable recipes. The Mediterranean cuisine offers so much variety with the different produce of the region and the variety of herbs and spices that it really is easy to dine healthfully. As a Registered Dietitian, I want readers to know the facts behind the Mediterranean diet, but most importantly, I want you to see that it is easy to adopt, a lifestyle that fits your routine, and a diet that helps you live longer and healthier.

Following the Mediterranean diet will boost your fruit, vegetable, and whole grain intake, making it easy for you to get the fiber you need for health and satiety; the vitamins and minerals needed to maintain a healthy body and an active lifestyle; and the phytonutrients that seem to help with the promotion of health and prevention of disease.

I hope you take time to assess your eating patterns, compare them to the Mediterranean pattern, and then decide how to change your diet for the healthier. I also hope you find trying the delectable recipes great fun and a wonderful enhancement to your current menu.

Connie Diekman, MEd, RD, LD, FADA

Welcome to the EVERYTHING® Series!

These handy, accessible books give you all you need to tackle a difficult project, gain a new hobby, comprehend a fascinating topic, prepare for an exam, or even brush up on something you learned back in school but have since forgotten.

You can choose to read an Everything® book from cover to cover or just pick out the information you want from our four useful boxes: e-questions, e-facts, e-alerts, and e-ssentials.

We give you everything you need to know on the subject, but throw in a lot of fun stuff along the way, too.

We now have more than 400 Everything® books in print, spanning such wide-ranging categories as weddings, pregnancy, cooking, music instruction, foreign language, crafts, pets, New Age, and so much more. When you're done reading them all, you can finally say you know Everything®!

QUESTION

Answers to
common questions

FACT

Important snippets
of information

ALERT

Urgent
warnings

ESSENTIAL

Quick
handy tips

PUBLISHER Karen Cooper

DIRECTOR OF ACQUISITIONS AND INNOVATION Paula Munier

MANAGING EDITOR, EVERYTHING® SERIES Lisa Laing

COPY CHIEF Casey Ebert

ACQUISITIONS EDITOR Katrina Schroeder

ASSOCIATE DEVELOPMENT EDITOR Hillary Thompson

SENIOR DEVELOPMENT EDITOR Brett Palana-Shanahan

EDITORIAL ASSISTANT Ross Weisman

EVERYTHING® SERIES COVER DESIGNER Erin Alexander

LAYOUT DESIGNERS Colleen Cunningham, Elisabeth Lariviere, Ashley Vierra, Denise Wallace

Visit the entire Everything® series at *www.everything.com*

THE
EVERYTHING®
MEDITERRANEAN DIET BOOK

All you need to lose weight and stay healthy!

Connie Diekman, MEd, RD, LD, FADA
and Sam Sotiropoulos

adamsmedia
Avon, Massachusetts

*This book is dedicated to those who love food
and who enjoy experimenting with it. The
Mediterranean diet will not only meet those
needs but will also help you be healthier.*

An Everything® Series Book.
Everything® and everything.com® are registered trademarks of F+W Media, Inc.

Published by Adams Media, a division of F+W Media, Inc.
57 Littlefield Street, Avon, MA 02322 U.S.A.
www.adamsmedia.com

ISBN 10: 1-4405-0674-4
ISBN 13: 978-1-4405-0674-1
eISBN 10: 1-4405-0675-2
eISBN 13: 978-1-4405-0675-8

Printed in the United States of America.

10 9 8 7 6 5

Library of Congress Cataloging-in-Publication Data
is available from the publisher.

The information in this book should not be used for diagnosing or treating any health prob-lem. Not all diet plans suit everyone. You should always consult a trained medical profes-sional before starting a diet program. The author and publisher disclaim any liability arising directly or indirectly from the use of this book.

Many of the designations used by manufacturers and sellers to distinguish their products are claimed as trademarks. Where those designations appear in this book and Adams Media was aware of a trademark claim, the designations have been printed with initial capi-tal letters.

*This book is available at quantity discounts for bulk purchases.
For information, please call 1-800-289-0963.*

Contents

Introduction ix

1 Introduction to the Mediterranean Diet 1

What Is the Mediterranean Diet? 2 • The Mediterranean Diet Pyramid 3 • Foods of the Mediterranean 8 • Important Nutrients 9 • Getting and Staying Active 10

2 The Science Behind the Mediterranean Diet 13

Why It Works 14 • When It Doesn't Work 17 • Who Should Use It 19 • How to Use It Effectively 20 • The Role of Wine 21

3 Focus on Plant-Based Foods 25

Whole Foods 26 • Grains 28 • Fruits and Vegetables 32 • The Nutrition of Fruits and Vegetables 35 • Beans, Nuts, and Seeds 37 • Olive Oil 40

4 Rounding Out Your Meals 43

Fish and Seafood 44 • Meat, Poultry, and Eggs 46 • Dairy Foods Do Fit In 49 • Herbs and Spices Make Mediterranean 52 • Sweets Flavor Mediterranean Meals 54 • Balancing Out the Mediterranean Diet 55

5 Lose Weight with the Mediterranean Diet 57

Start Shedding Pounds 58 • The Science of Weight Loss 58 • Why Is Activity Important 60 • Eating Balanced Meals 62 • Keeping the Weight Off 64

6 Get Healthy with the Mediterranean Diet 67

Fight Disease and Ailments 68 • Keep Your Skin Healthy 70 • Prevent
Cancer 72 • Impact on Diabetes 73 • Reverse Aging Effects 75

7 Meal Planning 79

Grocery Shopping 80 • Stocking Your Pantry 83 • Planning
Weeknight Meals 85 • Feeding Picky Kids 86 • Planning Holiday
Meals 87

8 Appetizers 89

9 Salads, Salad Dressings,
and Sauces 103

10 Pies 121

11 Soups 127

12 Pasta, Rice, and Grains 135

13 Vegetables and Legumes 147

14 Poultry 161

15 Meats 171

16   Fish and Seafood 183

17   Desserts 195

Appendix A: Bonus Recipes: Breakfast and Lunch 211
Appendix B: Glossary of Terms 247
Appendix C: Resources 257
Appendix D: Farmer's Markets by State 260
Standard U.S./Metric Measurement Conversions 286
Index. 287

Acknowledgments

My thanks go out to Katrina Schroeder for her kindness, positive comments, and her great support in the writing of this book. I also thank Sam Sotiropoulos for the wonderful recipes that give proof to the ease of the Mediterranean diet as well as the enjoyment of the foods of the region.

Introduction

THE MEDITERRANEAN REGION IS known for its beauty, diversity, the variety of fish that come from the sea, and the diet that takes its name from the region. The region encompasses the countries that ring the Mediterranean Sea. On the north side of the sea are Albania, Bosnia-Herzegovina, France, Greece, Italy, Malta, Monaco, Serbia, Slovenia, and Spain. The southern part of the region includes Algeria, Cyprus, Egypt, Israel, Lebanon, Morocco, Libya, Palestinian Authority, Syria, Tunisia, and Turkey. Despite the wide range of countries that comprise the Mediterranean region, when the Mediterranean diet is referenced the most common countries discussed include Spain, southern France, Italy, Greece, the isle of Crete, and the Middle East. When reviewing the diets in these countries there are differences in what constitutes the Mediterranean diet, but the common factors are the same: a focus on whole grains, fruits, vegetables, and fish.

The Mediterranean diet has been enjoyed for centuries, but within the last sixty years it has been the subject of much interest. People in the southern Mediterranean countries tend to have less heart disease, even though they consume more fat than many dietary guidelines recommend. In addition, a core element of diet in many of the Mediterranean countries is the consumption of wine. These two factors together seem to contradict the concept of healthful eating, but for people in the Mediterranean they are a part of life. Another factor that characterizes the diet is the use of oils, nuts, and seeds. The use of oils, in place of animal fats, seems to provide not only more healthy fats but also provides a variety of phytonutrients, which help in the prevention of disease.

Understanding the role of diet in the health of the Mediterranean people has been a topic of much research with studies looking at components of the diet; is it the fruits and vegetables, the wine, or is it the total diet? These questions still perplex researchers, and have caused other researchers to look at the overall lifestyle as a contributor to health. People in the

Mediterranean region spend more time walking, tending to gardens, and biking for recreation and transportation, so this movement could also be a factor in the health of the region.

Another lifestyle factor is the importance of time with family and friends. Mealtime is often long and slow paced. The midday meal is a time for everyone to take a break, savoring the meal and the company of others. Taking time to smell, taste, and savor the flavors of a meal improves the feeling of satisfaction, a factor that makes it easier to enjoy smaller portions. Taking time to savor foods requires a plan, and that plan needs to include an understanding of why changes in your eating patterns are important, tips for making small, gradual changes along with recipes, and suggestions for how to make foods more enjoyable. Whether you're headed to the grocery store, fixing a new recipe, or trying a new type of whole grain, this book will provide you with the tools you need to make Mediterranean eating your way of eating.

As you embark on this journey into healthier eating, think about the excitement new foods can provide and follow the advice of the 2010 Dietary Guidelines and shift your food choices to a more plant-based diet that emphasizes vegetables, dried beans and peas, fruits, whole grains, nuts, and seeds.

Enjoy! Bon Appétit! Buen Appetito!

CHAPTER 1

Introduction to the Mediterranean Diet

The Mediterranean diet is recognized as a healthier approach to eating, but upon searching for "What is a Mediterranean diet?" you will likely find many different diets. This book outlines the components and health benefits of a Mediterranean diet and how to make it part of your lifestyle. Since developing a healthy eating plan is just one part of a healthy lifestyle, the role of an active lifestyle will also be discussed.

What Is the Mediterranean Diet?

The Mediterranean diet is the name given to eating plans typical of countries of the Mediterranean, with Greece, Crete, Italy, and Spain being the main points of reference. These countries are built on agricultural, religious, and cultural traditions, and one of those traditions is making meals from current available crops. Before reviewing the agriculture of the Mediterranean, it's important to understand the culture and religion of the region. The Mediterranean region, often referred to as the Mediterranean basin, is made up of Muslims, Christians, and Jews, all of whom have different traditions. Muslims do not eat pork or drink wine or other alcoholic beverages. Jews avoid shellfish and pork, and Jews who keep kosher don't mix dairy products with beef, lamb, or veal. Greek orthodox populations avoid eating meat two days per week and during Lent will also often avoid it. Christians often avoid eating meat on Fridays, but do drink wine. These varying religious traditions change the dynamics of what is often called the Mediterranean diet. One common aspect of all of these cultures is the importance of enjoying a meal. Mediterranean countries enjoy their big meal midday and most take several hours out of the day to enjoy the meal with family.

Agriculture in the Mediterranean

With the balmy climate of the Mediterranean, people in these countries build their meals largely around plant foods, which enhance variety, nutrition, and flavor. Wild greens are often used in salads, soups, and with eggs. Vegetables, including greens, carrots, peppers, cucumbers, and onions are served at all meals, with several Mediterranean countries using vegetables as a main part of their breakfast and lunch. Animal foods are typically smaller contributors to the meal plans and appear more as an accompaniment than as the entrée. In countries where meat or poultry is used as an entrée, portions are traditionally three ounces or smaller. For many in the Mediterranean area a meal might be a large pot of beans, vegetables, bread, and olive oil that cooks together on the stove to yield a rich stew-like dish. The Italians call the dish ribollita, and it is a mainstay on the stove of many families. While many traditions of the Mediterranean remain, changes in portions are resulting in higher calorie intakes. As the Mediterranean region becomes more westernized, portions are increasing in size as is the inclusion of meat and poultry. The region is also trying to adapt to meet the palates of Western tourists losing some of the traditional cuisine.

Popularity of the Diet

Interest in the Mediterranean diet grew when scientists noted that people in the Mediterranean area had lower incidences of several diseases, but especially heart disease. Searching for the source of this lowered risk resulted in the examination of the lifestyles of those who live in the Mediterranean. Upon observation of lifestyle, the diet was an obvious point of review. The Mediterranean diet, while plant plentiful, is also rich in olive oil, a good source of omega-3 fatty acids. In addition to using olive oil for cooking, the Mediterranean diet has limited intake of solid or animal fats like lard. These factors are the likely cause of the diet's impact on reduced risk of heart disease. While the diets of people in Mediterranean countries vary, the evidence related to health promotion is consistent throughout the region. To accommodate the varying eating patterns of the different countries, a multitude of Mediterranean food pyramids exist. The pyramids all reflect a similar look, with lots of plant foods, but each has a unique twist to represent the cuisine of the country. With this variety of pyramids, what constitutes a Mediterranean diet can be confusing, but a close look makes it clear that Mediterranean diets, no matter which cuisine they represent, are built around plant foods.

ESSENTIAL

Omega-3 fatty acids in fish provide more heart-health benefits than those found in plant foods like walnuts and flax. Try to include at least ten ounces of fatty fish per week and use walnuts and flax to add variety and small omega-3 benefits.

The Mediterranean Diet Pyramid

The Mediterranean diet pyramid is one that includes a variety of fruits, vegetables, and grains with limited amounts of fish and poultry. The most famous Mediterranean diet pyramid is one developed in 1993 by the Harvard School of Public Health, the European Office of the World Health Organization, and Oldways Preservation Trust.

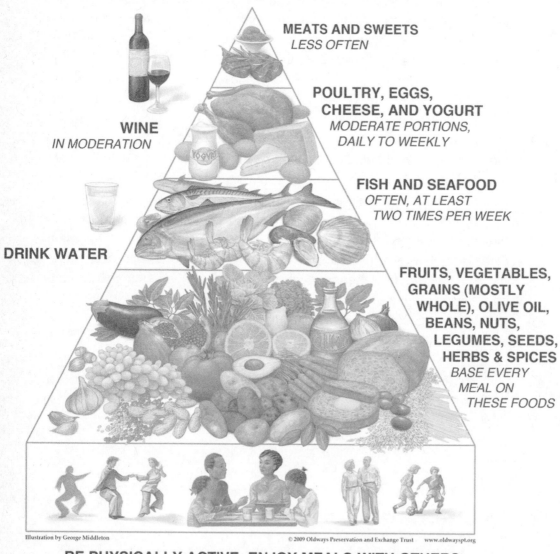

Mediterranean Diet Pyramid
A contemporary approach to delicious, healthy eating

MEATS AND SWEETS
LESS OFTEN

WINE
IN MODERATION

POULTRY, EGGS, CHEESE, AND YOGURT
MODERATE PORTIONS, DAILY TO WEEKLY

FISH AND SEAFOOD
OFTEN, AT LEAST TWO TIMES PER WEEK

DRINK WATER

FRUITS, VEGETABLES, GRAINS (MOSTLY WHOLE), OLIVE OIL, BEANS, NUTS, LEGUMES, SEEDS, HERBS & SPICES
BASE EVERY MEAL ON THESE FOODS

Illustration by George Middleton   © 2009 Oldways Preservation and Exchange Trust   www.oldwayspt.org

BE PHYSICALLY ACTIVE; ENJOY MEALS WITH OTHERS

As with all pyramids, the Mediterranean pyramid is built from the bottom up. The base of the pyramid reflects the domination of grains, fruits and vegetables, beans, nuts, and olive oil. If you look at the bottom of the pyramid, you'll see that this layer is in fact at least one-half of the entire pyramid, in order to make visually clear that plant foods come first. A close look at the bottom layer shows an abundance of whole grains like wheat, oats, rice, barley, rice, and corn. The vegetables range from dark green ones like broccoli, asparagus, wild greens, and spinach to dark red, orange, or purple vegetables such as pumpkin, eggplant, and peppers. The fruits in this layer also reflect the colors of the rainbow with apricots, cherries, olives, peaches, dates, and figs among them. This layer is also where you will find beans, nuts, and seeds used with all meals. Building on top of this layer, you'll find fish and seafood, poultry, eggs, cheese, yogurt, and finally meats and sweets. Placing these foods at the top of the pyramid conveys the importance of eating them less often and in smaller amounts. In addition to the sweets at the top of the pyramid, other processed foods are generally included here as well. This placement makes it clear these foods don't contribute to the overall health benefits of a Mediterranean diet and should be used as complements to the lower sections of the pyramid and not as first choices. In most Mediterranean countries, the use of sweets is portion appropriate, so they are used in the balance suggested by the pyramid. A common dessert in Italy is gelato, which is milk based, thus providing some protein, calcium, phosphorus, and potassium with the sweet. Fruit tarts are common throughout the region and allow for use of the current in-season fruit.

One Pyramid vs. Another

The Mediterranean pyramid conveys a very different picture than the U.S. pyramid. The Mediterranean pyramid clearly shows the importance of family, friends, and activity by including pictures to depict these components as the strong foundation of the pyramid. Putting these components at the base visually emphasizes that the Mediterranean diet is about lifestyle, not just foods. The food part of the pyramid clearly shows a majority of plant foods with animal foods pictured as complements to the foundation. The fruit and vegetable layer of the pyramid also contains nuts, beans, and seeds as these foods are important sources of protein and in many cuisines, a foundation of their dishes. In addition to the foods in the pyramid the inclusion of water and wine again shows the importance of all aspects of life in achieving health.

Tips for Making Your Diet Mediterranean

In addition to choosing the right foods, the traditional Mediterranean diet is very focused on the right balance of these foods. If you want to make the Mediterranean pyramid work for you, consider the following tips.

- Choose your fruits and vegetables by their season
- Focus on whole grains and whole fruits and vegetables
- Choose fish or shellfish twice a week
- Enjoy red meat once or twice a week
- Choose low-fat or fat-free dairy choices
- If you drink alcohol, keep portions moderate

It's Not Just Foods

The Mediterranean pyramid also includes visuals to encourage activity and time for sharing meals with others. In reviewing studies related to disease incidence, it is clear that the overall lifestyle of those who live in the Mediterranean is almost as important (in some studies *as* important) as the foods. Conveying this message of overall lifestyle is one the Mediterranean pyramids do with visuals of people sharing time together and enjoying activities and meals with each other. Given the warm environment of most Mediterranean countries, all the pyramids include the importance of two beverages as well. Water is often depicted at the base of a pyramid, but it might also appear alongside the pyramid.

FACT

Current guidelines state that adequate hydration is a minimum of 91 ounces, 8½ 8-ounce glasses, of fluids per day for women and 128 ounces, 16 8-ounce glasses, for men. These amounts include all the fluids you consume, even beverages containing caffeine. If you can, make half the total intake water, but most importantly, get adequate fluids.

Along with water, most Mediterranean diets aren't complete without the inclusion of wine, particularly red wine. The inclusion of wine in a pyramid may seem odd to you, but for those in Mediterranean countries this is a reflection of lifestyle. Wine is enjoyed with meals and is often shared with all family members. Wine is viewed as an enjoyable part of the meal, something that enhances the flavors of other foods. Mediterranean pyramids do state that wine should be used in moderation, just as it has always been used in the countries of the Mediterranean region.

QUESTION

What benefit does wine provide?
The evidence for inclusion of wine is associated with studies that have found that moderate amounts of red wine can help reduce the risk of heart disease. Studies seem to indicate that the phytonutrient content of the wine is the source of heart-disease protection. Phytonutrient content is higher in more darkly colored fruits, thus the connection to red wine.

It is important to note that on the Mediterranean diet pyramid pictured here, water and wine are off to the side of the pyramid. This placement shows their connection to the diet of the Mediterranean, but it also makes it clear that the true benefits of the diet are found in the foods within the pyramid. While adequate hydration is important for health, the addition of wine can be a matter of choice.

FACT

Remember that wine is a source of calories, and the scientific evidence indicates that moderate portions of wine are all that are needed for health benefits. In addition, it is important to remember that wine by itself is not a magic weight loss or healthy eating tool, so consume it in conjunction with an overall healthful eating plan.

Foods of the Mediterranean

Mediterranean countries are known for their wealth of produce and fish, but many also produce a variety of grains and great cheeses. Meals in the Mediterranean are built around fruits and vegetables with smaller amounts of protein foods. Some of the grains found in the various Mediterranean diets include:

- Whole-grain breads
- Couscous
- Rice
- Polenta
- Bulgur

In addition to the variety of grains found in Mediterranean diets, vegetables and fruits fill many breakfast, lunch, and dinner plates. Some of the frequently consumed fruits and vegetables include:

- Artichokes
- Arugula
- Beets
- Dandelion greens
- Eggplant
- Avocados
- Apricots
- Oranges
- Pomegranates
- Olives

Beans are often used as entrées or side dishes, with the most common being chickpeas, cannellini, fava, and green beans. Nuts and seeds complement many Mediterranean dishes, with the most common being pine nuts, pistachios, sesame seeds, and walnuts.

Complementing the plant foods are dairy foods like yogurt, Parmesan, and mozzarella cheese. Animal proteins are mainly from chicken and fish with salmon, sardines, shrimp, and tilapia being most common. And finally, olive oil and herbs and spices boost the flavor of Mediterranean cuisine, with basil, cloves, oregano, parsley, sage, and savory being some of the more commonly used herbs and spices.

Important Nutrients

While the foods of the Mediterranean make the pyramid unique, the health ...s are likely due to the nutrients found in the foods that make up the ...se of olive oil provides a good source of monounsaturated fats. ...tables, and beans boost the fiber content of the diet along ...nts, potassium, and B vitamins.

...that helps with regulation of fluids, maintenance ...sure, transmission of nerve impulses, and muscle ...required on a daily basis. Current guidelines recom- ...grams per day, with oranges or milk providing good ... this daily requirement by eating the following: two ...e orange, three cups of dairy, six ounces of fish, and three ...ark-green vegetables each day.

...mega-3 fatty acids are also plentiful in the Mediterranean diet due to ...e inclusion of fish, especially fatty fish like salmon, tuna, and sardines. The diet is also rich in complex carbohydrates, which can help maintain blood sugar levels longer, making it easier to control frequency of eating as well as foods consumed. Complex carbohydrates are found in the beans, vegetables, and grains.

FACT

Monounsaturated fatty acids are fats that in their chemical structure have one carbon-to-carbon link doubled, making the fatty acid more unstable and sensitive to light, heat, and air. Monounsaturated fats do not increase or decrease blood cholesterol, making them healthy options. The main monounsaturated fats are olive oil, peanuts, and peanut oil.

Phytonutrients are plant compounds that provide health benefits above and beyond those provided by proteins, carbohydrates, fats, vitamins, and minerals. Phytonutrients are the compounds that make a plant food what it is; in other words, the phytonutrients in beets account for the red color and in broccoli the green color and the strong flavor. Phytonutrients have been linked to lowered risk for a variety of diseases including heart diseases, diabetes, and several forms of cancer.

ALERT

Complex carbohydrates are carbohydrates with very long chains of sugars. All grains, whether they are whole grain or not, are complex carbohydrates. Their chemical structure doesn't change, despite the grain being processed.

B vitamins play a variety of roles in keeping the body healthy by converting carbohydrates and protein into energy, promoting the health of red blood cells, and many other functions. Because B vitamins are water soluble, we need to consume them every day, so building an eating plan around plant foods is a simple way to meet this nutritional need.

Getting and Staying Active

While people in the Mediterranean region consume healthful foods, they also include movement or activity in much of their day. The original Mediterranean routine was built around tending to farms, so walking, plowing, and raking were everyday activities. In addition, mode of transport was often walking or biking, so again, a boost to calorie burning, an aid to cardiovascular health, and a regulator of overall body functions. For most Americans, physical activity is not a part of the daily routine and for many it is not even a part of their lifestyle. While guidelines recommend two and a half hours of aerobic activity every week, fewer than 60 percent of Americans meet this guideline. In addition to this aerobic activity, the Centers for Disease Control and Prevention also recommends that you do some type of muscle-strengthening activity two or more days a week.

If you're finding it difficult to add activity to your routine, you might find it easier to start with small steps and build from there. If you can walk for ten minutes a day, you can slowly build this to twenty minutes and then thirty minutes. Some ways to get started are to park your car a little further away from work, walk one more stop when catching the bus or train, or take the stairs when you get to work. As your endurance increases, you will find that you don't breathe as heavily during activities and this will be your clue that it might be time to increase the length of time. As your daily length of time gets closer to thirty minutes, you can add more days. The important thing is that you make activity a regular part of your routine.

FACT

Aerobic activity or cardio activity gets your heart beating faster, thus helping to strengthen your heart. Aerobic activity is also a good calorie-burning activity, so walking, biking, swimming, or dancing are all good ways to add aerobic activity to your routine.

Muscle-strengthening exercise is important to bone and muscle health. As we age our bones thin, and if the muscles surrounding them are not strong enough, the bones become more susceptible to breaks. Muscle-strengthening exercises, also called resistance training, develop stronger muscles, which can help keep fragile bones stable and strong. All muscles need regular activity to keep them functioning at their best, and many groups get little workout on a daily basis. Strength training can improve muscles in the core or central part of the body, helping you not only look better but aiding your balance and mobility. Tips for starting a muscle-strengthening program include:

- Develop a plan for 2 days a week
- Work all body parts
- Use a weight you can lift for 8–12 repetitions
- Repeat the activity 2–3 times

If you aren't sure you can lift weights or you don't want to join a gym, you can get similar benefits by using some things you have in your home. Jugs of milk can serve as arm weights, cans of food allow you to do arm curls, and placing your feet under chairs or sofas can offer resistance for your legs. Working outside is also a way to get muscle-strengthening benefits. Consider the following:

- Cut the yard with a hand mower
- Rake leaves instead of blowing them
- Shovel snow
- Dig and plant in your garden

ESSENTIAL

Before starting any physical activity plan, even walking, make sure you check with your physician about your overall health and get approval to start your new routine.

It's not uncommon to worry about how to fit activity into an already busy day, but developing a plan is the first step. First, assess your current day and see where you might have some time to get started with activity. Next, decide what type of activity you would like to do (remember, if you don't like it you won't keep it up) and then get started. It may take some time for activity to be a comfortable part of your routine, but just as you have a routine for getting out of the house in the morning, soon physical activity will also be a routine.

CHAPTER 2

The Science Behind the Mediterranean Diet

Observing what populations eat and how they live is one way to assess if lifestyle plays a role in the risk for a variety of diseases, but having concrete evidence is important for recommending a diet or eating plan. Over the last fifty years, a variety of studies have looked at the Mediterranean lifestyle to assess what role it plays in health, what role the foods of the Mediterranean play, and whether this eating plan can yield the same results in other countries and populations.

Why It Works

The Mediterranean diet first evolved as a result of studies by Dr. Ancel Keys. Dr. Keys was a physiologist who first became interested in the diets of Italians when he was stationed in Italy and observed differences in diet and in overall health. One population group that was of particular interest to him was the inhabitants of Crete, who had a diet that consisted of 40 percent of calories from fat, but had the lowest levels of cholesterol and heart disease versus other Mediterranean countries. In 1958, in response to this observation, he started the fifteen-year Seven Countries Study. The Seven Countries Study looked at the eating patterns of more than 12,000 men in Finland, Greece, Italy, Japan, the Netherlands, the United States, and Yugoslavia. The study found that the more saturated fat people consumed, the higher their blood cholesterol levels and the rate of death from cardiovascular disease. The study found that the higher the saturated fat intake, as a percent of calories, the higher the disease rate. The fact that saturated fats were reviewed based on percent of total calories is important to the outcomes, since several Mediterranean countries consume high-fat diets but the percent of calories from saturated fat is low. Of the seven countries, Greece, Italy, and Japan had the lowest cholesterol levels and the lowest number of deaths from cardiovascular disease.

FACT

The diet of the island of Crete at the time of the study was high in olive oil, olives, grains, beans, nuts, vegetables, and minimal amounts of fish. One of the key factors of the diet was that the foods were consumed in their natural or whole form and not in more processed forms. In addition, they consumed wine on a daily basis. It is the diet of Crete that led to the use of the term Mediterranean diet.

Diet Benefits

Dr. Keys observed that the use of fats like olive oil, along with a low intake of saturated fat, must be the main factors in the reduction of cholesterol, even though the fat intakes were often much higher than what would be expected to be a healthful intake. Along with this focus on unsaturated fats, he observed that in Crete and Japan the intake of fruits, nuts, and legumes, all very rich in folate, calcium, and vitamins E and C, might also be factors. Animals in the Mediterranean region generally feed on grass rather than grain, so they were higher in the healthier polyunsaturated fats. The same could be said for dairy products, since dairy cattle also fed on grass rather than feed. Diet patterns in the Mediterranean were also rich in nuts, with walnuts often served as part of a meal; again, boosting the intake of healthier fats. Dr. Keys continued his work with his colleague, Dr. Henry Blackburn, at the Minnesota Heart Health Program, which also looked at switching sources of fats to boost the healthier unsaturated fats while decreasing the cholesterol-raising saturated fats.

The Lyon Diet Heart Study

The Lyon Diet Heart Study built on the outcomes of the Seven Countries Study. The Lyon Diet Heart Study was a clinical trial that compared a standard American Heart Association diet to a traditional Mediterranean diet with the goal of determining if one was more effective in reducing the rate of recurrences of heart disease after a first heart attack. The study, which lasted for five years, involved more than 600 patients who had had a previous heart attack. Key components of the Mediterranean diet group were:

- Use of olive oil and canola oil margarine
- Wide variety of fruits and vegetables
- Moderate intake of chicken, fish, and wine

The study found that those in the Mediterranean-type diet group had a 72 percent reduction in deaths from heart disease and heart attacks versus the other diet group. The study also found a 61 percent reduction in incidence of cancer in the Mediterranean diet group. This study was followed by other studies in men and women with mixed outcomes, but the overall outcomes continued to support the benefits of a Mediterranean-type diet in reducing risk of heart disease. The common factors associated with reduced risk seem to be the large portion of vegetables, fruits, and beans as well as the use of olive oil. The high antioxidant content of plant foods is one assumed factor in reduced disease risk, but the folate content of fruits and vegetables may also be an important aspect. Other studies have indicated the benefit might be due to the combination of the foods as opposed to any one food or food group.

North Karelia Study

Another study that followed the Seven Country Study was the North Karelia Study, conducted by the country of Finland to determine if the Mediterranean diet could reduce the very high levels of heart disease in Finland. The diet of Finland was traditionally very high in saturated fat, due to the high consumption of full-fat dairy foods like cheese, cream, and whole milk. At the same time, and due to the climate of Finland, the diet was very low in vegetables and fruits. The North Karelia Study involved community education for diet change, incorporating community tips for healthier eating, steps to boost availability of produce, and guidelines on how to reduce full-fat dairy intake. Study outcomes showed a 50 percent drop in deaths from heart disease. The North Karelia Study has remained a point of reference for healthy eating in Finland, with current dietary guidelines using the same types of community education, policy development, and efforts toward food availability.

QUESTION

What is folate?
Folate, or folic acid, is a B vitamin that helps control blood levels of homocysteine. Homocysteine is a compound that has been linked to increased risk for heart disease. Folate is found in orange juice, broccoli, spinach, beans, avocados, and enriched grain foods. For maximum health, consume 400 micrograms each day; this is equal to about one and a half cups of cooked spinach.

Evidence Consolidated

For many people, all of these studies are more overwhelming than they are helpful, so what do they actually say? The studies done on the traditional Mediterranean diet all clearly show a connection to better health and less death from heart disease. While questions continue about the *exact* mechanism for this improvement in health and the reduction in death rate, the benefits of the diet outweigh the unknown. The Mediterranean diet is an excellent source of a wide variety of vitamins, minerals, and phytochemicals. It adds plenty of healthy fats and the fiber content is excellent. Whatever each study proves about the Mediterranean diet and how it connects to health promotion, the one point that is very clear is that it is an eating plan that will keep you feeling good and support your health.

When It Doesn't Work

The Mediterranean diet has been the focus of many clinical studies to assess if the diet pattern and its role in heart disease prevention can be duplicated in other populations; outcomes from these studies have varied. Many studies look at single components of the diet as the cause of improved health or changes in blood levels but what is unique about the Mediterranean diet is how all of the foods, along with lifestyle, impact overall health so the whole diet has been a focus of much research. Studies have looked at adherence to the diet and impact on weight loss; some studies have shown a connection between the Mediterranean diet and weight loss while others have seen little connection. The studies that failed to show a connection have indicated that the overall Mediterranean lifestyle might be the important connection to disease prevention and weight loss. The message from these studies is that diet, social support systems, activity, and overall approach to life may all combine to yield the outcomes often associated with the Mediterranean diet. Other review articles have found that adherence to the diet may be a key factor in achieving outcomes. For many people, the content of the Mediterranean diet is quite different than they're used to, so making the change to more vegetables, fruits, and beans is more difficult to maintain than might be expected. Availability of produce is often an issue for people who live in colder climates, and when available in winter, cost can be a barrier.

Another area of potential problems for the Mediterranean diet is the issue of overconsumption of fats. One common myth is that if a little is good more must be better; but when it comes to foods and the calories they contain, this myth is a potential pitfall. While the Mediterranean diet is built around olive oil, nuts, seeds, and olives, the traditional diet includes these foods in moderate amounts, thus keeping the calories from fat to a healthy balance. In the traditional Mediterranean diet, these foods were used as accents to other foods or as flavor enhancers, so they improve the enjoyment of the diet but the small portions keep the calories balanced. Mediterranean diets can have a high percentage of calories from fat—some are as high as 40 percent—but as long as the total daily caloric intake does not exceed the calories burned, this high intake of fat is healthful.

In addition to overconsumption of fat another area that poses a problem for some people is overconsumption in total. No matter what diet people follow the bottom line should be is it healthy and will it maintain your body weight is if the calories consumed equal the calories you burn. While consuming larger portions of vegetables might not be a problem, too much intake of grains, even whole grain, beans, dairy foods, and of course sweets and alcohol will lead to an increase in total calories. Portion control is essential to following even a healthy diet like the Mediterranean diet and for many Americans portion sizes have gotten a bit large. An example of portions out of control include the current size of bagels, which are about double an actual portion or a 16-ounce bottle of juice versus a 4-ounce serving. These two examples result in consumption of 330 more calories than the appropriate portions.

The fact that the people in Mediterranean countries live very active lifestyles cannot be overlooked when assessing why a Mediterranean diet reduces disease risk or helps with weight management. Since factors that cause disease aren't totally clear, it is important to look at the whole lifestyle when determining how to reduce your risk of disease. If you want to adopt the Mediterranean diet, remember that the diet is part of a lifestyle that includes time with family and friends, regular activity, and a healthy perspective on life and the stress that comes with it. Changes in diet are just one part of developing a healthful lifestyle.

Who Should Use It

When it comes to healthy eating, the Mediterranean diet jumps to the top of most people's lists of diets to follow. Often, diets are geared to adults only—those who are healthy or those with special diet needs—but the Mediterranean diet meets the nutritional, health, and growth needs of everyone. Studies on the effects of the Mediterranean diet have been conducted on men and women, adolescents and the elderly, those with previous history of heart disease, and those who want to prevent disease. While study designs may be different, the nutritional status in all studies shows the positive nutritional benefits of the diet. The abundance of fruits, vegetables, grains, and beans ensures a good variety of carbohydrates, vitamins, minerals, and phytonutrients. With small portion complements of fish, dairy foods, and olive oil, protein, fat, and other nutrient needs can be easily met.

Meeting such a variety of nutritional needs is a plus for families wanting to prepare meals for the entire family. The focus on plant foods ensures a good variety of nutrients needed for growing children while the inclusion of low-fat or fat-free dairy products means that kids will get the nutrition they need for development of strong, healthy bones. At the same time the occasional inclusion of meat, poultry, and eggs allows for variety that kids often enjoy. Preparing the Mediterranean diet at home is also a great opportunity for families to get kids involved with food at young ages. This involvement boosts the odds that kids will feel comfortable trying new foods, that they will have a higher interest in foods and therefore improved nutrition. The Mediterranean diet offers variety, enjoyment, nutrition, and a family friendly menu base.

How to Use It Effectively

Following the Mediterranean diet is simple if you approach it as a life-long eating pattern that you are willing to take time getting used to. The best way to approach the diet is to assess your current intake and then compare it with the Mediterranean pyramid in Chapter 1. If your diet is lacking in plant foods, which tends to be the case for most Americans, set a plan to boost your intake. A good plan might be to try one new food each week until you reach the point where your eating plan looks like the Mediterranean diet. Another important part of using the diet well is to use more plant protein foods, so look for recipes with beans, nuts, or seeds. Using canned beans is an acceptable option, so don't feel that you need to use dried beans and soak them, cook them, and then prepare them. If you use canned beans, drain some of the liquid to reduce the amount of salt you consume.

Another aspect of the Mediterranean diet that might make it a more healthful routine is the pace with which people in the region eat. People who live in the Mediterranean region take time for their meals. The midday meal is often enjoyed as a break from work, lasting several hours. Families share the meal together and courses are lingered over rather than quickly grabbed from a drive-through. Learning to eat more slowly takes time and requires adjustments to your schedule.

QUESTION

Does eating more slowly help you eat less?
Studies show that it takes about twenty minutes for the stomach to signal the brain that it is full. Eating more slowly allows you to recognize the feeling from this signal. Slower eating also allows you to taste and savor your food, leading to taste satisfaction, another part of the process of feeling full.

It is also important to recognize that no one element of the diet is the key to the health benefits the diet provides. Therefore, if you decide to give the Mediterranean diet a try, make sure you achieve the right balance of all the foods outlined in the pyramid and that you don't rely on one food or food group to provide the "magic" answer.

The Role of Wine

How often does someone tell you that consuming something you really enjoy is in fact healthful? Well, that is the case with wine in the Mediterranean diet. Wine, and often red wine, is a common part of the diet of many in the Mediterranean region. According to many of the studies on the diet of the region and its role in heart disease risk, the inclusion of wine is one of the possible reasons for this positive benefit. Wines are made from grapes, so just as other fruits and vegetables provide a variety of phytonutrients, so too does wine. White wine lacks the variety of phytonutrients of red wine, since it is made from the pulp of the grape only. Red wine is made from the whole grape, so the phytonutrients in the skin are also in the wine. Red wine is rich in a variety of phytonutrients called polyphenols. The two main types of polyphenols are flavonoids and nonflavonoids.

Flavonoids

Within the group of phytonutrients called flavonoids there are six smaller groups, with wine containing four of these compounds. The most influential flavonoid in terms of heart health is resveratrol. Resveratrol is found in the skins and seeds of grapes, so since the skins are used in making red wine, it contains more resveratrol than white wine. Flavonoids are also found in the following foods:

- Berries
- Cherries
- Chocolate
- Tea
- Broccoli
- Onions
- Peanuts

Nonflavonoids

The nonflavonoids in wine include the phytonutrient ellagic acid, which also acts as an antioxidant, and the tannin compounds found in most wines. These compounds, combined with the flavonoids, act in the body to help boost the "good" blood cholesterol HDL, while also helping to lower the "bad" cholesterol LDL. In addition, the antioxidant properties may help keep the blood from getting too sticky, which leads to more clotting, a cause of heart attacks and stroke.

FACT

Antioxidants are a variety of vitamins, minerals, and phytonutrients that slow or prevent oxidation of cells and tissues, thus preventing destruction of cells. Antioxidants can also work to keep the immune system healthy, helping to fight aging, infection, and disease.

Should I Drink the Wine?

Research studies on the heart-health benefits of red wine are mixed, without conclusive evidence indicating you should add wine to your meal plans if you don't currently consume it. Studies also show that other types of alcohol can provide these benefits for heart health, so the question remains if red wine is the best choice.

Wine in the Mediterranean Diet

You might wonder what benefit red wine played in the Mediterranean diet of old. Likely, the reason wine added to heart-health benefits was the same reason that other foods within the diet provided benefits, and that is how they all work together as a lifestyle. In reviewing the Mediterranean diet, no matter which type you review, the amount of wine included is small, around 4–5 ounces per day, and the wine is always part of a meal.

ALERT

Current guidelines recommend that if you choose to consume alcohol you limit your intake to no more than 5 ounces of wine or 12 ounces of beer per day for women and no more than 10 ounces of wine and 24 ounces of beer for men. Remember, if you choose to drink, do so responsibly.

While wine and other alcoholic beverages might provide some health benefits, they are of course a source of calories. Alcohol provides 7 calories per gram versus 4 calories per gram in carbohydrates and protein. In addition to the calories from the alcohol, any mixers you use will boost the calorie content of the drink. Alcohol is digested differently from protein and carbohydrates, so it can not only cause you to feel its effect more rapidly, it also means it is stored as body fat more easily. Moderate drinking might boost health benefits or increase enjoyment of your meals, but should always be monitored for its calories and how they fit in with the rest of your daily intake.

▼ TABLE 2-1

Alcoholic Beverage	Portion	Calories
Beer, regular	12 ounces	150
Beer, light	12 ounces	100
Wine, dry	5 ounces	100
Distilled spirits	1½ ounces	100
Liqueur	1½ ounces	160

Including wine in your diet can boost the enjoyment of a meal, but it's not a magic solution. If you want to add small amounts of wine to your meals, remember that your overall eating pattern must be similar to the Mediterranean diet if you hope to reap the health benefits.

CHAPTER 3

Focus on Plant-Based Foods

While there may be as many Mediterranean diets as there are countries in the Mediterranean, all of the diets from the region have one thing in common: they build the meals around plant foods. With the proximity to the sea and some of the most lush land for growing, whole foods are an everyday part of menus. Enjoying foods in their whole form not only provides a great diversity of tastes, it boosts overall nutrition and is certainly more environmentally friendly.

Whole Foods

Whole foods, or foods that are consumed without any processing, not only offer more nutritional benefits, they bring with them less added sugar, fat, sodium, or other compounds used in preparing packaged, processed, or quick-prepare items. While this might sound as if nothing processed can be used, the reality is that processed items like bread or cereal really are, in many cases, still whole foods. Consuming the whole plant food not only provides a greater diversity of vitamins and minerals, it ensures the full intake and availability of phytonutrients. The phytonutrient content of foods varies, so as we look at all the different plant foods that make up the Mediterranean diet, we will talk about specific phytonutrients and how they contribute to health.

Another advantage of whole foods is the fiber content. Plant foods are the only source of fiber in our diets and current guidelines recommend, for those under the age of fifty, 25 grams of fiber each day for women and 38 for men. For those over the age of fifty, the recommendation is 21 grams a day for women and 30 grams for men. For some ideas on boosting your fiber intake, use the following examples.

▼ TABLE 3-1: FIBER CONTENT OF FOODS

Food	Serving Size	Fiber (grams)
Whole Wheat Bread	1 slice	1.9
Brown Rice	½ cup	1.8
Oatmeal (cooked)	½ cup	0.5
Lentils	½ cup	7.8
Navy Beans	½ cup	9.6
Date (dried)	5	3.3
Spinach	½ cup	2.2

From U.S. Department of Agriculture Research Service Nutrient Data Laboratory, Release 22

Fiber increases the length of time it takes to eat by requiring more chewing of the food. The longer it takes to eat the easier it is for you to recognize feelings of fullness. Slowing down your eating by consuming more fiber means that time passes between ingestion and the elevation of your blood sugar, the signal to the brain to stop eating. In addition to this feeling of fullness, fiber stays longer in the digestive tract, so it helps you feel full longer, meaning you don't need to eat as often.

FACT

Phytonutrients are plant compounds that provide health benefits beyond those provided by vitamins, minerals, protein, carbohydrates, and fats. Phytonutrients promote health by helping the body fight the risk of disease and the aging process. Most commonly, phytonutrients act as antioxidants, immune boosters, and detoxifiers. The best source of phytonutrients is foods.

Two Types of Fiber

There are two main types of fiber, and they each provide different benefits. The two types are soluble and insoluble fiber. Plant foods tend to be a mix of both types of fiber, with some foods containing more of one than the other. Soluble fiber dissolves in water, so it tends to provide more of the gummy or gel-like consistency you might recognize in foods like oatmeal. Beans, barley, apples, oranges, and other citrus fruits are high in soluble fiber. Soluble fibers help reduce blood cholesterol and blood sugar levels.

ESSENTIAL

The U.S. Department of Food and Drug Administration has approved a health claim for the role of some soluble fibers in reducing the risk of cardiovascular disease. Food labels may state this claim if the product meets the requirements set forth by the FDA.

Insoluble fiber is the type of fiber that helps with regularity. Insoluble fibers trap water so that they can move waste products through the digestive system. Insoluble fibers are found mainly in wheat, corn, flax, and the skins of fruits, many vegetables, and beans. Insoluble fiber helps with feelings of fullness, so including it in each meal can help you manage portions and overall calories. Even though there are two main types of fiber, the average person doesn't need to worry about getting enough of each kind as long as you consume plenty of total fiber each day.

Grains

Grains are good sources of a variety of vitamins and minerals and, of course, the best source of carbohydrates in the diet. Grains include the more common grains wheat, rye, barley, oats, and corn but also include more than seven other grains including quinoa (pronounced KEEN-wah), which is becoming more popular. Grains also add flavor, texture, and variety to menus, and the use of whole grains can further boost nutritional value. Whole grains add more phytonutrients, vitamin E, magnesium, iron, and fiber than more processed grains. The Whole Grains Council (*www.wholegrainscouncil.org*), a nonprofit consumer advocacy group working to increase consumption of whole grains for better health, defines whole grains this way: "Whole grains, or foods made from them, contain all the essential parts and naturally occurring nutrients of the entire grain seed." A grain kernel has three layers: the bran, the endosperm, and the germ. The bran is the outer layer and this is where the fiber and B vitamins are found. Since this is the outer layer, this is also the part of the grain that is removed during processing, so processed grains lack much of the fiber of whole grains. Grains that have had outer layers removed not only lack the fiber, they also lack many of the essential vitamins and minerals. It is this lack of vitamins and minerals that resulted in the National Enrichment Act of 1942. The law states that all refined grain products must add back the nutrients that were removed during processing, which means niacin, thiamin, riboflavin, and iron are added back to refined grain products. In 1998, a law requiring grain foods to be fortified with folate was passed and remains in effect today.

ALERT

Adding folate to refined grain foods was designed to boost the intake of the vitamin that is so important to the prevention of birth defects. If you consume only whole grains, make sure you consume plenty of fruits and vegetables to get the folate you need.

Foods in the Grain Category

The foods in the grain category might seem obvious, but some might surprise you. For instance, did you know popcorn was a grain? And more importantly, a whole grain? Mypyramid.gov lists the following foods as grain foods that contribute to overall health, eating enjoyment, and the nutritional value of your meal plan:

- Brown rice
- Bulgur
- Oatmeal
- Popcorn
- Whole-grain cereals, breads, and crackers

- Barley
- Whole-wheat pasta
- Whole-wheat tortillas
- Quinoa
- Millet

How Much Grain Should You Consume?

The 2005 Dietary Guidelines for Americans recommends that you consume at least three servings of whole grains each day, but that your actual intake is one-half of your total grain intake. Most Americans consume plenty of grain foods, and in many cases, we consume too much, but the problem is that few Americans consume the recommended intake of whole grains. The International Food Information Council reports that studies show only 4 percent of Americans over the age of twelve meet the recommended levels for whole grain consumption.

▼ **TABLE 3-2: GRAIN SERVING SIZES**

Food	Serving Size (each equals a 1-ounce serving)
Whole-grain bread	1 1-ounce slice
Whole-grain bagel	1 mini bagel
Bulgur, rice, or pasta	½ cup (cooked)
English muffin	½
Muffin	1–2½" diameter
Oatmeal	½ cup (cooked)
Tortilla	1–6" diameter

From Mypryamid.gov

For most healthy adults, the amount of total grain needed each day is between 5 and 10 ounces. So, the average adult's whole grain intake should be between 3 and 5 servings each day.

Nutrition in Grains

Grains and foods made from grains are packed with nutrition, ranging from their bounty of carbohydrates to their diversity of phytonutrients. Carbohydrates are the body's main source of fuel and are needed on a regular basis to allow the body to perform most efficiently. The carbohydrates in grain are primarily starches, also referred to as complex carbohydrates, and fiber. Starches provide a slower release of blood glucose or blood sugar, so they can keep the body fueled longer than a simple sugar like fruit, sweets, or milk sugar. Grains are rich in B vitamins, especially thiamin, riboflavin, folate, and niacin. They also contain the minerals iron, magnesium, phosphorus, potassium, sodium, and selenium. Grains have a small amount of protein, but it is not high enough for it, or the foods made from it, to be considered good sources of protein. The one exception to this protein statement is the grain quinoa, which is a good source of protein. One-half cup of quinoa has more than 4 grams of protein and all of the essential amino acids, making it a complete and good protein source for vegetarians and nonvegetarians alike. As a point of comparison, one-half cup of rice has a bit less than 3 grams of protein. The B vitamins in grains are important to overall energy, while the minerals aid red blood cell formation, work as antioxidants in the body, and aid nerve and muscle functioning.

QUESTION

How do I consume grains if I have gluten intolerance?
Gluten intolerance or celiac disease requires the avoidance of all grains that contain gluten, so a person must avoid eating wheat, rye, and barley and sometimes oats, since they are often processed with these other grains. Quinoa, rice, corn, millet, and sorghum are a few examples of grains that do not contain gluten.

Phytonutrients in Grains

While the understanding of phytonutrients is still evolving, the science shows that grain foods provide at least three phytonutrients: lignin, phytic acid, and inulin. Lignins appear to help promote heart health and may keep the immune system healthy. Lignins are found in rye, wheat bran, oatmeal, and barley. Phytic acid appears to help promote health in several ways. The first function is control of blood sugar levels, where phytic acid seems to help keep them within a normal range. The second function is aiding in the promotion of heart health. Phytic acid also appears to help prevent oxidation, so it aids in keeping cells and organs healthy. Inulin, along with two other compounds that act as prebiotics, works to keep the gastrointestinal tract healthy by keeping healthy bacteria fed. Keeping the gastrointestinal tract healthy means that it can better fight disorders and diseases like colon cancer and irritable bowel and inflammatory bowel disease. Inulin and other prebiotics also aid calcium absorption, which helps keep bones strong.

QUESTION

What are prebiotics?
Prebiotics are nondigestible compounds in food that help normal, healthy bacteria grow in your colon. Prebiotics aid in digestion and help prevent bloating and gas.

Fitting in More Healthy Grains

If you've worked to boost whole grain intake but find you haven't been able to reach the recommended intake, a few simple steps might help.

- Identify one whole grain you'd like to eat more often.
- Add the grain at one meal a day.
- Boost portions gradually.
- Consume plenty of fluids.
- Increase once you are comfortably consuming this grain.

Adding grains to other dishes is an easy way to boost intake. For instance, add brown rice to stir-fry or barley to soups. Switching to oatmeal is an easy way to get some whole grain each day, and changing from chips or pretzels to popcorn is another simple step. Using one slice of whole grain bread and one of white is a slow way to make the switch as is going to whole wheat pasta. Prepare one half white and one half whole wheat pasta so that the taste difference won't be as obvious. Add marinara sauce before serving so that the color difference isn't noticeable. Prepare brown rice, quinoa, or barley on the weekends and place in small containers to use throughout the week in other dishes or as a side dish. Make sure you heat grains being used for side dishes slowly and thoroughly. Another simple whole grain addition is to top yogurt or fruit with toasted oats or low-fat granola. A green salad takes a new twist when topped with cooked barley or quinoa instead of croutons.

Fruits and Vegetables

The Mediterranean diet is rich in fruits and vegetables due to their availability but also due to the variety and flexibility they add to the diet. Fruit can boost the flavor of all meals and snacks and can be enjoyed cooked or in raw form. Fresh fruits are the best choice, but when they are not in season fruits canned in their own or other fruit juices are an option. Another option is to use frozen fruits, but if they are frozen in sugar remember to adjust recipes and monitor portions. If fruits are frozen without sugar, they are often a bit mushy when thawed, so they tend to work best in smoothies or cooking. Fruit juices can also be a part of a healthful eating plan, as long as you monitor portions.

ALERT

If you are going to add fruit juice to your meal plan, make sure you read the label and only purchase 100% juice products. Fruit drinks and beverages often have more added sugar, so they can lack many of the nutritional and health benefits 100% juices provide.

Vegetables also provide a source of variety to meals and are packed with nutrition both in the variety of vitamins and minerals they contain and from their richness of phytonutrients. When choosing vegetables it is best to choose fresh, if available. The next best option is vegetables frozen without any added sauces, and the other option is canned. Canned vegetables are typically higher in sodium and often a bit lower in fiber. If you use canned vegetables, remember to monitor your use of salt in other parts of the meal and try to boost fiber through the use of whole grains or other vegetables. One thing to be aware of is the fact that dried beans and peas are counted as vegetables. Dried beans and peas provide the same variety of vitamins, minerals, and phytonutrients as other vegetables, which is why they are in the vegetable group. Dried beans and peas, also referred to as legumes, are higher in protein, so this makes them different in their overall nutritional package and also means they have more calories.

How Much Fruit Should You Consume?

The 2005 Dietary Guidelines for Americans shows that fruits should be the smaller contributor of the two food groups. There are two main reasons why fruit should be a smaller part of your meal plans than vegetables. The first reason is that fruits are higher in calories than vegetables, so including them in larger portions has a bigger hit on overall calories. The second reason is that fruits don't have the diversity of phytonutrients that vegetables do, so their overall contribution to health is a bit different. The good news is that the guidelines recommend most adults consume at least 1½ cups of fruits each day.

▼ TABLE 3-3: FRUIT SERVING SIZES

Food	Serving Size (equal to 1 cup)
Apple	1–2½" diameter
Banana	1 8–9" in length
Fruit juice	1 cup
Canned fruit	1 cup
Dried fruit	½ cup

From Mypyramid.gov

How Many Vegetables Should I Consume?

If you're an adult who never really cared for your vegetables, the portions needed to promote health will likely leave you saying, "Do I have to?" The answer is, "Yes!" To promote health, you need to consume the amount recommended in the current Dietary Guidelines, and that amount, for most healthy adults, is at least 2 cups per day. Boosting vegetable intake often means trying them raw or cooked, adding them to other dishes, or learning new ways to season them. Another positive point is that serving sizes aren't as large as you might fear. Since vegetables are such good sources of phytonutrients, the 2005 Dietary Guidelines not only listed servings needed and serving sizes, it listed a breakdown for the frequency of certain types of vegetables. For the average healthy adult, vegetable intake should be broken down the following way:

- Dark green vegetables: at least 2 cups per week
- Orange vegetables: at least 1½ cups per week
- Legumes: at least 2½ cups per week
- Starchy vegetables: at least 2½ cups per week
- Other vegetables: 5½ cups each week

A legume is defined as a pod, such as a bean, that splits into two. The side the seed is attached to is used as food. Common legumes are black beans, navy beans, kidney beans, split peas, and lentils.

▼ TABLE 3-4: VEGETABLE SERVING SIZES

Food	Serving Size (equals 1 cup)
Lettuce, spinach, or other greens	2 cups
Chopped vegetables	1 cup
Bell pepper	1–3" diameter
Potato	1–3" diameter
Broccoli	3–5" long spears
Baby carrots	12
Tomato	1–3" diameter
Dried beans or peas	1 cup cooked
Green peas	1 cup

The Nutrition of Fruits and Vegetables

Fruits and vegetables duplicate many of their vitamins and minerals, including vitamins A and C, folate, potassium, and fiber. Dark-green leafy vegetables contain magnesium, iron, and calcium while corn, peas, and potatoes contain more niacin, zinc, and vitamin B6. Legumes provide the greatest diversity of nutrients, containing protein, thiamin, folate, iron, magnesium, phosphorous, zinc, potassium, and of course fiber. These nutrients obviously provide many health benefits, but the key nutrients, vitamins A, C, and folate, along with the mineral potassium, provide the following benefits:

▼ TABLE 3-5: ROLE OF THE NUTRIENTS

Nutrient	Function
Vitamin A	Keeps eyes and skin healthy
	Keeps immune system healthy
Vitamin C	Helps with wound healing
	Keeps teeth and gums healthy
	Aids iron absorption
Potassium	Helps with blood pressure
	Helps with fluid balance
Folate	Helps with red blood cell formation
	Helps prevent birth defects

In addition to the rich bounty of nutrients, fruits and vegetables can be good contributors of fiber. The fiber in fruits and vegetables is a mix of soluble and insoluble, so using a wide variety of fruits and vegetables will provide a good mix of the two.

Phytonutrients in Fruits and Vegetables

When it comes to sources of phytonutrients, no food groups are better than fruits and vegetables. The phytonutrients in fruits and vegetables include beta carotene in yellow-orange fruits and vegetables like apricots, carrots, sweet potatoes, and winter squash, but it also is found in spinach, broccoli, and kale. Lutein is found in green vegetables while lycopene is found mainly in red fruits and vegetables like tomatoes, pink grapefruit, and watermelon. The family of phytonutrients called flavonoids are found in blueberries, cherries, eggplant, cabbage, apples, grapes, citrus fruits, broccoli, and onions. Cruciferous vegetables like broccoli, cabbage, and cauliflower are rich in isothiocyanates.

ESSENTIAL

Cruciferous vegetables come from the Brassica family of vegetables. The cruciferous name, in Latin *Crucifer*, reflects the four sections of the plant that appear in the shape of a cross. They are sulfur-containing vegetables, which is why they all have a stronger taste.

Fruits and vegetables, especially citrus fruits, red grapes, and berries, are rich in phenols, which promote healthy vision and heart health and act as antioxidants in the body. The final group of phytonutrients known to be part of fruits and vegetables are the sulfides or thiols. Chives, garlic, onions, leaks, scallions, and the cruciferous vegetables belong in this category. These phytonutrients help with maintenance of the immune system as well as the health of the heart.

ALERT

Fruits and vegetables are essential to overall health and need to be a part of your daily eating plan. If you are struggling to consume the recommended intake of fruits and vegetables, make it a priority this week—and the rest of your life.

Making the Changes

Consuming enough fruits and vegetables seems to be a constant challenge for most Americans. Given their rich source of nutrients, this is unfortunate. If you fall into this group, start to make the shift by trying to add fruits and vegetables to more dishes like soups or stews, sneak them into other dishes, or try them as snacks. A few ideas to boost your intake include:

- Start the day with a fruit and yogurt smoothie.
- Throw dried cranberries or raisins into your cereal.

- Add fruits to green salads; strawberries, cherries, oranges, and mango work nicely.
- Make a trail mix from dried fruit, nuts, and whole-grain cereal.
- Sauté vegetables to add to meat or fish.
- Combine vegetables with pasta and marinara.
- Add shredded veggies to meat loaf.
- Mash steamed cauliflower and add to mashed potatoes.

In addition to these ideas, consider snacking on veggies with low-fat ranch dressing or hummus. Sliced apples or bananas with peanut butter are nice midday pick-me-ups. Think with creativity in mind and you will find that fruits and vegetables are easy and enjoyable to consume.

Beans, Nuts, and Seeds

The Mediterranean diet is rich in beans as a source of protein, due to their easy availability and low cost. Beans and peas, technically referred to as legumes, provide a rich nutrition package as well as great taste and texture variety. For many people, this taste and texture variety requires a bit of an adjustment, so adding beans and peas generally works best when it is done gradually. Another reason many people limit or avoid beans and peas is the side effect of gas.

ESSENTIAL

Reduce the amount of gas that occurs when eating beans by first rinsing the beans, then soaking them and rinsing again. This rinsing and soaking doesn't reduce any of the nutritional value, but it does help reduce some of the sugars in beans that trigger gas in the intestines.

The sugar in dried beans and peas that causes this intestinal reaction is oligosaccharide, which is actually a very positive phytonutrient. However, oligosaccharide requires healthy intestinal bacteria to break down the sugar, and during this process the healthy bacteria emit gas that triggers the bloating and gas many people experience when eating beans. But wait, there is good news! Not only will proper preparation help reduce the gas formation, but consistent consumption of beans and peas seems to boost the healthy bacteria in the intestine, resulting in less bloating and gas. Another option is to use canned beans, which tend to have fewer side effects. It is a good idea to rinse canned beans, since they contain more sodium than dried beans or peas.

Nuts and seeds are another source of protein that many people don't think about except for the use of nut butters. Nuts and seeds are excellent sources of protein, though they need to be used in moderation due to their higher calorie content. One benefit of nuts—one of many—is that they contain healthier fats. Nut butters are a common and easy way to shift from animal protein choices while still keeping the quantity of protein needed for a healthy body.

ALERT

Another way to reduce the gas that so often occurs when eating beans is to use a commercial product added during the cooking process. Commercial products such as Beano contain an enzyme that converts the oligosaccharide into simpler sugars, making digestion of beans easier.

How Much Beans, Nuts, and Seeds Should You Consume?

When using beans, nuts, and seeds as protein sources, the amount needed is different than if you are using beans as a vegetable or nuts and seeds as complements to your meals. The 2005 Dietary Guidelines recommends that most healthy adults consume the equivalent of 5–7 ounces of protein foods each day. This amount is generally much smaller than what most adults consume, often because we fail to consume enough of other food groups or because we don't feel as full as we would like after eating smaller portions. Beans, nuts, and seeds provide many benefits, one of which is they can help us feel full longer so that eating smaller portions is a simpler step. As you might imagine, portion sizes for beans, nuts, and seeds are very different than they are for protein sources like meat, poultry, and fish.

Food	Serving Size (equal to 1 ounce)
Cooked beans or peas	¼ cup
Tofu	¼ cup
Tempeh	1 ounce (cooked)
Soybeans	¼ cup
Hummus	2 tablespoons
Sunflower seeds	½ ounce or 1 tablespoon
Almonds	12
Peanut or other nut butter	1 tablespoon

From Mypyramid.gov

Nutrition of Beans, Nuts, and Seeds

Beans, nuts and seeds are similar to animal protein foods in that they provide a good source of protein, iron, magnesium, phosphorous, zinc, thiamin, niacin, vitamin B6, and B12, but they also contain fiber, and nuts and seeds provide vitamin E and selenium. While beans are fat free, nuts and seeds are high in healthier fats, making them good choices.

Soybeans are the one bean that provide all of the essential amino acids provided by animal-protein choices. Providing all of the essential amino acids means that soybeans are a complete protein and can be used without having to plan for a balance of other plant proteins to ensure a good protein intake.

The Phytonutrients of Beans, Nuts, and Seeds

The major phytonutrient in beans, nuts, and seeds is the presence of fiber, but they also contain a few other phytonutrients. Flaxseeds contain lignans, which help with heart health and the immune system. Nuts and seeds all contain phytic acid, which helps with blood sugar regulation, heart health, and acts as an antioxidant. Phytic acid can interfere with absorption of iron and calcium, but its health benefits make the intake of nuts and seeds worth it. Soybeans contain phytoestrogens, which might help reduce heart disease risk, symptoms of menopause, and promote brain health.

Working in More Beans, Nuts, and Seeds

If you're not ready to serve beans as an entrée, consider adding them to soups, casseroles, pasta, or rice in place of meat. Spaghetti and marinara tastes very nice when kidney beans are added, and black beans, brown rice, and salsa provide a bit of a kick. Beans, nuts, and seeds can all add texture and taste to green salads, and with the variety of beans and peas available, you can change which ones you use to vary the salad. Nuts and seeds can add crunch to salads, vegetables, stir-fries, or even sauces. Nut butters are great options for sandwiches all the time, but are especially nice when you can't refrigerate the sandwich.

Olive Oil

The final plant piece in the Mediterranean diet is olive oil. Olive oil is a monounsaturated fat, so it is a healthier choice than many other oils. Olive oil comes in varieties ranging from extra virgin to plain olive oil. The extra-virgin or virgin olive oils are the least processed, so they contain more of the plant compounds, making them better choices. These two varieties also have a stronger olive taste, so they may take some getting used to and may not work in baking.

QUESTION

What are monounsaturated fats?
Monounsaturated fats are a type of fat that can help reduce blood cholesterol. The term monounsaturated refers to the structure of the fat; it is this structure that affects how the fats work in the body. Key monounsaturated fats are canola and olive oils, along with peanuts and peanut oils.

How Much Olive Oil Should You Consume?

While olive oil may be a healthier choice, no fat should be used in unlimited quantities. Current guidelines suggest that healthy adults consume between 5 and 10 teaspoons of oil and oil-based foods each day. This portion may sound like a lot, but if you think about a teaspoon of margarine on toast, 2 tablespoons of salad dressing or 2 teaspoons of oil on your salad, and 2 teaspoons of oil for cooking, you've met the lowest amount of oil per day. Oils of all kinds provide about 40 calories in a teaspoon, so those 5 teaspoons per day account for 200 calories.

The Nutrition in Oil

The main nutrition found in oils of all types is fat. Oils vary in terms of type of fat, with some containing more monounsaturated fats and some more polyunsaturated fats. All oils provide both types of fat, so if you want to use olive oil for most of your cooking but corn, canola, or soybean oil for baking, you will still consume a healthier balance of fats.

Phytonutrients in Olive Oil

The main phytonutrient in oil is polyphenols, which work as antioxidants to promote heart health and may aid vision. The main phytochemical oleuropein is what gives olives their strong flavor. While this may be the only phytochemical in olives, they are rich in other compounds that provide some health benefits. Olive oil is rich in omega-3 and omega-6 fatty acids, both of which appear to be helpful in disease prevention.

Making the Switch

If you're currently using oils, switching to olive will be easy. If you're currently using sold fats like butter or shortening, you will need to adjust the recipes for baked goods, but otherwise the oil will work very well. Olive oil does carry a stronger flavor, so if you want a milder oil try canola oil.

CHAPTER 4

Rounding Out Your Meals

The Mediterranean diet is built around plant foods, but the diet also recognizes the nutritional and enjoyment value of fish, poultry, dairy foods, and even sweets. The important thing about the Mediterranean diet is that these foods are used in smaller amounts and represent complements to the plant foods, not the other way around. While animal sources of protein can fit well, the idea of sweets in a healthy eating plan might feel foreign. The key is the same as with animal-protein choices: balance.

Fish and Seafood

Given the proximity to the sea, Mediterranean countries rely on fish and shellfish for many, if not most, of their meals. Using more fish and shellfish is a good way to shift the intake of fat from less healthy saturated fats to more healthy unsaturated fats. Fish and shellfish also offer the convenience of quick cooking and flexibility in terms of flavoring. There are more than 400 varieties of fish in the Mediterranean region, with the most common being salmon, tuna, sardines, herring, smelt, seabream, squid, and a variety of white fish. Popular shellfish include mussels, shrimp, and clams. A current trend in choosing fish is to choose those that, when fished, do not harm the environment. The Monterey Bay Seafood Watch recommends catching fish that are not overfished or that do not harm other marine life or the environment when they are caught. A few of the fish that are considered the best choices for the environment but that also contain more of the healthy fats are wild Alaskan salmon, striped bass, farmed rainbow trout, and albacore or skipjack tuna.

ESSENTIAL

Saturated fats are fats that have hydrogen connected to all of the carbons in the structure of the fat. This structure makes the fat very stable at room temperature, but it also means that these fats cause the body to make more "bad" cholesterol, thus raising blood cholesterol levels. Main food sources are animal foods, coconut oil, and palm and palm-kernel oils.

How Much Fish Should You Consume?

The American Heart Association recommends consuming at least 7 ounces and up to 12 ounces of fish per week, with an emphasis on fatty fish like salmon, mackerel, herring, lake trout, sardines, and chunk light tuna. Consuming fish this often helps shift the intake of fats from the more heart-disease promoting saturated fats to the healthier unsaturated fats found in fish. While lean fish like tilapia, cod, whiting, and other white fish don't contain the amount of fat found in fattier fish, they are still a source of these healthier fats and can be used as often as your menu plan allows. The waters that fish swim in all contain a variety of compounds, but one that generates the most concern is mercury. Given the small amount in fish and the small amount of fish people consume, for healthy adults the consumption of mercury is of little concern, but for young children and pregnant women it can be an issue. Too much mercury can affect a developing nervous system, so for that reason the Food and Drug Administration has recommended that women and young children consume up to 12 ounces per week of fish in the low risk for mercury category including salmon, canned light tuna, shrimp, pollock, and catfish.

ALERT

The Food and Drug Administration has recommended that children and pregnant women avoid shark, swordfish, king mackerel, and tilefish due to their extremely high levels of mercury. Children and pregnant women can consume up to 12 ounces per week of other types of fish.

Nutrition of Fish and Shellfish

Fish and shellfish are excellent sources of protein and healthier fats. Fish and shellfish generally do not contain any carbohydrates, but clams, scallops, and oysters can contain very small amounts. In terms of vitamins and minerals, the content varies based on the type of fish, but the main nutrients found in fish and shellfish are Vitamin A, iron, potassium, and sodium. Fish and shellfish provide less saturated fat than other sources of animal protein and most of them contain more of the healthy unsaturated fats. Most fish contain about the same amount of cholesterol as meat, but shrimp is higher, containing about 130 milligrams in a 3-ounce raw weight portion.

The main nutritional value of fish is the fat content. Fish contain monounsaturated fats and polyunsaturated fats, especially omega-3 fatty acids. Omega-3 fatty acids help lower blood triglycerides and appear to keep blood vessels more pliable, therefore, more resistant to heart disease. Omega-3 fatty acids also help prevent irregular heartbeats, help slow the growth of plaque in arteries, and help keep blood pressure at a normal level. Omega-3 fatty acids are found in higher amounts in fatty fish, so try to consume salmon, mackerel, sardines, and herring more often, but all fish will provide some omega-3s. Remember, though, that omega-3 fatty acids alone won't reduce the risk of heart disease. They must be combined with a lower intake of saturated fats, plenty of plant foods, and healthier oils—basically, the combinations found in the Mediterranean diet.

FACT

The American Heart Association recommends you limit your daily cholesterol intake to less than 300 milligrams per day. If you have heart disease, you should limit your intake to less than 200 milligrams each day. The best way to lower blood cholesterol is to limit saturated fats. An easy way to limit saturated fats is to cut down on the amount of meat that you consume.

Adding More Fish to Your Meals

For many Americans, adding more fish and shellfish to their menus is a complicated step, but it doesn't have to be that way. Fish cooks very quickly, and depending on the fish, it works nicely on the grill, baked, poached, or fried. Before you can cook the fish, you need to know how to purchase good fish. Look for fresh fish that is firm to the touch and has a mild, not fishy, smell. When it comes to cooking fish, you want to start with small, simple steps. Canned tuna is an easy place to begin, but instead of the traditional heavy mayonnaise-based tuna salad, combine it with celery, carrots, capers, chopped eggs, and half low-fat plain yogurt and half low-fat mayonnaise. Another easy start is to grill salmon by oiling a grill and both sides of the fish (to maintain the healthfulness of the fish use olive or canola oil). Grill the fish, skin-side down, 5–7 minutes, turn carefully, and grill another 5–7 minutes. There are lots of other easy ways to prepare fish and shellfish, so start small, but give it a try.

Meat, Poultry, and Eggs

While the Mediterranean diet is built mainly around fish and plant foods, meat, poultry, and eggs are used within the diet. People within the Mediterranean region know how to keep portions of meat and poultry smaller so that the contributions of saturated fat are also smaller. Meat choices vary throughout the region from beef to lamb but the consistent aspect among all the countries is smaller portions. It is true that some restaurants in Mediterranean countries are beginning to cater more to American habits and are increasing portion sizes, but this is not the typical diet plan for the Mediterranean diet. Poultry is often found on the menu of the people of the Mediterranean, but it rarely appears fried and usually appears as a part of a dish so that the actual portion is smaller than what is consumed when the poultry is the main entrée. Eggs are often used in the Mediterranean region both as part of a breakfast meal and in cooking and baking.

How Much Meat, Poultry, and Eggs Should You Consume?

If you're trying to make the shift to a Mediterranean eating plan, the first place to make some changes is in the portions of red meats you eat. Red meats such as beef, veal, lamb, and pork contain more saturated fat than poultry, so they are more likely to boost your cholesterol levels. Use them sparingly; weekly or even every couple of weeks. In addition to limited usage, it is important to limit the amount you consume; a 3-ounce cooked-weight portion is a good amount to choose. Three ounces cooked means you start with about 4 ounces raw weight. When choosing red meat, make sure you choose leaner cuts like loin, flank, or round and avoid things like hot dogs, sausages, lunch meats, and bacon, which are all high-fat choices. Organ meats, while not commonly consumed, are high in cholesterol and should be avoided or only used on occasion. Poultry contains saturated fat, but because it has more unsaturated fat than red meats, it tends to be a better choice. The white meat of poultry has less total fat than the dark meat, thus having less saturated fat, making it a better choice. Poultry may be a better choice than red meat, but in the Mediterranean diet it is limited in usage. Common usages are within casseroles or soups, where it is combined with vegetables and often beans.

Eggs appear in a variety of foods throughout the region but are a common part of breakfast in many countries. Eggs do contribute saturated fat and cholesterol, but current guidelines indicate that one egg per day is acceptable, unless you have heart disease or a strong family history of heart disease. The most important thing about preparing eggs is that they not be fried in animal fat or bacon grease, and that they are enjoyed with lower-fat foods. A perfect example of a good way to enjoy eggs is a Spanish omelet loaded with veggies or an Israeli veggie quiche.

QUESTION

Is it all right to cook poultry with the skin left on?
The skin of poultry is 100 percent fat, so it should be removed before eating and ideally before cooking. Since the skin keeps the meat moist, if you cook poultry without the skin you will need to moisten the skin with some oil, fat-free chicken broth, or other liquid.

The Nutrition of Meat, Poultry, and Eggs

One of the best things about meat, poultry, and eggs is their wide nutritional package. These foods are excellent sources of complete protein, iron, zinc, a variety of B vitamins, and of course fat. The B vitamins found in them help the body use the calories consumed, enhance formation of blood cells and tissues, and help the nervous system function. The zinc in them is important to the immune system and the iron carries oxygen in the blood. Red meats, poultry, and eggs are a source of saturated fats that increase the bad or LDL cholesterol in the blood, so leaner choices are better.

FACT

Animal protein foods like meat, fish, poultry, eggs, and dairy foods provide all the essential amino acids the body needs in order to repair and rebuild muscle tissue. Plant proteins, except for soybeans, contain amino acids, but not all that are needed by the body, so they must be consumed throughout the day for adequate intake.

Adjusting Your Intake

Transitioning from a diet high in animal-based food to a more plant-food based diet not only takes time to learn recipes but also takes time to shift your palate. Learning to enjoy more plant foods is easier if you initially switch your menus to meals that contain meat or poultry. So instead of using all meat in marinara, add chopped veggies and decrease the amount of beef you use. Serving more casseroles and stir-fries is another way to slowly adjust to smaller portions of meat. If you enjoy grilling meat or poultry, the next time you grill try meat and veggie kabobs, where the veggies exceed the number of meat pieces. Reduce your intake of eggs by using egg whites for your omelet or scrambled eggs and in cooking. Egg-substitute products are also an option. Both options provide less saturated fat.

Dairy Foods Do Fit In

Cheese and yogurt are common in the diets of the Mediterranean, but they tend to be used in smaller amounts so the fat they add to the diet is lower. Traditional Mediterranean diets tended to use higher-fat cheeses and full-fat yogurt, so using these smaller portions helped. However, if you are adopting the Mediterranean diet now, choosing low-fat or fat-free options is advised. Milk is not used as much but does appear in cooking. Milk has a higher amount of the milk-sugar lactose, so for some people in the Mediterranean lactose intolerance limits their use of fluid milk. Fortunately, yogurt contains active culture bacteria that break down the milk sugar so digestion is easier.

ALERT

Lactose intolerance does not mean you must avoid dairy foods. People with lactose intolerance can add dairy foods if they make sure to use more yogurt or cheese and always consume milk in small amounts and with other foods. If discomfort from lactose continues, consider using milk designed for those with lactose intolerance.

Dairy foods often appear on menus as complements to other dishes, for instance yogurt tops fruit or is mixed with cereal. Yogurt often appears in place of sour cream to complement meat or poultry. Cheese is enjoyed in small amounts at breakfast or on top of a pasta dish. Mozzarella cheese, feta cheese, Parmesan, Manchego, kasseri, and Queso de Murcian are a few of the popular cheeses throughout the region. By keeping these foods in smaller amounts, they can continue to supply the valuable nutrition they contain. As you choose dairy foods for your meal plan, focus on low-fat or fat-free varieties and limit or avoid sour cream, cream cheese, cream, and butter.

How Much Dairy Should You Consume?

The 2005 Dietary Guidelines recommends 3 cups of dairy every day for those over the age of nine years. Studies show that most adults, and unfortunately many children, do not consume the recommended daily intake of dairy foods, meaning they may miss the nutrients found in dairy foods. The traditional Mediterranean diet actually had fewer servings of dairy each day, generally only 2 cups, but they also consumed large quantities of dark-green leafy vegetables, so they often matched the calcium content of dairy foods. With the higher bean intake, the protein that dairy provides was also matched. Using current nutrition guidelines to build your meals makes striving for 3 cups a day a good idea. Consuming 3 cups per day isn't difficult if you think about using milk, yogurt, cheese, cottage cheese, and all the foods that can be prepared with milk. Portion sizes for milk include:

▼ TABLE 4-1: DAIRY SERVING SIZES

Food	Serving Size
Milk	1 cup
Yogurt	1 cup
Cheddar cheese	1½ ounces
American cheese	2 ounces
Cottage cheese	2 cups
Frozen yogurt	1 cup

From Mypyramid.gov

Nutrition in Dairy Foods

Dairy foods naturally contain all three of the calorie nutrients: protein, fat, and carbohydrates. Dairy foods are also the body's best source of calcium and riboflavin, and are good sources of phosphorous, potassium, magnesium, and vitamins A and B12. Many dairy foods are also fortified with vitamin D. The protein in dairy foods is a complete protein, so using dairy foods as your major source of protein will not compromise the quality of your protein intake. The type of fat found in dairy foods is predominately saturated fat, so choosing low-fat or fat-free varieties will limit your intake of this less-healthful fat. Fortunately, when the fat is removed from dairy foods all the other nutrients remain and calcium actually increases slightly. Since milk naturally contains the simple sugar lactose, all dairy products except for cheese contain this sugar as the source of carbohydrates. Some dairy foods have added sugars to provide flavoring, so make sure you read the label on the products you choose.

QUESTION

If milk naturally contains sugar, why doesn't cheese have any sugar in it? During the processing of cheese, the fluid part of the milk, also referred to as the whey, is separated and removed from the solid part, the curds. The liquid whey contains the milk sugar and other nutrients, whereas the solid part contains much of the protein and fat.

Calcium is important to bone and teeth health, but it also aids muscle contractions and helps maintain normal nerve function. Riboflavin helps the body use the energy it consumes from food. One cup of milk contains more potassium than an orange and almost as much as a banana, making milk a very good source of potassium. Potassium plays a role in the fluid balance of the body, and phosphorous and magnesium are two of the main minerals in the body.

Making Changes in Your Dairy Intake

One of the biggest changes you might need to make in terms of dairy is consuming the recommended 3 cups each day. If you continue to struggle to get enough dairy, consider using it like those in the Mediterranean. Add yogurt on top of fruit for dessert; have a breakfast of whole-grain bread, low-fat cheese, and fruit; add cheese to pasta; or top falafel with yogurt-dill sauce. Boost your dairy intake gradually as you adopt all the behaviors of the Mediterranean diet and you will find that the changes are simple and yield an enjoyable menu plan.

Herbs and Spices Make Mediterranean

Just as there are as many variations on the Mediterranean diet as there are countries within the region, so, too, is the variety of herbs and spices used in Mediterranean cooking. One consistent factor is that herbs and spices are very much a core of the cuisine. Herbs are plentiful in the region for the same reason that other crops and plants are plentiful—the climate in the region. Which herbs grow in which country is a function of the climate in that area, but all of the regions have a plentiful supply of herbs. Spices are generally in the region as a result of trading and transport. Spices used in the area are often more typical of Asia, but have been used for so long they are now considered as Mediterranean as the native herbs that grow there. Some of the most common herbs and spices of the region include the following, with Northern Africa listed first, followed by Southern Europe, and then the Eastern Mediterranean:

- Cinnamon
- Cloves
- Ginger
- Nutmeg
- Saffron

- Basil
- Bay leaves
- Parsley
- Oregano
- Rosemary
- Sage
- Thyme

- Allspice
- Dill
- Mint
- Sumac

These herbs and spices might be the most common, but many others are used as well, including anise, chilies, fennel, lavender, marjoram, and vanilla. Black pepper and garlic are both used throughout the region.

Benefits of Herbs and Spices

Herbs and spices obviously provide flavor, but they also may provide some health benefits. Herbs, of course, are plants, so like fruits, vegetables, beans, and whole grains, they contain phytonutrients that can help promote health and prevent disease. How much of each herb or spice you need to use is less clear, as is whether cooking changes the phytonutrients. The plus of using herbs and spices is that they enhance the flavor of your foods and can make eating more enjoyable, whether or not they provide health benefits. Current research indicates that herbs and spices might provide the following health benefits in their role as antibacterials, antioxidants, digestive aids, and anti-inflammatory agents: oregano as an antibacterial; cinnamon as an aid to cholesterol reduction; ginger as an antinausea aid; garlic as an aid to reduce heart disease risk; and dill as a digestive aid.

Boosting Your Intake of Herbs and Spices

For many people, the first step in flavoring food beyond salt or pepper is a bit intimidating, so a couple of rules up front can help. First, always start with small amounts of the herb or spice and then determine if you enjoy the flavor; next time add a bit more. Second, if you are using fresh herbs, plan on adding them closer to the end of cooking, since the flavor in them is more sensitive to heat. Chop fresh herbs into smaller pieces so the flavor they release is more evenly distributed. Finally, when using dried herbs or spices, add them at the beginning of cooking, since they release their flavor as you cook, but make sure you crumble the leaves or grind hard seeds so they can release more of their flavor.

Herb or Spice	Foods to Flavor
Cinnamon	Carrots, meats, apricots
Cloves	Baked goods, stews, meats
Ginger	Sauces, cakes, stir-fry
Nutmeg	Pastries, soups, pasta, beans
Saffron	Paella, eggs, poultry
Basil	Pesto, salads
Bay leaves	Soups, stews, poultry
Parsley	Sauces, dressing, salads
Rosemary	Stews, sauces, vegetables
Sage	Poultry, seafood, stuffing
Thyme	Seafood, meats, marinades
Allspice	Sauces, baked goods
Dill	Salads, vegetables
Mint	Tea, carrots, jams
Sumac	Meat, poultry, berries

Sweets Flavor Mediterranean Meals

While the diets of the Mediterranean focus on healthful choices, they also include that small sweet touch that people look forward to at the end of the meal. With the abundance of fruits and vegetables, many of the meals in the Mediterranean end with fruits in some fashion. Fruit soaked or poached in wine, fruit crisp, fresh berries with whipped cream, or clafoutis, a baked fruit pudding, are all popular desserts. While sweets are a part of most dinner meals, the difference in the sweets of a Mediterranean diet is that the portions are smaller, so dessert really represents a taste of something as opposed to a large piece. In addition to fruits, dairy products and eggs are commonly used as part of dessert. Flan and crème brulee are two dairy- and egg-based desserts that appear throughout the region. While both can be high in fat and calories, portion sizes tend to be not much bigger than a small scoop of ice cream. Another common sweet in the region is a pastry flavored with nuts and honey. Whether the traditional Greek baklava, honey cookies, the Egyptian basbousa, or the Israeli tradition of figs or dates with honey and walnuts, nuts and honey are enjoyed throughout the area. When families dine at home, many Mediterranean families stick with simpler desserts like the fruit or cookies, but enjoying a sweet to signal the end of the meal is very much a tradition of the region. Choosing desserts that include fruits, dairy, or nuts boosts the nutritional value of the dessert, making it a part of the meal rather than a source of added calories.

FACT

The 2005 Dietary Guidelines includes an allocation of calories for sweets, alcohol, and other higher calorie options. The amount of discretionary calories you should have is based on your daily calorie need, but the range for healthy adults is 200–400 calories per day.

Balancing Out the Mediterranean Diet

With all of this information, it might feel that a good Mediterranean diet requires too much time thinking, planning, shopping, and preparing, but that doesn't have to be the case. Certainly, within the Mediterranean region families enjoy the close proximity of small grocers and city markets that allow them to shop daily so they can enjoy the best quality food choices, but even if you live in a big city you can make the Mediterranean eating plan work. The biggest changes for most people are shifting to more plant foods and fewer animal foods, so if you want to start there you should develop a plan that focuses on making small menu changes. A good first step might be serving a dinner meal with several types of vegetables and whole grains while decreasing the portion size of the meat, poultry, or fish. Another way to make the shift is to look for the fruits and vegetables that are currently in season and build meals around them. In the summer this might mean cantaloupe, berries, and peaches with whole-grain cereal and low-fat milk for breakfast; a green salad with kidney beans, blueberries, chopped nuts, and vinaigrette for lunch; and grilled salmon topped with a fruit salsa, brown rice with diced tomatoes, peppers, and asparagus, and poached peaches for dinner. However you decide to start your new eating pattern, remember that the goal is a pattern you can maintain for life, a pattern that you enjoy and one that is simple for you to prepare.

CHAPTER 5

Lose Weight with the Mediterranean Diet

When Dr. Ancel Keys first observed the lifestyle of those living in the Mediterranean region, he not only noted their lower incidence of heart disease and some forms of cancer, he noticed that many of the people in the region were at a healthy weight even though they ate more total calories from fat. Can the Mediterranean diet help with weight loss even if you don't live in the region? In this chapter, we look at how the Mediterranean diet can help with weight loss no matter where you live.

Start Shedding Pounds

With more than 67 percent of Americans overweight or obese, the goal of losing weight is a common one, but achieving that goal is challenging for most people. When it comes to weight loss, people often look for the fastest, easiest diet answer. The problem with this is that diet alone won't achieve lasting weight loss. For many people, the cause of their excess weight is their overall lifestyle, which consists of low levels of activity, inappropriate food portions, and more and more foods that are energy dense as opposed to nutrient dense, more recently termed nutrient rich.

QUESTION

What is nutrient density?
The 2005 Dietary Guidelines for Americans defines nutrient-rich foods as those foods that provide substantial amounts of vitamins and minerals and relatively fewer calories. Nutrient-rich foods allow you to meet nutritional needs while consuming fewer calories as opposed to energy-dense foods, which contain more calories than nutrients.

Weight loss occurs when lifestyle behaviors are changed and maintained. The Mediterranean diet can be a good option for those wishing to lose weight because it offers a variety of foods, focuses more on lower-calorie, higher-fiber plant foods, and recognizes the importance of activity. Before you take up the Mediterranean diet for your weight-loss plan, let's look at what the science says about its role in weight loss.

The Science of Weight Loss

The Mediterranean diet and its effect on heart disease prevention has been studied for years, but within the last ten years studies have looked for a connection between the diet and weight loss. A review of the evidence shows that the Mediterranean diet has a role in preventing obesity. The diet provides most nutrients needed for health, it is high in fiber, the source of fat is of a healthier type, and more of the protein comes from plant foods. The Mediterranean diet offers a higher fat content, which can aid in satiety, making it easier to follow the diet. At the same time, the fiber content also keeps you feeling full longer, so it is easier to space meals further apart. Another aspect of the diet that has been researched by several different researchers is the role of the fluid content of the foods. The fruits and vegetables in the diet provide a lot of water, and as Dr. Barbara Rolls has shown, high-volume foods aid feelings of fullness. In a study in the journal *Nutricion Hospitalaria* authors Marta Garaulet and F. Perez de Heredia reported that in addition to the benefits listed above, three other factors also make the Mediterranean diet a good choice for weight loss:

1. The diet has a high carbohydrate content, which helps avoid the triggers for hunger, thus reducing the frequency of binge eating.
2. The diet can be followed comfortably for long periods of time.
3. The diet is tastier than many low-fat diet options.

FACT

Every pound of body weight is equal to 3500 calories, so when you are trying to lose or gain weight you must make a change in calories consumed, or burned, equal to that amount. Consuming lower calorie foods makes it easy to stay full and reduce calories.

A recent study compared three different diets and weight loss. The two-year study, of more than 300 moderately obese men and women, was recently published in the *New England Journal of Medicine*. The three types of diets were the Mediterranean diet, a low-fat diet, and a low-carbohydrate diet. The study found that people reported having an easier time following the Mediterranean diet and that group also ended up losing an average of just under 10 pounds. Those in the low-carbohydrate group lost just over 10 pounds, and those in the low-fat group lost only 6 pounds. While none of the subjects lost large amounts of weight, those in the Mediterranean diet group also saw their blood sugar levels reach a healthier number.

Studies Show Mixed Outcomes

While several research studies show a connection between the Mediterranean diet and weight loss, one in the journal *Obesity* found mixed results. The study looked at more than twenty studies done on the Mediterranean diet and found that there is an indication that it may help with weight loss. The report showed that thirteen of the studies reviewed found a connection with weight loss, but eight did not. The article pointed out that one of the major challenges in assessing whether the Mediterranean diet is effective for weight loss is the variability in defining the diet. Given the differences in food consumed in the countries within the Mediterranean region, studies that look at diet need to be more specific about the foods being consumed in the particular area.

Why Is Activity Important

Regular physical activity is important to the body for several reasons. Regular activity provides the following benefits:

- Aids weight loss
- Strengthens the heart, lungs, and blood vessels
- Helps improve your mental state
- Can help lower blood triglycerides and cholesterol
- Reduces body fat and preserves muscle
- Helps lower blood pressure
- Lowers blood sugar levels

Regular activity keeps the body working at its peak, which then improves your overall quality of life. People who get regular activity find they have more energy to do the things they want to do.

How Much Activity Do You Need?

Current guidelines recommend adults get at least two and one-half hours of moderate-intensity activity every week. Moderate activity is defined as walking briskly, doing water aerobics, or riding a bike. Along with this activity, adults need to do muscle-strengthening activities two or more days a week. Muscle-strengthening activities include lifting weights, working with resistance bands, doing push-ups or sit-ups, or yoga. This activity should include all parts of the body, so make sure you work your arms, legs, back, chest, shoulders, and abdomen. If time is an issue and you are able to do more vigorous activity, the guidelines call for one hour and fifteen minutes of vigorous activity each week. Vigorous activities include jogging, running, swimming laps, riding a bike uphill, or playing tennis or other sports. In addition to the vigorous activity, you still need the muscle-strengthening activities each week.

ALERT

Before you embark on any type of physical-activity routine, make sure you get a physical and talk with your doctor about your plans for activity. Make sure you discuss both types of activities to be sure you are fit for both of them.

Getting Started

If you're a bit hesitant to jump right into this much activity, know that it is okay to start slowly. If your current activity level is little to no activity, you might want to start with ten minutes each day or even a couple of days each week and then increase as your fitness develops. Increase the length of time when the amount of time you are doing becomes too easy or you find you aren't breathing as heavy as you used to while exercising. The goal with activity is the length of time, so whether you choose the 150 minutes of moderate-intensity activity or the seventy-five minutes of vigorous activity, the important thing is to get to that level and continue with that plan. Physical activity only provides a benefit when it is a part of your routine. If you plan to do muscle-strengthening work by lifting weights, you might want to take a class or work with a trainer to learn proper form. Overall, the goal with muscle strengthening is to do 8–12 repetitions of each lift, 2–3 times. It is always best to do one set and then do another activity before returning to do the second set. Muscles tire very quickly, so doing too many reps can cause the muscle to tire and it won't be able to get as much benefit from the lifting.

When lifting weight, it is a good idea to work opposing muscles so that development of the muscle is even. If you are doing an arm curl where you roll the weight into your body, make the next activity a press so that you extend the arms out from the body.

Striving for Greater Health Benefits

If you're in good shape or if you want to lower cholesterol more or keep blood sugar low enough to avoid medication, you might want to raise your activity goals. The Centers for Disease Control and Prevention recommends that those who want a greater health benefit strive for the following:

- 5 hours or 300 minutes of moderate-intensity activity each week plus muscle strengthening
- 2½ hours or 150 minutes of vigorous activity each week plus muscle strengthening
- A blend of moderate and vigorous activity each week plus muscle strengthening

Whether you want to push for greater health benefits depends not only on your overall goal but on what you can realistically do over time. Remember, the goal with activity is just like the goal with food choices: it needs to be something you can do for life, not just a short-term fix.

Eating Balanced Meals

Balancing activity and food choices is not only important to weight control it is also important to muscle strength and development. Timing your meals to your activity will help your body work more efficiently and enhance the ability to build muscle. Choosing the right foods before and after a workout will ensure that muscles repair and rebuild. Physical activity burns calories, but if you are trying to lose weight you won't want to overeat before or after your activity; you will want to be sure you consume the right foods for activity. Muscles grow when they are fed with fuel and nutrients for building. The fuel for growth is carbohydrates and the fuel for building is protein. Planning meals or snacks that combine carbohydrates and protein is the best way to fuel your workouts.

Workout Meals

If you are just starting out and your workouts aren't very long, you won't need a lot of extra nutrition for your workouts and you won't have to be as focused on when you eat. The longer or more intense a workout, the more important it is to fuel in a timely manner. For those just starting out, focus on using the Mediterranean pyramid to guide meal planning, but also make sure that your meals and snacks combine some protein and some carbohydrates. An example of a morning meal might include the following:

- 1 cup of cooked oatmeal
- 2 tablespoons chopped dried apricots and raisins
- 2 tablespoons chopped nuts
- 1 cup skim milk used to prepare oatmeal
- 1 slice whole-wheat toast
- 2 teaspoons peanut butter on the toast

If you plan to work out first thing in the morning, you may not want to eat a big meal first, so consider grabbing something small like a piece of fruit with a touch of peanut butter; if you are only working out for thirty minutes, a piece of fruit might be enough.

FACT

For the best repair and development of your muscles, refuel with some protein and some carbohydrates within two hours of working your muscles.

As your workouts reach thirty to forty minutes, you will need to think about what to eat after a workout to replace the energy you used and allow your muscles to repair and grow. Remember that if you are trying to lose or maintain weight, you need to keep calories and portions in mind. When physical activity is a part of your daily routine, you will get the greatest benefit from your workouts if you try to space your meals three to four hours apart. In addition to this timing, try to do your heavy workouts three to four hours after a large meal so you don't get stomach cramps from having just consumed a meal. This timing also means that right after your workout you can have another meal, thus timing your hunger and your muscle-fueling needs together.

Working in High-Fiber Foods

The Mediterranean diet is built around beans, whole grains, fruits, and vegetables, which all provide lots of fiber. While this fiber is a plus to overall health and satiety, it can be a negative to physical activity. High-fiber foods require more digestion time, that is why they help you feel full longer, but this longer time can mean that when you are working out the fiber is still sitting in your digestive tract. This slower digestion can lead to stomach cramping, so some people find they need to consume higher-fiber foods at meals further away from their activity. In addition to needing more time for digestion, high-fiber foods require more fluid intake. If you plan to work out after a meal that is high in fiber, you might need to boost your fluid intake to help you stay hydrated during your workout.

QUESTION

How much fluid is needed for a 30-minute workout?
Hydration needs vary from individual to individual, but as a general rule, you need to consume 2 cups of fluid two hours before your activity, another cup one hour before, and 4–6 ounces of water or sports drink for every fifteen minutes of activity during your workout.

Keeping the Weight Off

While losing weight isn't an easy task, trying to keep it off is even harder for most people. Trying to keep weight off is often harder because quick-fix diets mean you haven't developed a new lifestyle around your eating habits. Trying different diets to lose weight sets you up for short-term fixes, not lifestyle changes. So how do you lose it and keep it off? Before embarking on the Mediterranean diet, take some time to assess if you are ready for long-term change by asking yourself these questions:

- Am I willing to commit time to making changes in my food and activity patterns?
- Am I losing weight because I want to do this, not to please someone else?
- Have I reviewed my eating patterns, time commitments, and physical activity to determine what I can change?
- Am I comfortable losing weight gradually?
- Is my life quiet and under my control at this time?
- Will I use occasional slips as lessons to help me make permanent changes?

If you aren't in a good place in your life to make changes in your eating, activity, and behaviors, it might be best to wait to make big changes until you can control what you are doing. If things are chaotic right now, it might be best to make some small changes, feel good about them, and then make more changes later. One of the pluses of changing to the Mediterranean diet is that it can provide health benefits whether you lose weight or not. The healthier fats in the diet, shift from animal foods to more plant foods, and high-fiber content are all factors that will promote health.

FACT

Making changes in your eating and activity habits takes time. Some research studies show that it can take between 90 and 120 days for a new behavior to become a habit, so be patient with yourself.

Once you have decided you want to make lifelong changes and have started the process, remember that healthy weight loss happens slowly, about 1 pound per week on average, so plot your goals with that in mind. In addition to healthy weight happening slowly, it is not uncommon for weight loss to go through stages of plateaus or periods where no weight loss occurs. Weight loss that represents changes in body fat is gradual, but with steady commitment to a long-term goal, you can make it through the plateaus. Building in rewards for your efforts is one way to get through a plateau. For example, allow yourself an hour a day of reading a favorite book for each day you follow your workout plan. Another reward might be taking some "me time" for each day you follow your meal plan. Whatever you decide on for your rewards, make sure you take them and recognize that they mean you are making changes that will make you healthier and leaner in the long run.

Planning for Special Treats

If you've dieted before, you know that many if not most diets have forbidden foods or rules about enjoying special treats. These rules can help you stay on the diet plan, but they also set up a definite feeling of good and bad foods, a feeling that can lead to strong urges to eat those bad foods. One of the best ways to develop healthy eating behaviors and stay on your plan for a healthier weight is to budget in special treats. When you look at the diets of some Mediterranean countries, it is very clear that sweets can fit very nicely into their overall healthful eating plan. The reason these sweets fit into the traditional eating plans of these countries is twofold. First, the people of the Mediterranean region traditionally have a better perspective on portions, with desserts generally being very small in size. Second, these foods are enjoyed after they consume fruits, vegetables, beans, and grains as opposed to cutting back on those foods in order to consume larger portions of dessert. This healthier perspective about sweets makes it easier for people to feel comfortable consuming sweets but limiting the portion. If you want to enjoy the foods you love but keep your weight in a healthy range, you must develop an appreciation for portion size knowing that all foods can fit in a healthful eating plan.

CHAPTER 6

Get Healthy with the Mediterranean Diet

The popularity of the Mediterranean diet originated with the finding that people living in the Mediterranean had a lower incidence of heart disease than people living in a variety of other countries. As more and more populations are studied, evidence continues to evolve showing that the Mediterranean diet may provide an even wider variety of health benefits. This chapter will look at these health benefits in terms of what is known and what still needs to be learned.

Fight Disease and Ailments

The Mediterranean diet is probably one of, if not the most, studied diet; it has been reviewed in terms of prevention of a variety of diseases and overall promotion of health. Recent studies have looked at not only the impact of individual foods within the diet but the combination of all the foods; in other words, the synergy of the whole diet. Evidence continues to evolve in terms of *how* the Mediterranean diet impacts health, but the evidence continues to show it *does* promote health. The wide variety of foods included in the diet is likely the main reason for the diet's ability to promote health. Studies currently indicate that the Mediterranean diet plays a role in the prevention of several types of cancer, diabetes, dementia, metabolic syndrome, and heart disease. In addition, some studies show it helps fight inflammation, which could be an underlying contributor to the diseases listed above (or an independent risk factor). A recent review in the journal *Current Opinion in Lipidology* looked at the Mediterranean diet as an anti-inflammatory agent. Many researchers feel that the start of many diseases is inflammation. So, if the Mediterranean diet works as an anti-inflammatory that would explain how it helps promote health and prevent disease. Another study out of the University of Florence noted a similar outcome, but this study went on to say the whole diet pattern, not just a single nutrient or food, was likely the cause of the health benefit.

FACT

Inflammation is a normal reaction of the body to foreign bodies or matter. Inflammation helps the body protect itself while healing occurs. Inflammation that goes on all the time, called chronic inflammation, is not a healthy process and is the cause of damage to the body leading to aging and disease. Studies show diet plays a role in triggering and eliminating inflammation but the how it does it, as well as the why it does it are points that aren't clear.

How the Mediterranean Diet Fights Disease

Much of the evidence on the benefits of the Mediterranean diet has been obtained by observing populations or conducting smaller, short-term studies. A study was conducted about five years ago to determine if the diet can impact mortality from a variety of diseases. The study, published in the *Archives of Internal Medicine*, looked at the eating patterns of more than 300,000 men and women and found that the diet did lower death rates. The benefits of the diet were better in those who smoked, but showed a positive outcome in all subjects. The study looked at deaths due to cancer, heart disease, and other causes. A conclusion of this study was similar to the previous study in that the benefit seemed to be from the whole diet pattern, not a specific component of the diet. Research studies have looked at the Mediterranean diet in connection with longevity, Alzheimer's disease, Parkinson's disease, several forms of cancer, skin health and allergies, heart disease, and diabetes.

QUESTION

What components of the Mediterranean diet seem to be the most valuable for disease prevention?
Studies seem to indicate that the high usage of plant foods along with the low intake of animal foods provides a wider variety of nutrients and a healthier intake of fats. This combination, along with the overall pattern of phytonutrients, seems to be the connection to health and disease prevention.

Adoption of the Mediterranean Diet

While evidence continues to show that the Mediterranean diet promotes health and prevents disease, it continues to be challenged by the Western diet, which focuses on more animal foods than plant foods. People who live within the Mediterranean region are maintaining their eating habits, but even those habits are becoming tempered with a Western flair. Fast foods, snack foods, and large portions are invading the cuisine of many Mediterranean countries.

The 2005 Dietary Guidelines for Americans indicates that more plant foods are desirable for overall health, and all indications are that the next guidelines will reinforce this message even more strongly. Yet the consumption data shows this is not the pattern Americans are consuming. In an effort to collect data that would strongly convince people to maintain or adopt a Mediterranean diet, researchers in Florence, Italy studied adherence to the diet and the connection to health. Outcomes of the study showed that people who more closely adhered to the traditional Mediterranean diet had significant reductions in death from heart disease and cancer and a lower incidence of Parkinson's disease and Alzheimer's disease.

ESSENTIAL

All major scientific associations, as well as the Dietary Guidelines of the United States, encourage consumption of a Mediterranean-type diet to reduce risk of a variety of diseases. Shifting your diet to a Mediterranean-type diet can help reduce health care costs and improve quality of life.

Keep Your Skin Healthy

The Mediterranean region is known for its sunshine. In some of the countries of the region the sun shines for 300 or more days each year. With this much sun, and with the amount of time people spend outside, you would think the incidence of skin cancer would be high in the region. While statistics vary depending on the country, the average incidence of skin cancer in the Mediterranean region is 3 out of 100,000 versus an incidence of 20 out of 100,000 men and 17 out of 100,000 women in North America. The reason for these differences has been the focus of research studies, and one factor that has generated much interest is the role of diet. A comprehensive review of the role of diet appeared in the journal *Nutrition Reviews*. In this review, the components of diet that may help prevent skin changes were reviewed. While the review identified individual diet components, as a whole the individual components represent the foods of the Mediterranean diet.

Role of Antioxidants

The skin uses many antioxidants to offset the challenges to its health from the environment around it. The skin, at least on the face, arms, and legs, receives constant exposure to sunlight, which is helpful for the production of vitamin D; however, excess sunlight is known to trigger changes in the skin leading to skin cancers. Antioxidants in the skin that can help offset this challenge include carotenoids, tocopherols, glutathione, and others. Consuming foods that are rich in these and other antioxidants can set up a defense against the sun. Foods that provide antioxidants include vitamin C- and E-rich foods, selenium, flavonoids, and polyphenols. At the same time, proinflammatory compounds seem to help offset some of the dangers of the sun. Proinflammatory foods are mainly the fatty acids found in oils. Vitamin C-rich foods include citrus fruits, peppers, broccoli, dark leafy greens, tomatoes, and potatoes. Vitamin E-rich foods include vegetable oils, nuts, and seeds, and selenium is found in seafood, grains, and seeds. Flavonoids and polyphenols were discussed in Chapter 2, but they are both found in fruits and vegetables. A quick look at those food groups shows that they are components of the Mediterranean diet.

ALERT

Protecting your skin from the sun goes beyond choosing foods to keep it healthy. Make sure you talk with your physician about how much time in the sun is safe as well as ways to protect your skin from the sun, including wearing light layers and using sunscreen.

The Mediterranean Diet and Skin Health

Over the last ten years, a variety of studies have looked at skin cancer and diet. All have found that higher intakes of fruits, vegetables, legumes, olive oil, and tea provided protection against the damages of the sun. A recent study also found that consuming fish, especially fatty fish, on a weekly basis proved beneficial to skin health. While it may seem that the effect of the diet is only a positive within the Mediterranean region, a group of researchers did conduct a study on Americans who had the most serious form of skin cancer, melanoma, and found that those who consumed the most fruits and vegetables were at a lower risk from the disease. These studies all give support to the benefit of the Mediterranean diet in keeping skin healthy. Some claims exist related to the Mediterranean diet and acne, dryness, and overall skin health but thus far there is not significant scientific evidence to indicate the diet plays a role in prevention of acne or dry skin or that it improves overall smoothness or health of the skin.

Prevent Cancer

According to the American Cancer Society, the lifetime risk of developing cancer in the United States is 1 in 2 for men and 1 in 3 for women. Cancer is the second most common cause of death in the United States, with more than 1,500 people expected to die from it each day this year. While the causes of cancer are multifaceted, including both external causes such as tobacco and internal factors like heredity, making changes in lifestyle behaviors can help prevent several types of cancer. The American Cancer Society says that about one-third of the cancer deaths expected to occur in 2010 will be related to being overweight or obese, physical inactivity, and poor nutrition—behaviors which can be changed if people want to improve their odds at longevity. Recent studies have shown that switching to a Mediterranean-type diet can help with weight loss and help prevent several types of cancer. One very large study, published in the journal *Nutrition Reviews*, looked at almost 40,000 subjects over the course of twenty years. The review involved a variety of cancers and looked at the consumption of specific foods along with a few specific nutrients. The study looked at the intake of fruits and vegetables, red meat, fatty fish, grains, and fats. The following outcomes were noted.

▼ TABLE 6-1: DIET AND CANCER PREVENTION

Food	Impact on Cancer
Vegetables	Reduced risk for epithelial cancer
Fruits	Reduced risk for stomach, urinary tract, and upper GI cancers
Red meat	Increased risk at highest intake levels
Fish	Decreased risk of gallbladder, larynx, breast, and ovarian cancers
Whole grains	Decreased risk for colorectal and stomach cancers
Refined grains	Increased risk for stomach, breast, colorectal, thyroid cancers
Olive oil	Decreased risk of breast and colorectal cancers

From *Nutrition Reviews* Vol. 67 (Suppl. 1)

The same study also found that the higher the consumption of flavonoids found in fruits and vegetables the lower the risk of breast cancer. Similarly, they looked at antioxidant compounds in fruits and vegetables and found that those with higher levels of carotenoids, selenium, and vitamin E helped reduce the risk of breast cancer. Carotenoids, found in carrots, along with vitamin C reduced the risk of cancers of the upper gastrointestinal tract. The study also noted that tomato intake is associated with a lower risk of prostate cancer; the connection is likely the phytonutrient lycopene. Finally, this study noted that several nutrients combined together seem to reduce the risk of colorectal cancer. The study found that those who consumed higher amounts of calcium, vitamin D, vitamin E, and the carotenoids had a lower risk compared to those who consumed below-recommended intakes.

Connection with Diet

A review of the outcomes of this large study and of several other smaller studies shows that a diet rich in fruits, vegetables, whole grains, and olive oil can reduce the risk of developing several types of cancer. The mechanism that results in this effect isn't totally clear, and it may be a function of all of these foods together rather than one single cause; thus, the concept of the whole diet is important. Focusing on the key aspects of the Mediterranean diet shows how it can be a good choice for reducing your risk. The Mediterranean diet emphasizes the importance of plant foods and encourages the use of olive oil and fatty fish. Evidence from the recently updated 2010 Dietary Guidelines for Americans supports the positive health benefits of the Mediterranean diet.

Impact on Diabetes

Approximately 24 million Americans have diabetes, and this number is projected to double within the next fifteen years. Ninety percent of those with diabetes have type II diabetes, which can be avoided with proper lifestyle behaviors and managed through diet and activity. Scientific evidence shows that adherence to a Mediterranean-type diet is one good way to reduce the risk of developing type II diabetes. Studies over the last several years have looked at the impact of diet on the disease as well as management of the disease. One study set out to compare a lower carbohydrate Mediterranean diet with a low-fat diet to assess control of blood sugars, changes in weight and blood cholesterol, and management of blood pressure. The study looked at almost 300 people who were recently diagnosed with type II diabetes. While the diet was called a low-carbohydrate diet, one-half of the calories still came from carbohydrates. The diet provided a higher level of fat, much like the Mediterranean diet, and the main source of fat was olive oil. The study lasted for four years, and during this time people who lost weight the first year were able to maintain the loss throughout the study. The outcome of the study was improved control of blood sugars beyond the control achieved by the weight loss. The researchers found the Mediterranean-type diet improved the action of insulin and this was a function of less inflammation in the body. The reduced inflammation may have been a result of weight loss, increased intake of fruits and vegetables, or a combination of factors. The important outcome of the study was that after a four-year period of time people were able to maintain their weight and the changes in their lifestyle.

What is the difference between type I and type II diabetes?
Type I diabetes occurs when the body can no longer make insulin, which releases blood sugar into cells of the body. Type I is more common in children and young adults. Type II diabetes is the most common, and it occurs when the body can't make enough insulin. Being overweight and inactivity are key causes of type II diabetes.

Metabolic Syndrome

Metabolic syndrome is a name for a group of risk factors that exist together and increase the risk for heart disease and diabetes. The main risk factors associated with the syndrome are excess body weight around the midsection of the body and insulin resistance. Factors that lead to diagnosis are a combination of any three of these risks:

- Elevated blood pressure
- Elevated blood sugar
- HDL level below 40 mg/dl in men and 50 mg/dl in women
- Triglyceride above 150 mg/dl
- Waist circumference over 40" in men and 35" in women

The components of metabolic syndrome are best managed by making changes in diet and getting physical activity.

FACT

A normal blood sugar level is between 80 mg/dl and 120 mg/dl when you haven't had anything to eat for more than eight hours (fasting). Learn your blood sugar levels by visiting your physician. While you are there, ask about the other risk factors for metabolic syndrome.

The Mediterranean diet has been studied extensively to determine if it can reduce the effects of the syndrome and in fact prevent it. Several large studies have looked at the Mediterranean diet in a variety of populations and the overall outcome is that the diet is associated with a lower risk for developing metabolic syndrome. One large-scale study, done in Greece, found that one-third of the coronary events that led to hospitalization could have been prevented if the subjects had followed the traditional Mediterranean diet.

Reverse Aging Effects

Aging is often viewed as a natural part of life, but new research indicates that aging really is a result of damage to cells and tissue that over time leads to the death of cells, changes in organ functioning, and ultimately death. While this process of cell change is a normal part of life, the rate at which cells change is determined by genetics, environment, and lifestyle. Genetics, at this time, are factors that can't be modified or changed, but environment and lifestyle can both be changed to impact the aging process. The one environmental factor that can impact how cells change—and one that is easily modified—is diet. Changes in cells and tissues that lead to aging are typically a result of oxidation.

The oxidative process impacts cell membranes more than it affects other parts of cells, due to the high concentration of fatty acids in cell membranes. Once a cell membrane is damaged, it exposes the cell to more insult and harm. Given that cell membranes are high in fatty acids, one way to modify or change the oxidative process, and possibly the aging process, is to consume more healthy fats. Studies have looked at the intake of olive oil as a means of maintaining the health of cell membranes. Olive oil is high in monounsaturated fatty acids and especially oleic acid. Oleic acid interacts with the fatty acids in cell membranes better than other fatty acids, so it can help re-establish the membrane. Olive oil is, of course, the oil of choice in the Mediterranean diet, so it is a potential link to a slower aging process in many Mediterranean countries.

FACT

Oxidation is a chemical process that causes a change in cells, resulting in free radicals. Free radicals are compounds that then enter cells and can cause damage to the cells. Free radicals as a result of oxidation are the triggers for aging and damage to cells and tissues.

A study in adults ages seventy to ninety found that a Mediterranean diet and the traditional, healthy lifestyle is associated with a more than 50 percent lower risk of all causes of mortality. The mechanism for this lower risk is not clear, but outcomes of the study clearly showed an advantage to those who adhered to the Mediterranean eating pattern. One of the largest and most-often referenced studies on the effect of the Mediterranean diet and longevity is the EPIC study.

QUESTION

What are monounsaturated fats?
Monounsaturated fats are types of fat that, along with polyunsaturated fats, can help lower blood cholesterol when used in place of saturated fats. Monounsaturated fats are found in oils, nuts, seeds, and fatty fish.

The European Prospective Investigation into Cancer and Nutrition study followed people aged sixty and older for an average of six years. The study found that a healthy man of sixty years who adheres to a Mediterranean diet can expect to live one year longer than a man of the same age who does not follow this diet. The same study found that those who maintained a consistently high intake of fruits and vegetables had a reduction in mortality.

Another study, conducted by the AARP in the mid 1990s, followed a group of more than 500,000 people for ten years. Outcomes of the study showed that those who most closely followed a diet like the Mediterranean diet were 20 percent less likely to die from heart disease, cancer, or any other cause than those who did not follow the diet.

Nervous System Disorders

Oxidation is known to not only change the membranes of cells in the body but change the functioning of neurons or cells in the brain as well. Researchers have shown that an increased intake of plant foods can provide protection to the brain neurons. Several studies have looked at the role of the Mediterranean diet in preventing diseases of the brain and central nervous system including dementia, Alzheimer's, and Parkinson's disease. Studies have shown the link between the Mediterranean diet and lower risk of Alzheimer's, but outcomes for Parkinson's are less conclusive.

ALERT

Many factors, including the role of heredity, contribute to the development of diseases of the central nervous system. Studies may show a benefit to reducing the risk for these diseases, but a change in diet is not a guarantee of prevention.

The large EPIC study looked at the Mediterranean diet and cognition as well as longevity, and it found that following the diet, especially consumption of olive oil, improved cognitive function. A recent study in the *Journal of the American Medical Association* looked at the Mediterranean diet, physical activity, and risk of Alzheimer's. The study followed close to 2,000 older adults in New York for about a year and a half. The study found that those who more closely followed a Mediterranean diet had a lower risk of developing Alzheimer's. The study also found that physical activity reduced the risk as well, making the two factors independent variables in reducing risk for Alzheimer's.

Studies related to Parkinson's disease have not yielded such conclusive evidence. Some large studies have shown a connection with the Mediterranean diet and reduced risk but others have not, making more research an important step. The Mediterranean diet has also been studied in cases of depression, and while a connection was observed between specific nutrients in the Mediterranean diet, no overall connection to the diet has been observed. This lack of connection is a good reminder that the Mediterranean diet is not a magic solution to improved health; it is a part of a healthier lifestyle that can help reduce risk of several diseases and may enhance overall health.

CHAPTER 7

Meal Planning

Healthy eating is easy if you know what you want to achieve, have a plan for your meals, and have the right foods on hand. As you get ready to adopt a Mediterranean diet, take time to figure out what foods you need to have on hand to prepare healthy meals that sound good to you.

Grocery Shopping

Grocery shopping today is nothing like it was in Greece or Crete of old. Today, supermarket shelves are filled with a variety of foods and a multitude of brands of each food. Working your way through the supermarket can be overwhelming unless you know how to navigate the aisles. First thing to do is make sure the store is clean. Look at the floors, the shelves, and all of the display cases.

Next, make sure that products look fresh. Produce should be crisp and fresh, meat should be bright red in color and carry use-by dates that are reasonably far away, dairy foods should be dated for maximum usage, and the dairy cases should be cold. In the freezer section, make sure foods are frozen solidly and that there aren't any ice crystals on the exterior of the packages. Ice crystals can mean that packages have been exposed to warmer temperatures, which can compromise the quality of the food.

In addition to checking the cleanliness of the store and quality of the products, make sure workers who are stocking fresh produce, meat, and dairy are wearing gloves to protect the food from any food-borne bacteria.

FACT

When food is not handled properly, food-borne bacteria can result, leading to food-borne illnesses or food poisoning. Food-borne illnesses can result in chills, stomach cramps, dehydration, and in severe cases, death. Keeping cold foods below 40°F and hot foods above 140°F can help keep food safe.

Preparing to Shop

Before heading to the store, determine what you want to purchase. The Mediterranean diet pyramid outlines which foods need to make up your meal plan, but portions determine how much you need to buy.

▼ **TABLE 7-1: MEDITERRANEAN PORTION GUIDE**

Food Group	2,000 Calories per Day for Average Adult	Examples
Grains, preferably whole grains	6 ounces	2 slices of bread, 1 cup of pasta, 1 cup oatmeal
Vegetables	2½ cups	1½ cups cooked vegetables, 1 med. sweet potato
Fruits	2 cups	1 apple, 1 orange
Beans, nuts, seeds	3½ ounces	1 cup beans, 1 ounce nuts, 1 tablespoon sesame seeds (per week)
Olive oil	6 teaspoons	Olive oil in cooking and at the table
Dairy	3 cups	1 cup milk, 1 cup yogurt, 2 ounces low-fat cheese
Fish	3.5 ounces	At least twice a week
Poultry	3 ounces	A small chicken breast
Red meats	2 ounces	Limit red meats to once a week

Active adults and adolescents will need more calories while young children will need less. The portion table provides a good guideline to determine what you will need to purchase, but every family is different, so plan your meals based on the energy and eating needs of your family. After determining what you need, take a look at what you have on hand and then develop your shopping list to fill in the gaps. With your list in hand, head to the store and start the process of choosing the foods you and your family will enjoy.

Reading the Food Label

Once you have your list in hand you know what you want to purchase, but deciding which brand to buy involves picking up and inspecting produce; checking meat, fish, poultry, and dairy for freshness; reading food labels; and checking prices. Packaged foods must contain a label that not only tells you what you are buying, but provides the list of ingredients, where the product was produced, and the nutrition-facts panel. The nutrition-facts panel is the best place to look to determine if the product provides the right nutritional value. While the ingredient list provides a good glimpse of what is in the food, from major ingredients down to the smallest ingredient, the nutrition-facts panel tells you about the calories, protein, carbohydrates, fat, sodium, fiber, and several vitamins and minerals. The nutrition-facts panel is the best tool for comparing brands.

ESSENTIAL

The nutrition-facts panel lists nutrition information for a specified serving size. The serving size is listed on the label along with the number of servings in the product. Check this information before comparing different brands so you are truly comparing based on the same serving size.

Knowing how to read a nutrition-facts panel is important when purchasing packaged foods, but meat, poultry, and produce don't usually have a nutrition-facts panel, so judging them is a bit different.

Judging Produce

In the produce department, look for produce that is fresh, colorful, and at its best quality. For the best nutrition and overall health benefits, look for darkly colored and strongly flavored fruits and vegetables. The dark color and strong flavor of things like broccoli, apricots, cantaloupe, and spinach indicate the presence of more phytonutrients, great health-promoting benefits. A few tips for choosing the best produce include:

▼ **TABLE 7-2: PICKING THE BEST PRODUCE**

Fruit or Vegetable	Characteristics
Apricots	Plump and golden orange
Beets	Smooth skinned with fresh, dark-green leaves
Broccoli	Tightly closed, dark-green florets
Cabbage	Firm heads that are deep green and somewhat heavy
Cherries	Plump and bright-red color
Cucumbers	Firm and dark-green color
Greens	Fresh, tender leaves
Peaches	Creamy or yellow background color, slightly soft
Peppers	Bright, shiny, and firm
Sweet potatoes	Firm with bright skin

Avoid buying produce with cuts or bruises, since food-borne bacteria can enter these areas, making the produce a potential risk for food-borne illnesses.

Choosing Fresh Fish

Making your menus more Mediterranean means learning how to cook using more fish and beans. All fish fit into the Mediterranean eating plan, even though fatty fish are more common in the Mediterranean region. If you've avoided cooking fish, some simple steps can help:

- Choose cod, flounder, or other white fish for baking or poaching.
- Grill fatty fish like salmon, tuna, or trout.
- Look for fish that is shiny with bright eyes and doesn't smell fishy.
- Make sure frozen fish is free of ice crystals and is firm.
- Check for sell-by dates.

Deciding on Dairy

When shopping for dairy foods, the most important thing is to choose products with the longest use-by date so the product stays safe and fresh until you use it. In addition to choosing the freshest dairy, build your meals around low-fat or fat-free dairy foods. Low-fat or fat-free milk or yogurt is easy to find and both work well in place of full-fat products. Lower-fat cheeses have some limitations due to the absence of fat; low-fat cheeses can lack some of the taste and versatility of full-fat cheeses, but some, like part-skim mozzarella, offer good options. If you do use full-fat cheeses, limit the portions and use them mainly to accent dishes, not as the center of the meal.

Stocking Your Pantry

Building a menu around plant foods means choosing lots of fresh fruits, vegetables, and unprocessed beans and grains, but for practical reasons canned or packaged choices are sometimes needed. Whole-grain cereals, pasta, rice, and other grains are often good to keep in the pantry for those times when you need a fast meal. Choosing wheat berries, brown rice, whole-wheat pasta, and oatmeal are a few ideas to provide variety and ease for your meal plans.

QUESTION

How much whole grain should be consumed each day?
The 2005 Dietary Guidelines for Americans recommends that healthy adults consume a minimum of three servings of whole grains each day, with a goal of one-half of the daily intake of grains coming from whole grains.

Another item to purchase for your pantry is canned fish. Canned tuna or salmon provides good sources of the healthy omega-3 fatty acids in an easy way. Canned fish can be enjoyed with vegetables in a salad, on top of whole grains for a sandwich, or as an entrée with pasta, rice, or other whole grains. When preparing dishes with canned fish, limit the salt you add to the dish, since the canned fish will contain more salt than fresh fish.

ALERT

The oil used to pack canned tuna, salmon, and many other fish is generally vegetable oil, not the oil from the fish. This oil can add extra calories, so consider buying fish canned in water. The oil is a source of healthy unsaturated fats, but since it is often drained, it is better to buy the water pack and get oil from other sources.

When purchasing canned fruits, look for those canned in their own juice to limit the intake of added sugars and the calories found in those sugars.

Canned vegetables tend to be a bit lower in fiber and are generally higher in sodium, so limit their usage to rare or occasional times only. Draining canned vegetables will help reduce the sodium content, but avoid washing the vegetables since the water will draw out many of the water-soluble vitamins.

Planning Weeknight Meals

Menu planning can often sound like an overwhelming task. The idea of planning many menus in advance doesn't have to be difficult, and if done correctly can actually save time. Meal planning is a good way to save time and use leftovers. Start your meal planning by assessing the family schedule and deciding which nights will need to be "fast" meals and which will allow time for cooking.

Soups, stews, and casseroles are good choices for fast-meal nights. Soups and stews can be prepared in a slow cooker so they are ready when you get home or they can be prepared in large portions on one day and then enjoyed again on another day or even more than one other day. Soups and stews are also easy ways to cook beans and to work in more vegetables. If you are using dried beans, remember they need time to soak overnight; if you use the quick method they need about an hour or two to cook and sit before adding other ingredients. If you are preparing a soup with lots of water, you may find that dried beans will cook to tender in the slow cooker, but it will take more time. You might even try the Italian ribollita by combining greens, beans, tomatoes, bread, and other seasonal vegetables.

Casseroles can often be prepared ahead of time and serve as the meal for several nights. Vegetable lasagna, pasta with beans and veggies, and beans, vegetables, and rice are a few examples of casseroles that can be prepared in large portions. Round out these fast meals with a salad, cooked vegetable, or if the meal includes vegetables, slice up some fruit for a fruit salad. Whole grain bread can add some texture as well.

For nights that offer plenty of time to cook, stay with the plant-foods theme by preparing whole-grain pasta, brown rice, quinoa, or other grain to which you add sautéed vegetables. For the entrée, choose fish more often, followed by poultry, and then rarely by red meat. Bake white fish in olive oil and season with herbs and vegetables. Thin white fish will cook very quickly, so in eight to ten minutes your entrée will be ready. Chicken often takes longer to cook, but it also allows for combining with vegetables and even pasta or rice, so even a longer cooked meal can be easy. Side dishes for any of these meals are good opportunities to boost plant-food intake:

- Quinoa and sautéed squash
- Brown rice with mixed herbs and olive oil

- Sautéed eggplant combined with bulgur
- A cucumber, tomato, parsley, and yogurt salad

If your family doesn't feel a meal has ended until they've had dessert, make the shift to healthier desserts by switching first from high-fat cakes and pies to angel food cake, fruit crisp, or cupcake-size portions of these favorite desserts. As the family becomes more comfortable with different desserts, slowly move to fruit with yogurt, fruit with a drizzle of honey, or sorbets or gelatos. Another way to keep desserts on the menu is to serve them less often, so talk with your family about what would make their meals enjoyable.

Feeding Picky Kids

Most parents know the challenge of getting one or more of their children to eat broccoli, spinach, peaches, or any of a number of foods that kids decide they don't like. Picky eaters not only challenge parents' resolve, they trigger concerns about adequate nutrition and just how hard a parent should push kids to eat. As kids grow, they develop likes and dislikes, which are often different than what their parents might experience. Just because parents enjoy a food doesn't mean their child will automatically like that food. Picky eaters are developing their own personal palate, which is a natural part of growth and development, and parents can deal with the process more comfortably if they remember the following:

- Relax! Avoiding a food or meal won't lead to starvation.
- Don't prepare foods just for your picky eater.
- Offer small portions of a variety of foods.
- Encourage trying some of each food, but don't force it.
- Avoid serving very hot or cold foods; warm foods work best.
- Skip the meal schedule.
- Avoid fighting over food.

One of the biggest temptations for parents is to force their children to try a food or to clean their plate, but these actions can start bad eating habits. Let your child be the guide in determining how much they want to eat so they learn to recognize feelings of fullness and when to stop eating. Starting with smaller portions, about a tablespoon of each food served for each year of your child's age, avoids overwhelming your child and allows them to ask for more if they are still hungry.

A Good Eating Role Model

While all children will develop their own likes and dislikes, one way parents can help their children develop a variety of food likes is to model good eating behaviors. If you aren't a good vegetable eater or if you skip dairy, don't be surprised if your kids follow your lead. If there are foods you don't like, that is okay, but avoid turning up your nose when the food is served and at least try a small amount. Demonstrating these positive behaviors can help children develop good eating habits, no matter which foods they may never end up liking.

QUESTION

How often should a two- or three-year-old eat?
Young children have smaller stomachs, so they can only eat small amounts at each meal, making three meals a day impossible for them to meet their nutritional needs. Plan to feed young children every three to four hours to make it easier for them to meet their nutritional needs.

Picky eaters can often be encouraged to eat more when they feel more comfortable with their food. Involving children in meal preparation is a good way to encourage them to try new foods. Having children help with mixing, stirring, and as they get older, cutting and serving, are a few ways to expose them to new foods in a comfortable way.

Planning Holiday Meals

Holiday meals are often built on family traditions, with many foods served every year. If you're like many families, some or many of these recipes are high in fat and possibly even low in fruits, vegetables, and whole grains.

Trying to shift traditional holiday meals to healthier meals needs to be viewed as a process. First, you must make adjustments slowly so that you don't change what the family views as the holiday meal. Next, you need to review which recipes would be easiest to change; for example, switch from cream to evaporated skim milk in a sauce or for a cream pie. Finally, you need to consider smaller serving sizes for things that just can't be changed.

FACT

Vegetable oils can be used in pastries in place of solid fats, but they don't bring in as much air as solid fats, so the texture of the crust will be crisper rather than flaky. While the texture might be different, the use of oil helps lower the saturated fat.

If your holiday meals contain more cream sauces and gravies than fruits and vegetables, this might be the first place to make some changes. If your Thanksgiving stuffing is mainly bread, meat, and meat drippings, consider switching to whole-wheat bread, adding sautéed carrots, celery, onions, and mushrooms in place of the meat, and using fat-free chicken broth for the drippings.

Planning a Fourth of July picnic around potato salad, hot dogs, and baked beans can be converted to a healthier option by leaving the skins on your potatoes, using one-half light mayonnaise and one-half low-fat, plain yogurt for the dressing, and adding chopped vegetables. If the hot dogs are key to the celebration, you can either switch to low-fat or turkey dogs or leave them in the meal and shift other higher-fat options. The baked beans could actually be a main dish, but prepare them without added meat, limit any sugar or honey, and boost flavor with grilled pineapple or apples.

Involve the Family

Just as involving young children gets them to feel more comfortable with new foods, getting the family involved in holiday meal preparation is a good way to shift traditions to healthier options. Sharing traditional recipes and having family members work to make them healthier can add some fun to the mix as well. In addition to having family members prepare items, they can bring the recipes for sharing with the rest of the family.

CHAPTER 8

Appetizers

Scorthalia
90

Feta and Roasted Red
Pepper Piquante
91

Feta Fritters
92

Cheese Saganaki
93

Gigantes Tiganiti (Pan-Fried Giant Beans)
94

Kalamarakia (Pan-Fried Calamari Rings)
95

Village-Style Zucchini Fritters
96

Baked Feta Cheese
97

Sfougato (Aegean Omelette)
98

Tomato Fritters
99

Dolmades (Stuffed Grape Leaves)
100

Garlic Feta Spread
101

Scorthalia

This dip is a cousin to the famous garlic yogurt dip known as tzatziki and is an excellent accompaniment for vegetable and fish dishes.

INGREDIENTS | SERVES 4–6

6–7 garlic cloves, peeled and finely shredded

3 large potatoes, peeled

⅓ cup Greek extra-virgin olive oil

⅓ cup vinegar

1 tablespoon dried Greek oregano

Salt and pepper to taste

1. Fill a medium-sized saucepan with water and dash of salt. Bring to boil.

2. Cut peeled potatoes into eighths and add to boiling water. Boil potatoes until soft; drain and put in medium- to large-sized mixing bowl.

3. Using a potato masher or large fork, thoroughly mash potatoes. Add garlic, olive oil, vinegar, oregano, salt, and pepper; resume mashing and stirring to incorporate all ingredients.

4. Ensure there are no lumps of potato remaining. When uniform and creamy, set aside to cool. Serve at room temperature.

PER SERVING Calories: 171 | Fat: 12g | Sodium: 4mg | Carbohydrates: 15g | Fiber: 1.5g | Protein: 1.5g

Feta and Roasted Red Pepper Piquante

This dip should be refrigerated until needed, and is best served with some warm pita bread.

INGREDIENTS | SERVES 4–6

½ pound Greek feta cheese

1–1½ tablespoons dried chili pepper flakes

2 roasted red peppers

4 tablespoons extra-virgin olive oil

1 teaspoon fresh-ground black pepper

Love of Olive Oil

The most characteristic aspect of the Mediterranean diet is the ubiquitous presence of the olive and its juice in the foods that comprise the traditional cuisines that evolved under its influence.

1. Crumble feta into a food processor or blender.

2. Add chili pepper flakes to processor. (This dip ought to be spicy but not red hot, so adjust the amount of chili pepper flakes accordingly.)

3. Remove seeds and skins from roasted red peppers; add to processor.

4. Add olive oil and 1 or 2 pinches of pepper to processor.

5. Purée until smooth throughout.

PER SERVING Calories: 186 | Fat: 17g | Sodium: 427mg | Carbohydrates: 3g | Fiber: 0g | Protein: 6g

Feta Fritters

Sprinkle these fritters with lemon juice and use some chopped fresh mint as a garnish when serving.

1. Peel potatoes and cut into quarters; boil in salted water until soft (approximately 20 minutes). In large mixing bowl, mash potatoes thoroughly. Add 1 tablespoon olive oil, onions, dill, mint, oregano, fresh-ground pepper, and bread crumbs; mix well.

2. Let mixture stand 5 minutes to cool slightly. Add feta and eggs; mix until everything is well incorporated. Put bowl in freezer 20 minutes to chill mixture.

3. Remove from freezer; spoon out small portions and roll with fingers into balls (about the size of ping pong balls). Place balls on a flat baking pan covered with wax paper; slightly flatten each ball into a little cake with fingers.

4. Roll each fritter in flour to cover completely and arrange on pan; place pan in freezer for another 5 minutes to firm before frying.

5. Heat a couple tablespoons of olive oil in a large frying pan; start frying fritters in batches over medium-high heat about 1 minute per side, until golden brown. Use a small spatula or fork to turn in pan. Sprinkle generously with lemon juice and serve immediately.

PER SERVING Calories: 429 | Fat: 26g | Sodium: 372mg | Carbohydrates: 41g | Fiber: 4g | Protein: 10g

Cheese Saganaki

This classic cheese flambé is seen at Greek restaurants. The flaming of the cheese, which does not alter the flavor in any way, is not recommended for home cooks for safety reasons.

INGREDIENTS | SERVES 4

¼ pound Greek Kefalotyri cheese (or Italian Pecorino)
2 tablespoons all-purpose flour
2 tablespoons extra-virgin olive oil
1 lemon

Appetizer Culture?

Whether it's *tapas* at one end of the Mediterranean, or *mezes* at the other, there is no mistaking the popularity of numerous small dishes as an entrée among the nations that live in and along the shores of "Earth's Middle Sea."

1. Slice cheese into ½" thick slices.

2. Put flour in a clear plastic bag. Wet cheese slice under running tap, shake off excess water, and drop into bag. Twist bag shut; shake to coat thoroughly with flour.

3. Heat olive oil in shallow pan on medium-high heat. When oil is hot, place cheese in pan; cook until cheese starts to melt along bottom edge.

4. Carefully turn slice over; cook to melting point again. Remove when golden, repeat with remaining cheese, sprinkle with lemon juice, and serve immediately.

PER SERVING Calories: 163 | Fat: 14g | Sodium: 239mg | Carbohydrates: 4g | Fiber: 0.5g | Protein:6 g

Gigantes Tiganiti (Pan-Fried Giant Beans)

You should be able to find the Greek gigantes beans at any well-stocked European market. If not, giant butter beans will do as a substitute.

INGREDIENTS | SERVES 4

1 cup dried gigantes (Greek elephant beans)

Pinch of salt

¼ cup milk

1 egg, beaten

½ cup all-purpose flour

Salt and pepper to taste

1 cup vegetable oil

½ cup bread crumbs

Lemon juice to garnish

Is That a Legume in Your Pocket?

The large-scale consumption of legumes and pulses has been an integral part of the Mediterranean diet since time immemorial.

1. Soak beans in water overnight to rehydrate them. Drain and rinse beans well.

2. Add to pan with enough cold water to cover beans by 1" or so. Add pinch of salt to water; bring to a boil then simmer 10 minutes.

3. Drain beans, rinse with cold water, and return to pan. Add fresh cold water to pan along with some salt; once more bring to a boil. Lower heat to medium-low; simmer 25–30 minutes, until beans are tender. Remove from heat, drain water, and set aside.

4. Beat milk and egg well in small bowl. Sift flour into another small bowl; add salt and pepper.

5. Heat oil in small pan. Dredge beans in flour in small batches, dip in egg mixture, then cover with bread crumbs. Fry in small batches and be ready to turn them over quickly to cook both sides evenly. Watch carefully as they don't require very long and you don't want them to burn. Remove from oil when a uniform golden brown outer color is achieved, approximately 5 minutes or so. Sprinkle with lemon juice and serve warm.

PER SERVING Calories: 711 | Fat: 59g | Sodium: 270mg | Carbohydrates: 36g | Fiber: 4g | Protein: 10g

Kalamarakia (Pan-Fried Calamari Rings)

*Make sure not to overcook the calamari rings; they will become
rubbery if you leave them in the oil too long.*

INGREDIENTS | **SERVES 4**

4 large frozen squid tubes
3 heaping tablespoons all-purpose flour
1 heaping tablespoon corn flour
Vegetable oil for frying
Juice of 1 lemon

1. Defrost and wash squid tubes; slice into ring segments approximately ¼" in width.

2. Put flour and corn flour in clear plastic bag; shake to mix thoroughly. Add squid; shake in flour to ensure a complete coating.

3. Heat oil in frying pan over medium heat. Make sure to use enough oil to completely immerse rings for frying.

4. Loop some floured ring segments over the handle of a wooden spoon, until you have a good batch for frying; add rings to oil one by one in a clockwise fashion until pan is full. Keep an eye on the time—at the 2½ minute mark, start removing rings in clockwise order from your starting point in the pan.

5. Place cooked rings on plate lined with paper towels to drain until all squid has been cooked. Serve immediately. Be sure to sprinkle the fried calamari liberally with fresh-squeezed lemon juice and serve it with either scorthalia or tzatziki.

PER SERVING Calories: 120 | Fat: 8g | Sodium: 14mg | Carbohydrates: 7g | Fiber: 0.5g | Protein: 6g

Village-Style Zucchini Fritters

You do not need to peel the zucchini, but you must peel the potato for use in this recipe.

INGREDIENTS | YIELDS 12–14 PIECES

1 medium-sized zucchini

1 medium-sized potato

½ white onion

Olive oil for frying

2 eggs

2 tablespoons fresh mint leaves, finely chopped

1 tablespoon dried oregano

1 large fresh garlic clove, pressed or finely shredded

1 tablespoon Greek extra-virgin olive oil

½ cup dried bread crumbs

2 tablespoons all-purpose flour

Salt and pepper to taste

Pinch of baking soda or ½ teaspoon baking powder

1. Wash zucchini and potato; shred entirely into large mixing bowl using grater or shredder. Finely chop onion; add to bowl.

2. Heat frying oil in large pan—depth of oil should be no more than ½"—and set burner to medium heat. Allow 3–4 minutes for oil to heat thoroughly.

3. Beat eggs well; add to mixing bowl along with mint, oregano, garlic, 1 tablespoon extra-virgin olive oil, bread crumbs, flour, salt and pepper, and baking powder or soda. Mix well, until thick batter-like consistency is achieved. Zucchini will begin to seep water immediately upon shredding—work quickly so mixture does not become watery. If it is thin, add more bread crumbs or flour to thicken slightly. Note: If using baking soda, make sure to only use a slight pinch so fritters won't be bitter.

4. Using large spoon, add portions of mixture to hot oil in small clumps, making sure to form them as small pancakes. It is easier to make this dish with a large frying pan so you can control the shape of the clumps.

5. Cook about 3–4 minutes on one side; carefully turn with small spatula or large fork and cook on other side and cook for another 3–4 minutes.

6. Remove from pan when golden brown; set aside on plate/tray lined with paper towels or napkins to drain.

PER SERVING Calories: 62 | Fat: 2g | Sodium: 53mg | Carbohydrates: 9g | Fiber: 1g | Protein: 2g

Baked Feta Cheese

For a spicy variation, you can add a teaspoon of chili pepper flakes to this recipe.

INGREDIENTS | SERVES 4

2 tablespoons extra-virgin olive oil

1 medium-sized onion, sliced

1 large green pepper, seeded and chopped

1 large red pepper, seeded and chopped

½ pound Greek feta cheese (1 thick slice)

1 teaspoon dried oregano

Fresh-ground pepper

1. In frying pan, heat oil; sauté onion and peppers until soft.

2. Place feta in small clay baking vessel; add onion and peppers. Sprinkle oregano and pepper over top. Cover with foil or lid and place in preheated oven at 350°F; bake 15 minutes. Serve hot with fresh crusty bread or warm pita bread.

PER SERVING Calories: 235 | Fat: 19g | Sodium: 640mg | Carbohydrates: 8g | Fiber: 1g | Protein: 9g

Sfougato (Aegean Omelette)

For Greeks, eggs are not limited to a breakfast food; they often make an appearance at the lunch or dinner table as an appetizer or main course.

INGREDIENTS | SERVES 4

1 cooking onion, finely diced
4 tablespoons all-purpose flour
¼ cup bread crumbs
2 tablespoons fresh mint, finely chopped
½ cup crumbled Greek feta cheese
Salt and pepper to taste
1 tablespoon dried thyme
6–8 eggs
2 tablespoons extra-virgin olive oil

1. In mixing bowl, add onion, flour, bread crumbs, mint, cheese, salt, pepper, and thyme; mix well.

2. In separate bowl, add eggs; beat well.

3. Add olive oil to large frying pan; heat to medium-high. When oil is hot, add eggs to cheese and bread crumb mixture; combine well then pour into pan.

4. Using wooden spoon, stir until thickened; cook one side 4–5 minutes. Flip it, turn down heat to medium, and cook for another 4–5 minutes, until done.

5. When omelette is cooked, turn off heat and place pan in oven preheated to 350°F for 5 minutes. Serve immediately.

PER SERVING Calories: 285 | Fat: 19g | Sodium: 353mg | Carbohydrates: 15g | Fiber: 1g | Protein: 13g

Tomato Fritters

Peel tomatoes by dropping them in boiling water until their skins start to shrivel. Then remove from water and carefully peel away the skins, as tomatoes will be hot.

INGREDIENTS | **YIELDS 24 PIECES**

8 whole, cooked tomatoes, peeled and diced

½ pound Greek feta cheese, crumbled

1 egg, beaten

¾ cup of all-purpose flour

2 onions, grated

¼ cup fresh mint, finely chopped

1 teaspoon dried oregano

¼ cup dry bread crumbs

Salt and pepper

1. Dice peeled tomatoes into cubes. Separate and remove as many seeds as possible; place in colander and set aside to drain 15 minutes.

2. In large mixing bowl, combine tomatoes, feta, egg, flour, onions, mint, oregano, bread crumbs, salt, and pepper; mix together thoroughly until smooth and fluffy. Refrigerate and chill mixture 1 hour.

3. Heat oil in saucepan; take spoonfuls of chilled mixture and carefully drop into oil. Turn using spatula until both sides are nicely browned, approximately 5–6 minutes; remove with slotted spoon and place on platter lined with paper towels to drain. Serve immediately on their own or with some tzatziki sauce.

PER SERVING Calories: 60 | Fat: 2g | Sodium: 120mg | Carbohydrates: 7g | Fiber: 1g | Protein: 3g

Dolmades (Stuffed Grape Leaves)

You can also add some black raisins to this recipe for a whole new dimension to the dish.

INGREDIENTS | YIELDS APPROXIMATELY 28 PIECES

30 medium-sized grape leaves
⅓ cup extra-virgin olive oil
2 onions, diced
1 cup white/Italian style/Arborio rice
¼ cup fresh parsley, chopped
¼ cup fresh mint, chopped
¼ cup fresh dill, chopped
¼ cup pine nuts
1 teaspoon dried oregano
Salt and pepper
½ cup water
Juice of 2 lemons

How Did They Spread?

The olive, vine, fig, date, and pomegranate are propagated only by cuttings and not by seeds. Their spread throughout the Mediterranean region was purely the result of agriculture.

1. Blanche grape leaves in boiling water until soft; remove from pot and set aside to drain.

2. In frying pan, add 2 tablespoons olive oil; sauté diced onions until soft. Add rice, parsley, mint, dill, pine nuts, oregano, salt, and pepper along with ½ cup water. Cook over medium heat until water is absorbed, about 8–10 minutes or so; remove from heat.

3. Place a grape leaf shiny-side down on flat surface. Put teaspoonful rice mixture in center; fold two sides of leaf inward. Roll up bottom edge to complete small package. Set aside on plate; use up filling using as many leaves as required.

4. Line bottom of deep pan with any remaining leaves; place dolmades closely packed in pan, layering as necessary. Place plate on top of dolmades to prevent them from opening/floating.

5. Add enough boiling water to cover pan contents completely. Pour in lemon juice and remaining olive oil, cover and cook over low heat 30 minutes. Drain any remaining water from pot; set aside to cool slightly before removing. Serve at room temperature and garnish with olive oil and lemon slices.

PER SERVING Calories: 29 | Fat: 2g | Sodium: 1mg | Carbohydrates: 3g | Fiber: 1g | Protein: 1g

Garlic Feta Spread

This dip is best refrigerated until needed and accompanied by some fresh crusty bread.

INGREDIENTS | SERVES 6–8

½ pound Greek feta cheese, crumbled

3 garlic cloves, pressed

2 tablespoons extra-virgin olive oil

2 tablespoons fresh parsley, finely chopped

1 teaspoon dried oregano

Fresh-ground pepper

1. Combine all ingredients; mash and mix well. Or put everything into food processor and blend at low speed until smooth.

2. Refrigerate before/after serving. Serve with warm pita bread.

PER SERVING Calories: 108 | Fat: 9g | Sodium: 320mg | Carbohydrates: 2g | Fiber: 0g | Protein: 4g

CHAPTER 9

Salads, Salad Dressings, and Sauces

Amaranth Salad
104

Cretan Dakos (Rusk Salad)
105

Grilled Eggplant Salad
106

Lahanosalata (Cabbage Salad)
107

Ladolemono (Olive Oil and Lemon Sauce)
108

Taramosalata/Tarama (Fish Roe Salad)
109

Village Greek Salad
110

Béchamel Sauce
111

Grilled Halloumi Salad
112

Melitzanosalata (Eggplant Dip)
113

Parsley Spread
114

Tzatziki (Yogurt-Garlic Sauce)
115

Santorini (Fava)
116

Grilled Banana Pepper Salad
117

Lemon Mustard Sauce
118

Dandelion Greens
119

Sliced Tomato Salad with Feta and Balsamic Vinaigrette
120

Amaranth Salad

This salad is best served alongside grilled fish. If amaranth leaves are not available, use Swiss chard or rocket greens.

INGREDIENTS | SERVES 4–6

Tender amaranth leaves and shoots (no stalks), a large bunch

Dried Greek oregano

Salt and pepper to taste

Greek extra-virgin olive oil

Wine vinegar

1. Add amaranth leaves and shoots to pot; boil 5–8 minutes, until leaves are a dark green color and shoots are noticeably tender. Remove from pot and place in colander; run under cold water and set aside to drain 15 minutes.

2. Serve with a sprinkling of dried Greek oregano and salt and pepper and drizzle with olive oil and wine vinegar. It is also good served with a dollop of scorthalia over the top.

PER SERVING Calories: 23 | Fat: 2g | Sodium: 3mg | Carbohydrates: 0.5g | Fiber: 0g | Protein: 0g

Cretan Dakos (Rusk Salad)

If you cannot find cretan barley rusks, use the largest barley rusks you can find.

INGREDIENTS | SERVES 4

4 cretan barley rusks
3 tomatoes, diced
¼ pound Greek feta cheese, crumbled
4 tablespoons extra-virgin olive oil
2 tablespoons fresh mint, finely chopped
1 tablespoon dried oregano
2 tablespoons wine vinegar
¼ cup red wine (optional)
4 kalamata olives
1 garlic clove, peeled and pressed

If It's Not Greek, It's Not Feta . . .

Greek feta cheese has a lower overall fat content and is more nutritionally beneficial than most other commercially available cheeses, including imitation cow's milk "feta" cheeses being produced and sold in North America and elsewhere.

1. Soak barley rusks slightly with water or splash or two of red wine; set aside for a couple minutes.

2. Drizzle rusks with olive oil. Let sit for another couple minutes until oil is absorbed; drizzle another tablespoon or so over top of each rusk.

3. Combine tomatoes with chopped mint, garlic, and vinegar. Top rusks with equal portion of mixture; add feta, pinch of oregano, and another touch of olive oil over top of each rusk. Finish by placing an olive on top of it all. Serve immediately.

PER SERVING Calories: 388 | Fat: 22g | Sodium: 372mg | Carbohydrates: 40g | Fiber: 9g | Protein: 11g

Grilled Eggplant Salad

This salad is best served cold and is even tastier the next day after the flavors of the eggplant and tomato mixture have a chance to coalesce. Do not add salt to the tomato mix until you are ready to serve.

INGREDIENTS | SERVES 4

1 large eggplant

2–3 tomatoes

Small bunch of parsley, finely chopped

2 garlic cloves, pressed or very finely diced

Salt and pepper to taste

1 tablespoon dried oregano

¼ cup extra-virgin olive oil

1. Slice eggplant into discs along length—not too thin and not too thick, about ¼" thickness is ideal. Fill large mixing bowl or pot with salted water, add 2 tablespoons of salt and mix well; place eggplant discs in salt bath and set plate over top to weigh them down. Soak 20–30 minutes. Mix periodically to ensure salty water soaks them completely.

2. Dice tomatoes; place in bowl. Add parsley, garlic, salt, pepper, oregano, and 2–3 tablespoons olive oil; mix well and set aside.

3. Light grill and set on high temperature. When grilling surface is ready, spray or wipe with vegetable oil.

4. Using your hands and working quickly over grill, brush (or spray) downward-facing side of each slice of eggplant with a little olive oil; place across grill, starting from top left rear section and filling entire surface in rows. Once all eggplant discs are on grill, give upward-facing sides brush (or spray) of olive oil. Grill until visibly softened around the edges and centers, approximately 6–8 minutes. Allow each side a few minutes to cook through and absorb oil, but watch them carefully.

5. Brush with olive oil again; turn over. Grill another few minutes; give final brushing of oil. Leave on grill another minute or so; remove onto platter or dish.

6. Arrange several eggplant discs on serving plate, top with chopped tomato mixture, sprinkle with oregano, and serve with crusty bread.

PER SERVING Calories: 166 | Fat: 14g | Sodium: 7.5mg | Carbohydrates: 11g | Fiber: 4g | Protein: 2g

Lahanosalata (Cabbage Salad)

If you do not have any yogurt on hand, you can use a couple tablespoons of mayonnaise as a substitute for the dressing in this recipe.

INGREDIENTS | **SERVES 4**

⅓ of a white cabbage

2 large carrots

½ cup Greek-style strained yogurt

¼ cup extra-virgin olive oil

2 tablespoons fresh lemon juice (or vinegar)

½ teaspoon dried oregano

1 tablespoon chopped fresh dill

Salt and pepper to taste

Long Before Caffeine . . .

Dill seeds were chewed by the ancient Greeks as a form of stimulant to wakefulness, as well as to freshen breath.

1. Wash cabbage well; peel carrots. Shred cabbage finely with sharp knife. Shred carrots into ribbons using mandolin or large holes on a grater; add to shredded cabbage.

2. Toss shredded cabbage and carrots well.

3. In food processor/blender, add yogurt, olive oil, lemon juice, oregano, dill, salt, and pepper; blend together until smooth and creamy.

4. Pour dressing over top of individual servings or mix well into entire salad before serving. Garnish with chopped dill and a kalamata olive or two.

PER SERVING Calories: 182 | Fat: 15g | Sodium: 71mg | Carbohydrates: 13g | Fiber: 3g | Protein: 2g

Ladolemono (Olive Oil and Lemon Sauce)

This is the classic Greek sauce used on grilled meats, vegetables, and fish.

INGREDIENTS | **YIELDS 1 CUP**

½ cup extra-virgin olive oil

½ cup fresh lemon juice

1 tablespoon dried oregano

1 teaspoon salt

1 teaspoon fresh-ground black pepper

Combine ingredients and mix well.

PER TABLESPOON Calories: 61 | Fat: 7g | Sodium: 146mg | Carbohydrates: 0.5g | Fiber: 0g | Protein: 0g

Antioxidants for Everyone

Lemon juice, which is an ingredient in almost every Greek dish, is not only a good source of Vitamin C, but it also packs a respectable dose of antioxidants. Sprinkle it liberally!

Taramosalata/Tarama (Fish Roe Salad)

The pink coloring of the carp roe in this recipe is a food dye. In Greece, taramosalata can often be beige in color, as undyed roe is often used.

INGREDIENTS | SERVES 6–8

½ loaf 2-day-old white bread
½ cup carp roe
1 large onion, grated
Juice of 2 lemons
2 cups extra-virgin olive oil

1. Remove outside crust and soak inner bread in water; squeeze well to drain and set aside.

2. Place fish roe in food processor/blender; mix a minute or so to break down eggs.

3. Add grated onion to processor; continue mixing.

4. Add moistened bread in stages to processor/blender; mix well.

5. Slowly add lemon juice and olive oil while constantly mixing. Note: When adding olive oil and lemon juice, add in slow and alternate fashion by first adding some lemon juice then some olive oil and so on, until both are incorporated into the tarama.

6. Refrigerate before serving to firm up the tarama. Garnish with cucumber, tomato slices, and/or olive(s); serve with warm pita bread.

PER SERVING Calories: 591 | Fat: 57g | Sodium: 125mg | Carbohydrates: 18g | Fiber: 1g | Protein: 5g

Village Greek Salad

Lettuce is rarely used in salads in Greece, as it requires a great deal of water to cultivate lettuce as a commercial crop.

INGREDIENTS | SERVES 4–6

3 medium-sized ripe tomatoes, cut into quarters or sixths

½ yellow onion, sliced

½ cucumber, peeled, halved, and sliced

Several pepperoncini (squeeze to drain brine before using)

Kalamata or wrinkled black olives (as desired)

½ cup crumbled Greek feta cheese

¼ cup Greek extra-virgin olive oil

2 tablespoons wine vinegar (optional)

1 teaspoon dried oregano

Fresh-ground black pepper

1. Wash and cut tomatoes, cucumbers, and onions; put into salad bowl.

2. Add several olives and pepperoncini to bowl.

3. Sprinkle feta over the top of vegetables; follow with fresh-ground pepper, oregano, and olive oil.

4. Mix everything together a couple turns, but don't overdo it; serve.

PER SERVING Calories: 101 | Fat: 9g | Sodium: 5mg | Carbohydrates: 5g | Fiber: 1g | Protein: 1g

We Are What We Eat?

It is becoming increasingly clearer that general human health and well-being is in no small part based on dietary choices.

Béchamel Sauce

*Make the béchamel only when you need it, as it quickly starts to congeal
once it is prepared and cannot be stored for later use.*

INGREDIENTS | SERVES 6–8

4 cups scalded milk
1 cup all-purpose flour
¾ cup grated Kefalotyri (or Parmesan)
½ cup salted butter
3 egg yolks, well beaten
½ teaspoon ground nutmeg
½ teaspoon fresh-ground black pepper

1. Melt butter in deep saucepan over medium heat.

2. Using a whisk or immersion blender with a whisk attachment, slowly incorporate flour by briskly whisking; add to melted butter in stages while stirring continually to avoid formation of lumps

3. Once flour is fully incorporated, slowly add hot milk while continuing to constantly stir butter and flour paste to ensure smooth consistency.

4. Remove saucepan from heat; add grated cheese, nutmeg, pepper, and egg yolks in that order while continuing to rapidly whisk mixture. Set aside when smooth and well mixed. However, do not let it stand for too long without a good stirring, as you do not want the top to start congealing.

5. Use as topping for baked dishes such as pastitsio or moussaka (see Chapter 12).

PER SERVING Calories: 328 | Fat: 23g | Sodium: 374mg |
Carbohydrates: 17g | Fiber: 0.5g | Protein: 11g

Grilled Halloumi Salad

Halloumi cheese is a specialty from the island of Cyprus. It is a firm cheese that holds its shape well when heated. It is usually served grilled or fried and adds a wonderful chewy texture to any salad.

INGREDIENTS | SERVES 4

10–12 kalamata olives, pitted and finely chopped or ground to a pulp

¼ cup extra-virgin olive oil

2 tablespoons balsamic vinegar

1 tablespoon dried oregano

1 medium carrot, shredded

¼ of a small green cabbage, shredded

1 large tomato

1 bunch fresh rocket greens (arugula), finely cut

1 head romaine lettuce, finely cut

2 stalks fresh green onion, finely sliced (green stalk included)

½ pound halloumi cheese, thick sliced

Changing Diets

A growing number of people who inhabit the Mediterranean basin are eschewing their traditional eating patterns for a less healthy but more convenient "Western" diet. As a result, health issues are on the rise exponentially.

1. Prepare dressing by pitting and grinding or finely chopping olives; combine pulp with olive oil, vinegar, and oregano. Mix well; set aside.

2. Wash all vegetables well. Peel carrot; use mandolin to finely shred cabbage and carrot into large salad bowl. Chop tomato into sections; add to bowl. Finely cut rocket and lettuce; add to bowl. Finely slice green onions; add to salad.

3. Fire up BBQ; grill halloumi until it noticeably starts to soften and grill marks appear. Make sure to flip cheese so both sides are scored with grill marks. When cheese is done, remove from heat and immediately cut into cubes; add to salad. Pour dressing over salad; mix well. Serve immediately.

PER SERVING Calories: 362 | Fat: 30g | Sodium: 613mg | Carbohydrates: 13g | Fiber: 2g | Protein: 13g

Melitzanosalata (Eggplant Dip)

Look for eggplants with a noticeable round indentation at their fat end, as they tend to have fewer seeds.

INGREDIENTS | SERVES 6

2 large, plump eggplants
1 medium-sized yellow onion, grated
3 cloves of garlic, pressed or minced
2 tablespoons fresh parsley, finely chopped
¼ cup extra-virgin olive oil
2 tablespoons wine vinegar
1 tablespoon mayonnaise
1 teaspoon dried oregano
Salt and pepper to taste

Gifts of the Gods?

According to ancient tradition, the olive was the gift of the goddess of wisdom, Athena; the chickpea was the gift of the god of the sea, Poseidon; and the grape was the gift of Dionysus, god of wine.

1. Remove stalk ends of eggplants; pierce holes with a fork all over bodies. Bake in preheated oven at 350°F until well browned and soft to the touch, approximately 45 minutes.

2. Remove eggplants from oven; cool until you can handle them, then peel away skin using a spoon and place pulp in mixing bowl.

3. Add grated onion and garlic to eggplant; mix together thoroughly with fork until smooth. Add parsley, olive oil, vinegar, mayonnaise, oregano, salt, and pepper; mix until thoroughly combined.

4. Refrigerate 30 minutes before serving with some warm pita bread.

PER SERVING Calories: 140 | Fat: 11g | Sodium: 19mg | Carbohydrates: 11g | Fiber: 5g | Protein: 2g

Parsley Spread

A refreshing dip for summertime parties. Best kept refrigerated when not used immediately.

INGREDIENTS | SERVES 4

2 bunches of fresh parsley
4 slices stale bread, no crusts
3 green onions, diced
½ cup extra-virgin olive oil
¼ cup fresh lemon juice
1 tablespoon vinegar
1 teaspoon dried oregano
Salt and fresh-ground pepper

1. Wash and drain parsley well; remove all stalks.

2. Moisten bread; squeeze to drain excess water.

3. In a food processor on low speed, chop parsley and onion to combine well. Slowly and alternately add moistened bread, olive oil, lemon juice, vinegar, oregano, salt, and pepper until smooth. Serve cold.

PER SERVING Calories: 304 | Fat: 28g | Sodium: 77mg | Carbohydrates: 13g | Fiber: 1g | Protein: 2g

Tzatziki (Yogurt-Garlic Sauce)

Make sure to drain as much water from the cucumber as possible. The dip should be as thick as possible, so you don't want the cucumber leeching its water in the dip.

INGREDIENTS | YIELDS APPROXIMATELY 2½ CUPS

½ seedless cucumber

2 cups strained yogurt (see Chapter 17 for recipe)

3–6 cloves of garlic, pressed or grated

1 tablespoon fresh dill, finely chopped

1 tablespoon extra-virgin olive oil

Pinch of salt

¼ teaspoon white vinegar

1. Peel cucumber; grate onto clean kitchen towel. Wrap; squeeze towel to remove as much water as possible from cucumber. Set aside to drain on fresh towel.

2. In a mixing bowl, combine yogurt, garlic, cucumber, and dill; mix thoroughly until smooth.

3. Add olive oil, salt, and vinegar; mix well once more. Refrigerate at least 1 hour before serving.

PER TABLESPOON Calories: 10 | Fat: 0.5g | Sodium: 18mg | Carbohydrates: 1g | Fiber: 0g | Protein: 0.5g

Is Your Refrigerator Running?

Before the advent of some of the cooler modern conveniences, yogurt was the easiest way to preserve milk's freshness in the warm Mediterranean region.

Santorini (Fava)

*If you can find them, Santorini yellow split peas (known as favas to Greeks)
are far superior for this dish than commonly available varieties.*

INGREDIENTS | SERVES 4–6

1 pound dry yellow split peas
1½ teaspoons salt
1 onion, finely diced
Juice of 1 lemon
Extra-virgin olive oil
Dried oregano to taste

1. Wash split peas well in a basin with lots of water.

2. Put peas in pot; add water to cover by about ½" or so.
   Add onion and extra-virgin olive oil; bring pot to a
   boil and simmer approximately 40 minutes, stirring
   occasionally and skimming off any froth.

3. As peas start to soften, add salt to taste and stir more
   frequently. (Note: You may need to add some more
   water to the pot if peas soak it up before they are fully
   cooked, but don't add too much.)

4. When peas have thickened and are fully cooked,
   remove from heat and purée until smooth with a
   wand blender or other food processor.

5. Refrigerate or let stand for several hours so favas
   congeal. Serve with some lemon juice, olive oil, and a
   generous dose of oregano on top.

PER SERVING Calories: 267 | Fat: 1g | Sodium: 593mg |
Carbohydrates: 48g | Fiber: 20g | Protein: 19g

Grilled Banana Pepper Salad

If you don't like hot peppers, make sure to choose sweet banana peppers for this recipe.

INGREDIENTS | SERVES 6

6 hot banana peppers (aka Hungarian or wax peppers)

½ cup Greek feta cheese, crumbled

2 tablespoons extra-virgin olive oil

2 tablespoons wine vinegar

1 teaspoon dried oregano

1. Grill peppers until they are soft and their skins are charred, approximately 8–10 minutes; peel.

2. Spread peppers flat on serving dish; add feta over top of peppers.

3. Drizzle a little olive oil and some wine vinegar over everything.

4. Finish with a sprinkle of oregano, and serve.

PER SERVING Calories: 82 | Fat: 7g | Sodium: 143mg | Carbohydrates: 2.5g | Fiber: 1g | Protein: 2g

Lemon Mustard Sauce

This sauce goes well with grilled fish as well as a dressing for green salads.

INGREDIENTS | YIELDS APPROXIMATELY ⅔ CUP

¼ cup fresh lemon juice

2 cloves of garlic, pressed

1 tablespoon lemon rind, grated

1 tablespoon prepared mustard

¼ cup extra-virgin olive oil

1 teaspoon thyme honey

Salt and pepper

Combine all ingredients; mix until smooth. Serve immediately.

PER TABLESPOON Calories: 54 | Fat: 5.4g | Sodium: 2mg | Carbohydrates: 1.4g | Fiber: 0g | Protein: 0g

Dandelion Greens

Be sure to wash these greens well and cut away all of the root stalk when cleaning, as it is tough and does not become tender when cooked.

INGREDIENTS | SERVES 6

4 pounds dandelion greens
½ cup extra-virgin olive oil
½ cup fresh lemon juice
Salt and pepper to taste

1. Cut away and discard stalks of dandelion greens; wash thoroughly.

2. Bring large pot of water to rolling boil; add greens and stir. Cook over high heat until greens are tender, about 8–10 minutes; remove and drain well.

3. Combine olive oil, lemon juice, salt, and pepper; use as a dressing for greens. Can be served warm or cold, as a side for grilled fish, or on their own with some crusty bread, kalamata olives, and feta. Garnish with fresh minced garlic.

PER SERVING Calories: 300 | Fat: 20g | Sodium: 231mg | Carbohydrates: 30g | Fiber: 11g | Protein: 8g

Sliced Tomato Salad with Feta and Balsamic Vinaigrette

*This dish is all about presentation, so take your time with it and your guests
will be pleased with the way it looks as well as how it tastes!*

INGREDIENTS | SERVES 4–6

4 large tomatoes, washed and sliced into round slices

¼ pound Greek feta cheese, crumbled

1 teaspoon dried oregano

¼ cup extra-virgin olive oil

2 tablespoons balsamic vinegar

Fresh-ground black pepper

Everything Has Its Time

Traditional eating patterns are based on seasonal availability of fresh ingredients and do not rely on canning, preservatives, and refrigeration.

1. Wash and slice tomatoes into rounds approximately ¼" thick. Arrange slices in a slightly overlapping circle pattern on large presentation platter.

2. Cover tomatoes with layer of feta cheese, making sure to spread cheese over all tomato slices then sprinkle oregano over top of the cheese.

3. Combine olive oil and balsamic vinegar; pour over cheese and tomatoes. Sprinkle with fresh-ground pepper and serve.

PER SERVING Calories: 151 | Fat: 13g | Sodium: 217mg | Carbohydrates: 6g | Fiber: 1g | Protein: 3.6g

CHAPTER 10

Pies

Prassopita (Leek Pie)
122

Patatopita (Potato Pie)
123

Bougatsa (Minced Meat Pies)
124

Spanakotyropita (Spinach and Cheese Pie)
125

Aegean Tyropita (No-Pastry Cheese Pie)
126

Prassopita (Leek Pie)

I prefer serving this on the following day to allow the flavors time to meld. I usually refrigerate the pie once it has cooled to room temperature and then cut and warm the slices as needed.

INGREDIENTS | SERVES 6

½ cup extra-virgin olive oil

3–4 large leeks, sliced thinly (upper dark-green stalks removed)

¼ cup green onion, finely chopped

3 large eggs

1½ cups milk

1 cup crumbled Greek feta cheese

¾ cup all-purpose flour

¼ cup fresh dill, finely chopped

1 teaspoon dried oregano

Fresh-ground pepper and pinch of salt

1. Preheat oven to 350°F.

2. Heat olive oil in pan; sauté leeks about 5 minutes. Add onion; continue sautéing until both are soft and tender, another 3 minutes or so.

3. In large bowl, beat eggs well; add milk, feta, flour, dill, oregano, salt, pepper, and sautéed leeks and onions; mix well.

4. Grease sides of dish with olive oil; pour mixture into dish. Bake about 1 hour.

5. Allow to cool before cutting. Can be served warm or at room temperature.

PER SERVING Calories: 328 | Fat: 23g | Sodium: 74mg | Carbohydrates: 24g | Fiber: 2g | Protein: 7.5g

Patatopita (Potato Pie)

This recipe incorporates halloumi cheese. Halloumi is a traditional Cypriot cheese made from sheep and goat's milk that has a texture similar to mozzarella, though saltier in flavor.

INGREDIENTS | SERVES 6

2½ pounds white potatoes
1 cup finely crumbled Greek feta cheese
1 cup finely shredded halloumi cheese
1 tablespoon finely chopped fresh mint leaves
Slight pinch nutmeg
Salt and pepper to taste
4–5 eggs, well beaten
2 tablespoons extra-virgin olive oil
1 cup dried bread crumbs

Thank you, Columbus!

Potatoes, peppers, and tomatoes are all relatively recent imports to the Mediterranean region.

1. Preheat oven to 350°F.

2. Wash and peel potatoes; cut into small chunks. Boil in plenty of salted water until soft, about 30–40 minutes. Drain and place in large mixing bowl; mash well and leave to cool slightly a few minutes.

3. Add cheeses, mint, nutmeg, salt, pepper, and eggs; incorporate well with potatoes, until entire mix is smooth and creamy.

4. Using 1 tablespoon oil, grease pie baking pan well; spread a little less than half of bread crumbs evenly across bottom of pan. Pour potato pie mix into greased pan; spread evenly.

5. Evenly distribute rest of bread crumbs across top; spray remaining olive oil on top.

6. Bake 40–45 minutes, or until top is golden brown. Note: The pie will rise while in the oven and will settle when removed to cool, so don't be surprised by either state. Let stand 1 hour before slicing and serving.

PER SERVING Calories: 481 | Fat: 24g | Sodium: 807mg | Carbohydrates: 45 g | Fiber: 5g | Protein: 22g

Bougatsa (Minced Meat Pies)

Garnish these pies with a sprinkling of toasted sesame seeds when serving.

INGREDIENTS | YIELDS 6–8 PIES

2 tablespoons extra-virgin olive oil

1 large onion, finely chopped

2 pounds ground beef or veal

1 cup of diced and sieved tomatoes (fresh or canned)

1 tablespoon fresh parsley, finely chopped

1 small cinnamon stick

1 cup milk

½ cup grated Kefalotyri cheese (or Parmesan)

2 eggs, beaten well

½ cup salted butter

1 package commercial phyllo sheets (about 20 sheets)

Salt and fresh-ground pepper to taste

Where Is the Beef?

Until relatively recently, meat was festive fare for Greeks, Turks, Italians, Spaniards, Levantines, and North Africans; it was reserved for private or public occasions and was not consumed on a daily or even weekly basis.

1. Preheat oven to 350°F.

2. Heat olive oil in frying pan; sauté onions until soft. Add and brown meat.

3. When meat is thoroughly browned, add tomatoes, parsley, cinnamon stick, salt, and pepper; simmer until all liquid is absorbed.

4. Remove cinnamon stick; add milk and simmer another 5 minutes, until thick. Remove pan from heat; add cheese and eggs, making sure to mix thoroughly and set aside.

5. Melt butter and working quickly to avoid drying out pastry leaves, spread sheet of phyllo in large greased baking pan; using brush, spread some butter on phyllo sheet to cover completely. Add another sheet on top; spread with butter.

6. Place portion of meat mixture at one end of buttered sheets; spread slightly and fold phyllo over meat in rectangle pattern until completely folded over into a packet. Butter outside of packet; fold over open ends of phyllo to close packet. Butter outside of folded packet; set aside with folded ends facing down. Repeat process until all meat mixture has been wrapped.

7. Grease a large baking sheet; spread packets out. Bake about 30–35 minutes, until packets are golden brown. Remove from oven and cool about 20 minutes before serving.

PER SERVING Calories: 661 | Fat: 42g | Sodium: 654mg | Carbohydrates: 31g | Fiber: 1.5g | Protein: 38g

Spanakotyropita (Spinach and Cheese Pie)

Dandelion greens can be added to this recipe for a variation on the flavor.

INGREDIENTS | YIELDS APPROXIMATELY 20 PIECES

1 package commercial phyllo
2 pounds fresh spinach
½ cup fresh dill, finely chopped
½ cup fennel leaves, finely chopped
2 green onions, diced
2 large leeks, white part only, thinly sliced
½ cup extra-virgin olive oil
1 pound Greek feta cheese, crumbled
2 eggs, lightly beaten
Salt and fresh-ground pepper to taste

1. Preheat oven to 350°F.

2. Wash spinach well; chop coarsely and set aside to drain well. Wash, drain, chop, and combine dill and fennel in mixing bowl.

3. In large frying pan, sauté leeks and diced green onions in 2 tablespoons olive oil until soft; set aside in mixing bowl 10 minutes to cool. Add dill, fennel, feta, eggs, salt, and pepper; mix thoroughly.

4. Spread phyllo sheet. Lightly brush entirely with olive oil; spread line of cheese and vegetable mix along length of one edge. Roll lengthwise into long cigar shape with filling inside. Curl each cigar-shaped package into spiral; place on lightly greased baking sheet.

5. Bake 45 minutes, until golden brown. Serve hot or cold.

PER SERVING Calories: 190 | Fat: 12g | Sodium: 401mg | Carbohydrates: 15g | Fiber: 2g | Protein: 7g

Aegean Tyropita (No-Pastry Cheese Pie)

*Any fine or specialty cheese shop in most major cities will
stock the requisite Greek cheeses for this recipe.*

INGREDIENTS | SERVES 6

4 eggs
1½ cups grated kefalograviera (saganaki) cheese
1½ cups grated graviera cheese
1 cup strained/pressed yogurt
1 cup all-purpose flour
⅓ cup extra-virgin olive oil
1 teaspoon dried oregano
¼ teaspoon fresh-ground pepper
¼ cup dry bread crumbs

1. Preheat oven to 350°F.

2. In large mixing bowl, beat eggs. Add cheeses, yogurt, flour, all of the olive oil (except 1 tablespoonful), oregano, and pepper; mix thoroughly.

3. Grease shallow baking pan with a tablespoonful of olive oil. Evenly sprinkle bread crumbs to cover bottom; pour in and spread mixture evenly.

4. Bake 50–60 minutes, until top is slightly browned. Let cool slightly before cutting to serve.

PER SERVING Calories: 620 | Fat: 45g | Sodium: 994mg | Carbohydrates: 23g | Fiber: 1g | Protein: 30g

CHAPTER 11

Soups

Fasolada (White Bean Soup)
128

Revithosoupa (Chickpea Soup)
129

Kakavia (Fish Soup)
130

Fakkes (Lentil Soup)
131

Tahini Soup
132

Avgolemono (Egg-Lemon Soup)
133

Bakaliaros Avgolemono (Cod Egg-Lemon Soup)
134

Fasolada (White Bean Soup)

*This thick soup is considered one of the national dishes of Greece
and has been a staple food in that country for centuries.*

INGREDIENTS | SERVES 4

1 pound dried haricot (white kidney) beans

2 medium-sized carrots, sliced into discs

2 medium-sized cooking onions, diced

2 stalks celery, thinly sliced

1 cup tomato sauce or 3 finely diced tomatoes

1 medium-sized parsnip, thinly sliced

1 tablespoon dried rosemary

1 tablespoon dried thyme

3 bay leaves

¼ cup olive oil

4 tablespoons finely chopped fresh parsley

4–6 garlic cloves, whole or halved

Salt and pepper to taste

1. Soak beans overnight in roughly three times their volume of water. Dump beans into colander; rinse well before use.

2. Put 3 quarts of water in pot; add beans and bring to boil over high heat. Skim away surface foam as it develops. Boil beans 15 minutes, continuing to skim away surface foam using a wooden spoon. At 15-minute mark, skim off last bit of foam; dump into colander to strain and rinse the beans. Rinse pot well.

3. Put another 3 quarts of fresh water in pot; bring to a boil and add beans. After 5 minutes, skim any remaining surface foam that may develop; add all remaining ingredients. Stir well.

4. When it has resumed boiling, cover pot with lid slightly ajar; let simmer over low heat 2 hours, or until beans are soft. Stir occasionally and check to ensure ample liquid in pot to keep beans from sticking to bottom. Note: Though it is technically a soup, you do not want a very runny soup, nor do you want one that is thick and gooey, so monitor the water content of the pot and add a cup or so if necessary.

PER SERVING Calories: 310 | Fat: 15g | Sodium: 412mg | Carbohydrates: 39g | Fiber: 10g | Protein: 8g

Revithosoupa (Chickpea Soup)

Canned chickpeas can be used for this recipe, and they require less cooking time.

INGREDIENTS | SERVES 4

1 pound dried chickpeas
Salt and pepper to taste
Several strands of saffron (optional)
2 finely chopped onions
1 cup extra-virgin olive oil
1 teaspoon dried oregano
Juice of 1 lemon
2 tablespoonfuls of chopped parsley

When in Rome

In Mediterranean countries, meals mean sitting at a proper table with family or friends, not a sandwich at your desk in front of your computer.

1. Soak chickpeas overnight in double their volume of water.

2. In large pan, add drained chickpeas, salt, pepper, saffron, onions, olive oil, oregano, and enough water to cover chickpeas about 1".

3. Cover and simmer 2 hours, stirring occasionally, until chickpeas are soft and tender. Note: you may need to add some more water if you have to cook them longer than 2 hours, as dried chickpeas generally take longer to cook through.

4. Serve hot or cold with lemon juice. Garnish with chopped parsley and a lemon wedge.

PER SERVING Calories: 909 | Fat: 61g | Sodium: 30mg | Carbohydrates: 74g | Fiber: 20g | Protein: 22g

Kakavia (Fish Soup)

Feel free to add some shrimp, scallops, or any other favorite seafood to this recipe for variation.

INGREDIENTS | SERVES 6

2 medium-sized onions, diced

2 medium-sized potatoes, cubed

2 stalks celery, finely chopped

2 medium-sized carrots

1 tablespoon dried marjoram

Salt and pepper

2 pounds fresh cod, cut into pieces

2 pounds fresh grey mullet, deboned and cut into pieces

1 pound mussels, cleaned and bearded

¼ cup fresh parsley, roughly chopped

½ cup extra-virgin olive oil

Juice of 1 lemon

1. Put 6 pints water in large pot; bring to a boil. Add chopped vegetables, marjoram, salt, and pepper; cover and boil 30 minutes.

2. Wash and thoroughly clean fish and mussels. When pot has boiled 30 minutes, add fish and mussels and parsley; boil another 20 minutes.

3. Using slotted spoon, remove fish and mussels from pot; set aside on plate.

4. Strain stock through sieve; push softened vegetables through sieve using wooden spoon. Return strained stock to pot; add olive oil and lemon juice and bring to boil. Add fish and mussels; simmer 3–5 minutes. Serve hot.

PER SERVING Calories: 571 | Fat: 25g | Sodium: 385mg | Carbohydrates: 29g | Fiber: 4.5g | Protein: 57g

Fakkes (Lentil Soup)

Garnish this soup with a few kalamata olives and a splash of wine vinegar.

INGREDIENTS | SERVES 4

1 pound (2 cups) dry lentils

1 medium-sized onion, finely chopped

1 large carrot, peeled and grated

4 whole garlic cloves

1 cup minced and sieved tomatoes (fresh or canned)

1 teaspoon dried rosemary

2 bay leaves

½ cup extra-virgin olive oil

1. Soak lentils overnight in cold water. Rinse and add to large pot of boiling water 10 minutes; drain water. Add 6 pints fresh water; bring to boil.

2. Add onion, carrot, garlic, tomatoes, rosemary, bay leaves, and olive oil to pot; cover and cook 1 hour, or until lentils are tender. Remove bay leaves and serve hot or cold.

PER SERVING Calories: 688 | Fat: 28g | Sodium: 174mg | Carbohydrates: 80g | Fiber: 37g | Protein: 31g

Keep It Simple Silly (KISS)

Traditional Mediterranean food cultures are based on simple nonprocessed foods like fruits, vegetables, nuts, seeds, legumes, grains, olive oil, and wine.

Tahini Soup

Tahini is a ground sesame paste that has been used in cooking throughout the Eastern Mediterranean for many centuries. Most well-stocked supermarkets should carry a brand of tahini, or visit a Middle Eastern grocery where they are sure to have it in stock.

INGREDIENTS | SERVES 4–6

4–5 pints water

2 cups orzo pasta

Salt and pepper

½ cup tahini

Juice of 2 lemons

1. Bring water to boil in large pot. Add pasta, salt, and pepper; stir well. Cover and simmer until cooked, about 10 minutes. Remove pot from heat.

2. Add tahini to mixing bowl; slowly add lemon juice while whisking constantly. Once lemon juice has been incorporated, take about ½ cup hot broth from pot and slowly add to tahini-lemon mixture while whisking, until creamy smooth.

3. Pour mixture into pot with pasta; mix well. Serve immediately.

PER SERVING Calories: 249 | Fat: 10g | Sodium: 15mg | Carbohydrates: 34g | Fiber: 3g | Protein: 8g

Avgolemono (Egg-Lemon Soup)

You can use an equivalent amount of white rice in this recipe if you do not have any orzo pasta handy.

INGREDIENTS | SERVES 4

8 cups chicken stock

1 large carrot, peeled and sliced into discs

1 medium-sized potato, peeled and cut into small cubes

Salt and pepper

½ cup orzo pasta

3 eggs

Juice of 2 lemons

Soup for Dinner

Whether in Greece, Turkey, Italy, Morocco, Spain, Israel, or neighboring countries, a soup or broth can often be the main meal of the day.

1. In large pot, bring stock to boil. Add carrots, potatoes, salt, and pepper; cover and simmer 15 minutes.

2. Add orzo to pot; cover and cook another 10–12 minutes.

3. While soup is simmering, prepare egg-lemon sauce. Beat eggs well in mixing bowl; in a slow stream add lemon juice while briskly whisking eggs to incorporate citrus thoroughly. Using ladle, take 2 cups hot broth from pot and slowly add to egg-lemon sauce while whisking continuously.

4. When pasta has cooked, uncover pot and slowly pour in egg-lemon sauce while stirring as soup simmers. Cover pot and turn off heat; allow to stand 5 minutes before serving.

PER SERVING Calories: 1330 | Fat: 40g | Sodium: 3023mg | Carbohydrates: 175g | Fiber: 12g | Protein: 87g

Bakaliaros Avgolemono (Cod Egg-Lemon Soup)

If you're using salted cod, make sure to soak the cod in water for at least 24 hours, making sure to change the water several times, to remove the salt.

INGREDIENTS | SERVES 4

⅓ cup olive oil

2–3 celery stalks, sliced

1 medium-sized onion, diced

3 medium-sized potatoes, peeled and cubed

Salt and fresh-ground pepper to taste

½ tablespoon corn flour

1½ pounds fresh, frozen, or salted cod (thick-cut pieces)

2 eggs

2 lemons

Get It Up!

Olive oil is a monounsaturated fat which has been shown to raise HDL levels ("good" cholesterol) in blood.

1. In large pot, bring 4 cups of water to boil; add olive oil, celery, onion, potatoes, salt, and fresh-ground pepper. Cover and simmer 15 minutes.

2. Dilute corn flour in ½ cup of warm water. Add to pot; stir well. Immediately add cod to pot; cover and boil a further 5–6 minutes.

3. Separate egg whites from yolks; put whites in large mixing bowl. Whisk whites stiff; add yolks while continuing to whisk. Slowly add lemon juice while stirring mixture constantly with whisk.

4. Slowly mix 2 ladlefuls of hot broth from pot into egg-lemon froth in mixing bowl while continually whisking, to achieve a uniform creamy consistency.

5. Remove pot from heat and add contents of mixing bowl to pot; cover and let stand a few minutes before serving.

PER SERVING Calories: 548 | Fat: 22g | Sodium: 180mg | Carbohydrates: 53g | Fiber: 7.5g | Protein: 38g

CHAPTER 12

Pasta, Rice, and Grains

Domatorizo (Tomato Rice)
136

Grandma's Pligouri (Bulgur Medley)
137

Prassorizo (Leeks and Rice)
138

Spanakorizo (Spinach Rice)
139

Makaronada (Spaghetti with Meat Sauce)
140

Cypriot Orzo Yiouvetsi
141

Pastitsio
142

Pilafi (Rice Pilaf)
144

Sam's Greek Rigatoni
145

Domatorizo (Tomato Rice)

Add a few golden raisins and pine nuts to this recipe for some extra texture and varied flavor.

INGREDIENTS | SERVES 4

1 large onion, finely chopped

1 cup Arborio rice

1 cup fresh tomato juice (or strained tomato pulp)

3 tablespoons dry white wine

½ cup extra-virgin olive oil

2 cups water

1 tablespoon tomato paste

Salt and pepper to taste

¼ cup pine nuts and/or golden sultanina raisins (optional)

½ cup crumbled or cubed Greek feta cheese

1 pinch dried Greek oregano

1 green onion

1. In medium-sized saucepan, sauté onion in olive oil until soft; add rice and continue to stir into onion at high heat for 2 minutes.

2. Add tomato juice and wine to rice; let simmer a few minutes, stirring often to keep it from sticking to pan bottom.

3. In separate, smaller saucepan, mix 2 cups water with tomato paste and bring to boil. Add to simmering rice along with salt and pepper to taste (and the optional pine nuts and raisins); stir well. Cover; simmer over medium-low heat 15 minutes. Make sure to occasionally stir rice (about every 2–3 minutes or so) to ensure it does not stick to bottom of pan.

4. When rice is cooked, remove saucepan from heat; cover with a cotton cloth before covering with lid. Let stand 10–15 minutes.

5. Spoon rice into serving bowls and add some feta on top. Sprinkle feta with pinch of dried Greek oregano and garnish with finely slivered or chopped green onion.

PER SERVING Calories: 510 | Fat: 36g | Sodium: 252mg | Carbohydrates: 40g | Fiber: 3.5g | Protein: 12g

Grandma's Pligouri (Bulgur Medley)

Blanched almonds and raw walnuts can also be added as a garnish when serving this dish.

INGREDIENTS | SERVES 4

1 medium-sized onion, diced

1 tablespoon butter

1 tablespoon extra-virgin olive oil

½ cup chopped button mushrooms

1 small handful golden raisins (sultanas)

¼ cup pine nuts

2 cups vegetable or chicken stock (or water with a bouillon cube)

1 teaspoon ground cumin

Salt and pepper to taste

1 cup medium bulgur

1 tablespoon petimezi (concentrated Greek grape must syrup, called Sapa by Italians) or honey

½ cup roasted chestnuts, peeled and cut in half (approximately 12 chestnuts)

1 teaspoon sesame seeds (raw and/or black)

1. In medium-sized saucepan, sauté onion in butter and olive oil over medium heat until soft, 3 minutes or so.

2. Add mushrooms, raisins, and pine nuts to pan; continue to sauté another 2 minutes, stirring regularly.

3. Add stock, cumin, salt, and pepper. Turn heat to medium high and bring to boil; add bulgur and petimezi and cook while stirring well about 3 minutes. [Note: If you cannot find any petimezi, some Greek thyme honey makes a good substitute.]

4. Add chestnuts; stir well. Cover and lower heat to medium-low; allow to simmer 20 minutes or so, until all liquid is absorbed.

5. Uncover and stir thoroughly from the bottom and sides; cover with tea or paper towel before replacing lid (to eliminate any steam-water built up in lid from running back into pan when uncovered for serving). Remove from heat and set aside 10 minutes. Garnish with sesame seeds, both black and raw, then serve.

PER SERVING Calories: 282 | Fat: 11g | Sodium: 317mg | Carbohydrates: 41g | Fiber: 5g | Protein: 7g

Prassorizo (Leeks and Rice)

Try adding some crumbled feta cheese with a sprinkling of lemon over the top of this dish when serving.

INGREDIENTS | SERVES 4–6

6 large leeks
5 cups water
4 green onions, chopped
⅓ cup fresh dill, finely chopped
¼ cup fresh mint, finely chopped
½ tablespoon dried thyme
Salt and fresh-ground pepper to taste
1 cup white/Italian-style/Arborio rice
⅓ cup extra-virgin olive oil
1 lemon

Eat Your Veggies

In Mediterranean countries vegetables are not only used as garnishes or sides to mains, they also comprise entire meals in themselves.

1. Wash leeks well and cut white ends into thick slices; do not use green part of leeks.

2. Add 5 cups water to large saucepan and bring to boil. Add leeks, green onions, dill, mint, thyme, salt, and pepper; cook uncovered over medium heat about 20 minutes.

3. Once leeks are noticeably soft, add rice and stir well. Cover and simmer over medium-low heat about 20 minutes, stirring occasionally.

4. Add olive oil; cook 3–4 more minutes. Serve warm with lemon juice sprinkled over top.

PER SERVING Calories: 196 | Fat: 12g | Sodium: 19mg | Carbohydrates: 21g | Fiber: 2g | Protein: 2g

Spanakorizo (Spinach Rice)

Brown or wild rice can be used in this recipe instead of white rice, but you must cook it longer.

INGREDIENTS | SERVES 4–6

2 pounds fresh spinach

½ cup extra-virgin olive oil

1 large onion, diced

1 tablespoon tomato paste

2½ cups water

¼ cup fresh mint, finely chopped (or ½ cup fresh dill, finely chopped)

Salt and pepper to taste

1 lemon

1 cup white/Italian style/Arborio rice

The Silk Road

Long before Marco Polo travelled east, rice and spices flowed into the Mediterranean from India and beyond.

1. Wash spinach well; chop coarsely and set aside to drain.

2. In pot, heat olive oil and sauté onion over medium-high heat until tender; add spinach and reduce heat to medium. Cover and cook a few minutes to wilt spinach.

3. Dilute tomato paste in 2½ cups water; add to pot along with rice, mint, salt, and pepper and stir thoroughly. Bring to boil and cover; simmer over medium-low heat 20 minutes, until water has been absorbed, stirring occasionally to prevent any sticking to bottom of pot.

4. Remove from heat and let covered pot stand 10 minutes. Serve hot or cold with a sprinkling of fresh lemon juice over top.

PER SERVING Calories: 243 | Fat: 19g | Sodium: 143mg | Carbohydrates: 17g | Fiber: 3.5g | Protein: 6g

Makaronada (Spaghetti with Meat Sauce)

Well-stocked cheese shops should carry Greek myzithra cheese.
Use it if you can find it, for an authentic flavor.

INGREDIENTS | SERVES 4

⅓ cup extra-virgin olive oil

1 white onion, diced

1 pound lean ground veal

Salt and pepper to taste

¼ cup white wine

1½ cups strained tomato sauce or ¼ cup tomato paste diluted in 1½ cups water

1 medium-sized cinnamon stick

2 bay leaves

1 clove of garlic, whole

1 pound spaghetti-style pasta

Grated myzithra cheese (or Parmesan)

1. Heat olive oil in large pan; sauté onion until soft. Add ground veal; stir well to break up thoroughly. Keep stirring over medium-high heat 5 minutes, or until meat is browned.

2. Once meat is browned, add salt and pepper, wine, and tomato sauce; mix well. Bring to boil.

3. Add cinnamon stick, bay leaves, and garlic clove and cover with sauce; reduce heat to medium-low. Cover pot, leaving slightly uncovered to allow water to evaporate as steam; simmer 30 minutes. The sauce should reduce so that the water is steamed away and the tomato and cinnamon hinted olive oil is left behind with the meat. When ready, meat will have absorbed all liquid.

4. Boil and strain pasta. Sprinkle generously with grated myzithra cheese; spoon meat sauce over top. Make sure to stir sauce first to get some orange-tinted olive oil in each helping.

PER SERVING Calories: 539 | Fat: 35g | Sodium: 63mg | Carbohydrates: 30g | Fiber: 3g | Protein: 27g

Cypriot Orzo Yiouvetsi

*This dish tastes best when cooked in a stoneware casserole,
so if you have one available you will want to use it.*

INGREDIENTS | SERVES 4

3 tablespoons Greek extra-virgin olive oil

1 pound lean ground veal

1 onion, grated or finely chopped

2 garlic gloves, finely chopped or pressed

1 cup fresh strained tomato sauce or 2 tablespoons tomato paste diluted in 1 cup water

1 cinnamon stick

4 spice cloves

Salt and pepper to taste

4 cups beef stock

1½ cups orzo pasta

1 teaspoon butter

1. Preheat oven to 350°F.

2. Heat olive oil in large sauce pan over medium heat; add veal and break up with wooden spoon. Sauté 5–8 minutes, stirring constantly, until thoroughly browned.

3. Add onion, garlic, tomato sauce, cinnamon stick, cloves, salt, and pepper to saucepan with meat. Bring to a boil, stirring well; cover and simmer 15 minutes over medium-low heat.

4. In separate pan, bring stock to boil; cover and reduce heat to low.

5. When meat has cooked, remove cinnamon stick from pan. Add uncooked orzo pasta to hot beef stock for a couple stirs; add stock to pan with meat sauce. Stir to mix thoroughly.

6. Butter sides and bottom of casserole; add yiouvetsi mixture. Bake uncovered 50–60 minutes, until liquid has been absorbed by pasta.

7. Stir well with wooden spoon only once, at about 25-minute mark (making sure to get into corners of dish); let it cook undisturbed for remainder of time. Look for surface of yiouvetsi to form a crust-like top layer, especially near edges.

8. Remove from oven and let sit for 15 minutes before serving.

PER SERVING Calories: 454 | Fat: 28g | Sodium: 546mg | Carbohydrates: 20g | Fiber: 2g | Protein: 30g

Pastitsio

It is important to let this recipe cool sufficiently before cutting into it, or you will end up with bits and pieces instead of a nice neat serving.

INGREDIENTS | SERVES 6–8

¼ cup extra-virgin olive oil

1 large or 2 medium-sized yellow onion(s), finely diced

1½ pounds ground veal (or beef or minced lamb)

1 teaspoon dried rosemary

2 cloves of garlic, grated

¼ cup white wine

2 cups diced and sieved tomatoes (fresh or canned)

Salt and pepper

2 bay leaves

1 pound Greek No. 2 pasta (or bucatini or ziti pasta)

1 recipe Béchamel Sauce (Chapter 9)

3 egg whites, beaten

¼ cup grated Kefalotyri cheese (or Parmesan)

1. Preheat oven to 350°F.

2. Heat olive oil in large pan over medium heat; sauté onion until soft. Add veal; break up thoroughly. Stir constantly over medium-high heat 5 minutes, or until meat is browned.

3. Add rosemary, garlic, wine, tomatoes, salt, and pepper; mix well. Bring to boil; add bay leaves and reduce heat to medium-low. Cover, leaving slightly uncovered to allow excess water to evaporate. Simmer 30 minutes, stirring occasionally.

4. When ready, meat will have absorbed liquid in pan. Remove bay leaves and set sauce aside.

5. Bring large pot of water to boil. Add pasta to water; parboil until soft but not fully cooked (about ¾ of suggested cooking time on package).

6. While pasta is cooking, make béchamel sauce.

7. Drain pasta and return to pot with 2 tablespoons olive oil; mix well. Remove pot from heat; let stand for a few minutes to cool.

8. Add egg whites to pasta along with ¼ cup grated Kefalotyri cheese; mix well. Set aside.

Pastitsio

(*continued*)

9. Grease sides and bottom of medium-sized deep baking dish with olive oil; spread ⅔ of pasta evenly to form bottom layer. Spread meat sauce on top—distribute evenly without gaps. Add remaining pasta on top of meat; pour béchamel sauce over entire surface area of dish.

10. Bake uncovered about 30 minutes, or until béchamel sauce is golden brown. Let stand 30 minutes before cutting and serving.

PER SERVING Calories: 470 | Fat: 21g | Sodium: 114mg | Carbohydrates: 44g | Fiber: 2g | Protein: 27g

Pilafi (Rice Pilaf)

For presentation purposes, a bundt cake–style mold can be used for this recipe, and the cavity in its center may be filled with sautéed mushrooms and onions, or even cubed and lightly sautéed vegetables of your choice.

INGREDIENTS | SERVES 4–6

5 cups vegetable stock (or equivalent water and stock cubes)

2 tablespoons butter

2 tablespoons extra-virgin olive oil

1 bay leaf

Salt and fresh-ground pepper to taste

2 cups of white/Italian style/Arborio rice

1. In large saucepan, add stock, butter, olive oil, bay leaf, salt, and pepper; bring to a boil. Add rice and stir well; once it has resumed boiling, cover and reduce heat to medium-low. Simmer 20 minutes, stirring occasionally with wooden spoon so rice does not stick to bottom of pan.

2. Once water has been fully absorbed, uncover and fluff rice with fork. Cover and remove from heat; let stand 5 minutes.

3. Uncover pan and remove bay leaf. Spoon rice into mold; let stand a couple minutes before turning pilaf out onto presentation plate.

PER SERVING Calories: 156 | Fat: 8.6g | Sodium: 501mg | Carbohydrates: 16g | Fiber: 0g | Protein: 4g

Sam's Greek Rigatoni

Capers also make a good addition to this dish.

INGREDIENTS | **SERVES UP TO 4**

½ pound rigatoni shape pasta
¾ cup kalamata black olives
10 sundried tomatoes
½ pound Greek feta cheese
⅓ cup extra-virgin olive oil
1 tablespoon dried oregano
Fresh-ground black pepper

Serious Cheese Eaters!

Feta cheese accounts for well over half of the 27.3 kilos of cheese the average Greek consumes in a year. No other nation eats as much cheese, not even the French.

1. Bring salted water to boil; cook pasta according to directions on package.

2. Pit and chop olives into pieces (not too small). Chop sundried tomatoes into ribbons. Cut feta into small cubes.

3. Heat olive oil in large sauté pan.

4. Drain pasta well; add to heated olive oil in sauté pan. Add feta, and sundried tomatoes; heat through by tossing repeatedly for a couple minutes until cheese just starts to melt.

5. Season with oregano and pepper; give a couple more tosses in pan and serve hot.

PER SERVING Calories: 649 | Fat: 45g | Sodium: 1340mg | Carbohydrates: 50g | Fiber: 2.5g | Protein: 16g

CHAPTER 13

Vegetables and Legumes

Patates Lemonates
(Lemon Potatoes)
148

Imam Bayildi (Fainting Cleric)
149

Gemista (Stuffed Peppers
and Zucchini)
150

Fassolakia Moraïtika
(Peloponnesian Braised
Green Beans)
152

Revithia Sto Fourno
(Baked Chickpeas)
153

Melitzanes Yiahni
(Braised Eggplant)
154

Briami (Baked
Vegetable Medley)
155

Baked Giant Butter Beans
156

Chickpea Rissoles
157

Arakas (Stewed Green Peas)
158

Beets with Yogurt
159

Black-Eyed Peas and
Swiss Chard
160

Patates Lemonates (Lemon Potatoes)

Yukon Gold potatoes are preferable when preparing this recipe.

INGREDIENTS | SERVES 4–6

2½ pounds potatoes, washed and peeled

½ cup Greek extra-virgin olive oil

Salt and pepper to taste

Juice of 2 lemons

1 tablespoon finely shredded lemon rind

1 heaping tablespoon dried oregano

Health and Longevity

It has become common knowledge that certain elements of Mediterranean diets, especially olive oil, fresh vegetables, fruits, legumes, fresh fish, nuts, and cereals, offer considerable health benefits toward a vigorous and lengthy life.

1. Cut potatoes into thin wedges slightly bigger than fries but not too big, as you want them to cook through and crisp slightly on outside.

2. Spray or sprinkle olive oil to coat bottom and sides of deep-walled medium-sized baking pan (stone bakeware works best).

3. Spread potato slices evenly across bottom of pan; liberally sprinkle salt and fresh-ground pepper on top.

4. Add enough water to almost but not quite cover bottom layer of potatoes. Add lemon juice and lemon rind; using your hands, mix potatoes well in pan to ensure an even soaking and help spread salt, pepper, and lemon zest.

5. Pour remaining olive oil over top of potatoes, making sure to cover all of them; sprinkle oregano over everything. Bake approximately 50 minutes in a 375°F oven; mix potatoes well at halfway mark, to guarantee a thorough and even baking. When potatoes are visibly crisping at edges it is time to remove the pan or turn oven off.

PER SERVING Calories: 293 | Fat: 18g | Sodium: 12mg | Carbohydrates: 31 g | Fiber: 4g | Protein: 4g

Imam Bayildi (Fainting Cleric)

As with all oil-rich foods, this dish is best served cool to allow the flavors to coalesce, so let cool to room temperature before serving.

INGREDIENTS | SERVES 4

6 smallish eggplants
1 cup extra-virgin olive oil
1 pound yellow onions, chopped
3 tomatoes, pulped and strained or 1 cup fresh tomato sauce
3 garlic cloves, minced
2 tablespoons finely chopped parsley
Salt and pepper to taste
Slight pinch of nutmeg
2 tablespoons bread crumbs

Frying Is Popular

In olive oil producing countries fried foods are very popular. Olive oil is the healthiest and tastiest oil for frying.

1. Preheat oven to 350°F.

2. Wash eggplants well and remove stems and ends. Make 4 deep lengthwise slits in each eggplant; make sure each slit runs almost to but not through each end. Sprinkle salt inside each incision; place in saltwater bath 1 hour. Remove and wash eggplants; leave to drain 5 minutes.

3. Heat olive oil in large frying pan; add eggplants. Be sure to turn eggplants a quarter turn or so every couple minutes to ensure even cooking, and fry until they become soft and they begin to wilt. Remove and set side by side in a baking dish, always with 1 incision facing straight up.

4. In same oil eggplants were fried in, add onion. Sauté until golden; add tomato pulp. Bring to boil and simmer 10 minutes. Stir in garlic, parsley, salt, pepper, and nutmeg; simmer another 5 minutes. Remove pan from heat and cool slightly.

5. Using teaspoon, carefully spread open and fill top incision on each eggplant with generous portions of onion mixture, but be careful not to split eggplants through, as they will be very soft. Once eggplants have been filled, place leftover onion mixture in pan among or between eggplants. Pour any remaining oil from frying pan over everything.

6. Sprinkle some bread crumbs over top of each stuffed eggplant; bake 1 hour.

PER SERVING Calories: 253 | Fat: 9g | Sodium: 43mg | Carbohydrates: 47 g | Fiber: 22g | Protein: 8g

Gemista (Stuffed Peppers and Zucchini)

I do not use tomatoes in this recipe, as many people find it makes the recipe too acidic since tomato sauce is used in the stuffing mix. Feel free to stuff the tomatoes, too, if you'd like.

INGREDIENTS | SERVES 6

3 medium-sized ripe tomatoes

6 medium-sized red bell peppers

3 medium-sized zucchini

2–3 large potatoes

½ cup Greek extra-virgin olive oil

2 onions, finely chopped

1 cup white rice

¼ cup black raisins (or dried currants)

¼ cup pine nuts

2 tablespoons minced fresh mint leaves

2 tablespoons minced fresh parsley

Salt and fresh-ground black pepper to taste

Dry breadcrumbs to taste

1. Preheat oven to 350°F.

2. Wash all vegetables well. Peel, pulp, and strain tomatoes to remove seeds; set aside.

3. Using sharp knife, cut into tops of peppers and continue cutting around stem to create a cap, which will be used to close top of stuffed pepper. Using your fingers or small spoon, remove seeds and as much membrane as you can from peppers without cutting through walls or bottoms. Sprinkle a little salt and pepper inside each pepper; set aside.

4. Cut zucchinis in half and remove ends from each; slice thin cap from each end and set aside. Use melon baller or small spoon to hollow out zucchinis without going all way through to bottom or piercing walls. Sprinkle a little salt inside each zucchini half; set aside.

5. Cut potatoes into small cubes and set aside.

6. In large frying pan, sauté onions in half of olive oil until golden. Add tomato pulp and juice; mix with onions. Cook for 5–6 minutes; add remaining ingredients including zucchini pulp. Mix well in pan a few minutes over moderate heat.

7. Fill each pepper and zucchini half about ⅔ full with mixture using teaspoon. Note: Do not fill all the way to top, as rice will expand while cooking and overflow or break through skins of vegetables.

Gemista (Stuffed Peppers and Zucchini)

(*continued*)

8. In a deep-walled baking pan, place peppers in rows and zucchini halves standing upright among them. Add potatoes into empty recesses of pan; pour in small amount of water to cover bottom of pan, about ¼" or so. Place caps back on top of peppers and zucchini halves; pour rest of olive oil on top of everything.

9. Sprinkle dry bread crumbs on top of each pepper and zucchini; sprinkle salt and pepper over potato cubes. Cover pan with cover or aluminum foil; bake 1 hour. Uncover and bake additional 15 minutes, or until caps have browned, water has been cooked off or absorbed, and peppers are tender. Serve warm or at room temperature.

PER SERVING Calories: 345 | Fat: 21g | Sodium: 17mg | Carbohydrates: 37g | Fiber: 6g | Protein: 6g

Fassolakia Moraïtika (Peloponnesian Braised Green Beans)

Try using a bean slicer to remove the bean strings and cut the beans lengthwise.

INGREDIENTS | SERVES 4

2 pounds fresh green beans, washed and trimmed

½ cup extra-virgin olive oil

1 medium-sized cooking onion, finely chopped

1 large or 2 medium-sized red skin potatoes, washed and cut into eighths (optional)

1½ cups fresh tomato juice, sauce, or strained tomato pulp

4 tablespoons chopped fresh mint

Salt and pepper to taste

1. Wash and clean beans by trimming ends and removing strings.

2. Heat olive oil in cooking pot over medium-high heat; reduce heat to medium and sauté onion until slightly softened and translucent.

3. Add beans to pot; stir well to mix with olive oil and onion. Cover and let simmer 10 minutes.

4. Uncover and stir; add potatoes, tomato juice, mint, salt, and pepper along with 1 cup water. Stir well, but make sure potato pieces end up under beans.

5. Bring to boil; reduce heat to medium-low and partially cover pot, leaving it slightly open to allow steam to escape so sauce can reduce. Let simmer 45 minutes to 1 hour, or until beans and potatoes are tender enough to cut with fork. Stir occasionally if necessary, but avoid adding water to cover, as this will result in a runny, thin sauce; this dish is not meant to be soupy.

PER SERVING Calories: 401 | Fat: 27g | Sodium: 23mg | Carbohydrates: 37g | Fiber: 9g | Protein: 6.5g

Revithia Sto Fourno (Baked Chickpeas)

Canned or dried chickpeas can be used for this recipe. Dried chickpeas must be soaked overnight and boiled for 30 minutes before use.

INGREDIENTS | **SERVES 2–4**

1 (16.9-ounce) can chickpeas

¼ cup extra-virgin olive oil

4–6 whole garlic cloves

1 large bay leaf

1 cup water

1 tablespoon dried savory (or dried marjoram)

1 teaspoon dried thyme leaves

Salt and pepper to taste

1 large onion, quartered and thinly sliced

Juice of 1 lemon

Cooks and Poets

The ancient food writer, Athenaeus, claimed there was no difference between a poet and a cook as both were artists who enchanted the senses with their imagination and creativity.

1. Preheat oven to 325°F.

2. Add chickpeas, olive oil, garlic cloves, bay leaf, and water to small high-walled earthenware/Pyrex baking vessel. Sprinkle half of dried savory, all of thyme leaves, salt, and pepper over chickpeas; mix slightly to disperse herbs and seasonings.

3. Arrange sliced onion on top of chickpeas; sprinkle remaining dried savory on top.

4. Cover with lid or aluminum foil; bake 1½–2 hours.

5. Remove from oven and let cool 5–10 minutes while still covered. Remove lid; add lemon juice, mix well, and serve.

PER SERVING Calories: 495 | Fat: 20g | Sodium: 25mg | Carbohydrates: 64g | Fiber: 18g | Protein: 19g

Melitzanes Yiahni (Braised Eggplant)

This eggplant dish is best served over a bed of rice.

INGREDIENTS | SERVES 4

2 large eggplants

¼ cup extra-virgin olive oil

1 medium-sized yellow onion, diced

3 cloves garlic, minced or pressed

2 cups pulped fresh tomatoes

1 cup water

1 tablespoon dried oregano

Salt and pepper to taste

2 tablespoons finely chopped fresh basil

2 tablespoons sesame seeds

An Eggplant for Your Thoughts . . .

Though originally from India, the eggplant is likely the most widely used vegetable throughout the Mediterranean.

1. Wash eggplant and cut into small cubes; place in colander and sprinkle with salt. Place colander over plate; let stand 30 minutes to drain bitter juices.

2. Add 2 tablespoons of olive oil to pan; add onion and sauté over medium heat until soft, about 5 minutes. Add garlic; mix 30 seconds. Add tomatoes and water; bring to boil.

3. Rinse eggplant well and drain. Add to pan with boiling sauce. Partially cover; simmer over medium-low heat 30 minutes, until eggplant is soft and sauce has reduced. Stir occasionally; add oregano, salt, and pepper.

4. Add remaining olive oil to pan; stir well. Let simmer another 15 minutes over medium-low heat. Just before removing from stove, add basil and give a few quick stirs.

5. Serve hot over a bed of rice and garnish with sesame seeds.

PER SERVING Calories: 211 | Fat: 15g | Sodium: 8mg | Carbohydrates: 17g | Fiber: 8g | Protein: 4g

Briami (Baked Vegetable Medley)

Feel free to add radishes, peppers, sweet potatoes, or any other vegetable that takes your fancy to add more variety to this dish.

INGREDIENTS | SERVES 4

2 large eggplants, cubed

2 zucchini, cubed

2 large potatoes, cubed

2 large parsnips, peeled and thickly sliced

2 large carrots, peeled and thickly sliced

1 pound white button mushrooms, thickly sliced

1 large yellow onion, sliced

1 large red pepper, cut into strips

6 garlic cloves, cut in half

½ cup extra-virgin olive oil

1 tablespoon fresh rosemary, finely chopped

½ tablespoon dried oregano

Salt and pepper to taste

Religious Influences on Diet

Much of traditional Mediterranean food culture is informed by the fasting rules and dietary restrictions imposed by age-old religious observance.

1. Preheat oven to 400°F.

2. Wash eggplant and cut into small cubes; place in colander and sprinkle with salt. Place colander over plate and let stand 30 minutes to drain bitter juices.

3. Wash and cut remaining vegetables; set aside until eggplant has drained.

4. Rinse eggplant and combine all vegetables and garlic in large baking dish; add olive oil and mix well. Sprinkle with rosemary, oregano, salt, and pepper; add enough water to cover bottom half of baking dish and contents.

5. Bake uncovered 50–60 minutes, or until water has been absorbed. Make sure to stir vegetables at least once halfway through cooking time, or as needed.

6. Serve warm.

PER SERVING Calories: 537 | Fat: 29g | Sodium: 76mg | Carbohydrates: 68g | Fiber: 18g | Protein: 11g

Baked Giant Butter Beans

Try adding some fried bacon pieces to this dish as a final garnish for a nonvegetarian version.

INGREDIENTS | SERVES 4

½ pound dried Greek gigantes (or giant butter) beans
½ cup extra-virgin olive oil
1 medium-sized onion
3 garlic cloves, minced or pressed
1 red bell pepper, diced
1 tablespoon dried oregano
Salt and pepper
1 cup tomato sauce
1 cup water
Small bunch parsley, finely chopped
1 teaspoon chili flakes
¼ pound Cretan graviera cheese (optional)

Smelly and Good for You Too

Garlic and onions have been shown to protect against high-fat levels in the blood and are believed to be effective agents in the fight against heart disease.

1. Preheat oven to 375°F.

2. Soak dried gigantes beans overnight (use at least a 3:1 ratio of water to beans). Rinse and add beans to generous pot of boiling water; cook 45 minutes over medium heat, until beans are soft. Use large spoon to skim away any surface foam.

3. In large pan, add 2 tablespoons olive oil; sauté onion until soft. Add garlic and red pepper; mix well. Season with oregano, salt, and pepper.

4. Stir in tomato sauce, water, parsley, and chili flakes. Bring to a boil; lower heat to medium-low and let simmer 15–20 minutes.

5. Place earthenware/stoneware/clay baking vessel in oven to warm. When beans are cooked soft, drain and add to pan with sauce; combine.

6. Take heated vessel out of oven. Add beans; pour remaining olive oil over top and return to oven. Bake 35 minutes.

7. Remove baking vessel from oven; add cubed cheese over top of beans and bake another 10 minutes, until cheese has melted. Serve with some chewy sourdough village-style bread.

PER SERVING Calories: 325 | Fat: 27g | Sodium: 11mg | Carbohydrates: 17g | Fiber: 3.4g | Protein: 5g

Chickpea Rissoles

These rissoles can be served warm or at room temperature with a tomato sauce or dip of your choosing.

INGREDIENTS | SERVES 4

1 pound chickpeas (soaked overnight if dry)

1 egg

1 tablespoon dried oregano or finely chopped fresh

3 tablespoons finely chopped fresh mint

3 tablespoons flour

1 teaspoon pepper

½ teaspoon salt

3 tablespoons bread crumbs

Vegetable oil for deep-frying

The "Fainting Cleric"

The name of the dish "Imam Bayildi" is Turkish for "The Fainting Cleric" and as the legend has it, a certain "imam" (the Muslim term for a religious leader) had just completed a long fast and when this dish was set before him, he was so overcome with the mouth-watering aroma that he fainted.

1. Boil chickpeas 30 minutes, or until soft; drain and purée with egg, oregano, mint, flour, pepper, and salt.

2. Scrape chickpea purée into mixing bowl. Add bread crumbs; mix well.

3. Spread sheet of wax paper on counter/cutting board. Spoon about ⅓ of chickpea mixture in an even line along horizontal center of wax paper. Fold over bottom half of wax paper and using the flat of your hand, roll mixture into a long cylindrical shape (similar to using a sushi roller). Cut resulting cylindrical shape into 3 equal pieces or "sausages." Repeat to use up the rest of chickpea mixture.

4. Place rissoles into sizzling oil; fry 5–6 minutes, making sure to turn often if oil does not completely cover rissoles. Remove with slotted spoon; set on paper towel a few minutes to drain.

PER SERVING Calories: 504 | Fat: 12g | Sodium: 371mg | Carbohydrates: 78g | Fiber: 20g | Protein: 24g

Arakas (Stewed Green Peas)

Frozen peas are an excellent choice for this dish, as they do not require shelling and are ready at a moment's notice.

INGREDIENTS | SERVES 4

2 pounds shelled green peas (fresh or frozen)

2 medium-sized potatoes (optional)

½ cup extra-virgin olive oil

2 yellow onions, diced

1 cup diced and sieved tomatoes (fresh or canned)

½ cup fresh dill, finely chopped

1 teaspoon dried oregano

Salt and pepper to taste

1 cup water

1. Rinse peas in colander and drain well. Chop potatoes into sections.

2. Heat oil over medium-high and sauté onions until they begin to soften; add peas and potatoes and continue to sauté another 3–4 minutes, stirring constantly.

3. Add tomatoes, dill, oregano, salt, pepper, and water; stir and bring to boil. Cover; reduce heat to medium-low and simmer about 1 hour.

4. Can be served hot or cold.

PER SERVING Calories: 590 | Fat: 28g | Sodium: 166mg | Carbohydrates: 67g | Fiber: 16g | Protein: 17g

Beets with Yogurt

This recipe does not require the yogurt, as the beets can be eaten on their own.

INGREDIENTS | SERVES 2–4

2 pounds fresh red beets

3 cloves garlic, finely minced

¼ cup extra-virgin olive oil

¼ cup red wine vinegar

Salt and fresh-ground pepper

1 cup strained yogurt

Open-Air Markets

From Madrid to Athens, open-air markets bursting with seasonal produce are the preferred shopping sources for fresh vegetables, fruits, and herbs.

1. Remove leaves from beets, leaving approximately 1" of stem along with lower root, if still attached. Wash beets gently in cold water, making sure not to break skin.

2. Place beets in pot of cold water; cover and bring to boil. Cook on medium heat until beets are cooked yet still firm, usually about 45–50 minutes.

3. Drain beets and run under cold water to cool for handling. Peel skin away and slice into discs.

4. Combine beets, garlic, oil, and vinegar in mixing bowl; toss thoroughly. Add salt and pepper. Cover and refrigerate 2 hours. Serve with a good dollop of yogurt on the side.

PER SERVING Calories: 259 | Fat: 16g | Sodium: 206mg | Carbohydrates: 27g | Fiber: 7g | Protein: 6.5g

Black-Eyed Peas and Swiss Chard

*Though Swiss chard is usually used in this dish, it is possible
to substitute beet leaves when beets are in season.*

INGREDIENTS | SERVES 4

1 cup dry black-eyed peas
2 pounds Swiss chard
Salt and pepper
¼ cup extra-virgin olive oil
1 teaspoon dried oregano
1 lemon

1. Soak peas overnight. Drain and rinse before using.

2. Bring pot of water to boil; simmer peas 15 minutes.

3. Drain water from pot. Add fresh water, olive oil,
   oregano, and salt and pepper; bring to boil again.
   Simmer on medium-low heat 30 minutes.

4. Chop Swiss chard leaves into ribbons; add to pot after
   30 minutes. Simmer another 5 minutes.

5. Sprinkle with lemon juice. Serve warm or cold.

PER SERVING Calories: 329 | Fat: 14g | Sodium: 486mg |
Carbohydrates: 41g | Fiber: 11g | Protein: 14g

CHAPTER 14

Poultry

Roast Lemon Chicken
162

Chicken with Yogurt
163

Chicken with Egg Noodles and Walnuts
164

Stuffed Grilled Chicken Breasts
165

Chicken Livers in Red Wine
166

Chicken Galantine
167

Spicy Turkey Breast with Fruit Chutney
168

Grilled Duck Breast with Fruit Salsa
169

Roast Lemon Chicken

You can add potato wedges to the pan in this recipe, just make sure to add enough water to almost cover the potatoes, along with the juice of one more lemon and 2 more tablespoonfuls of olive oil.

INGREDIENTS | **SERVES 4**

1 whole chicken
Salt and pepper to taste
Juice of 2 lemons, shells retained
2 tablespoons extra-virgin olive oil
1 tablespoon prepared mustard
1 teaspoon dried oregano

Lemon History

The lemon is not native to the Mediterranean region. It is conjectured to have been brought from Asia sometime around the first or second centuries A.D. A first-century A.D. wall painting in Pompeii is the earliest available evidence of the lemon in Europe.

1. Preheat oven to 400°F.

2. Wash chicken well inside and out and pat dry. Sprinkle inside and out with salt and pepper and stuff squeezed out lemon halves into cavity. Place chicken breast down on rack in shallow roasting dish. Combine lemon juice, olive oil, mustard, and oregano; brush/pour over entire chicken.

3. Bake 60–70 minutes, making sure to turn chicken over at halfway point and basting it regularly with juices from pan.

4. To test if it's done, prick with fork and see if juices run clear, or test with meat thermometer for 350°F. When done, turn off oven and cover chicken in aluminum foil. Let rest in warm oven 10 minutes.

5. Serve hot with pan juices.

PER SERVING Calories: 483 | Fat: 30g | Sodium: 135mg
Carbohydrates: 0g | Fiber: 0g | Protein: 46g

Chicken with Yogurt

You don't need to use a whole chicken for this recipe; drumsticks, thighs, and breasts can all be used exclusively or in combination.

INGREDIENTS | **SERVES 4**

1 whole chicken

2 lemons

Salt and pepper

2 cups strained yogurt (see recipe in Chapter 17)

2 tablespoons milk

2 tablespoons fresh mint, chopped

2 cups dry bread crumbs

½ cup salted butter

Yogurt Lore

The oldest surviving reference to yogurt is a passage by Pliny the Elder, a Roman author and philosopher, who records that certain nomadic tribes were in the habit of thickening milk into a substance with a pleasing acidity.

1. Preheat oven to 350°F.

2. Wash chicken well inside and out and pat dry with paper towel. Cut chicken into sections; rub vigorously with lemon halves and sprinkle with salt and pepper. Place pieces in colander; let stand 1 hour.

3. Place yogurt in mixing bowl. Add milk and mint; mix well with whisk until smooth.

4. Dip each piece of chicken into yogurt mix then cover entirely with good sprinkling of bread crumbs. Place on greased roasting pan; drizzle melted butter over top.

5. Bake about 1 hour, until chicken pieces are golden brown.

6. Serve with a side of rice or fried potatoes.

PER SERVING Calories: 921 | Fat: 53g | Sodium: 816mg | Carbohydrates: 51g | Fiber: 5g | Protein: 58g

Chicken with Egg Noodles and Walnuts

*If you have a nut allergy, the walnuts are really an optional element
and not necessary for the success of this dish.*

INGREDIENTS | SERVES 4–6

1 whole chicken

½ cup extra-virgin olive oil

1 onion, diced

¼ cup butter

2 cups tomato pulp, minced and sieved

4 cups boiling water

1 tablespoon fresh mint, chopped

Salt and pepper

1 pound square egg noodles (Greek hilopites)

½ cup crushed walnuts

Grated myzithra or Parmesan cheese for garnish (optional)

1. Wash chicken well inside and out and pat dry with paper towel. Cut into sections.

2. Heat oil. Sauté onion slightly; add butter and chicken and sauté thoroughly on all sides.

3. Add tomatoes, boiling water, mint, salt, and pepper. Bring to boil; cover and simmer over medium-low heat 30 minutes.

4. Add egg noodles and crushed walnuts; give a good stir. Cover and continue to simmer another 30 minutes.

5. Stir before serving hot with some grated myzithra or Parmesan cheese over each helping.

PER SERVING Calories: 688 | Fat: 49g | Sodium: 175mg | Carbohydrates: 24g | Fiber: 1.5g | Protein: 37g

Stuffed Grilled Chicken Breasts

Make sure to pin the open end of the breasts closed tightly so the stuffing does not drip out into your barbecue and cause flare-ups.

INGREDIENTS | SERVES 6

6 large boneless, skinless chicken breasts
1 cup crumbled Greek feta cheese
½ cup finely minced sundried tomatoes
1 teaspoon dried oregano
2 tablespoons extra-virgin olive oil
Salt and pepper

Which Came First?

The question of which came first, the chicken or the egg, was a popular after-dinner conversation topic at ancient Greek drinking parties (symposia).

1. Wash chicken breasts well and pat dry with paper towel.

2. In bowl, mix feta with sundried tomatoes and oregano; combine thoroughly.

3. Place each chicken breast on flat surface; using sharp paring knife, carefully slit top edge of each breast and make deep incision that runs within length of each breast. Be careful not to pierce any holes that would allow stuffing to seep out while grilling.

4. Use small spoon to stuff an equal portion of cheese mixture into each breast; use poultry pins or toothpicks to close openings.

5. Sear breasts in heated frying pan with olive oil, approximately 2–3 minutes per side.

6. Sprinkle with salt and pepper; cook on prepared grill over high heat about 15 minutes, approximately 8 minutes per side. Serve immediately.

PER SERVING Calories: 267 | Fat: 11g | Sodium: 372mg | Carbohydrates: 3.5g | Fiber: 0.5g | Protein: 39g

Chicken Livers in Red Wine

For a nice (and sweet!) variation on this recipe, you can try using a fortified wine.

INGREDIENTS | SERVES 4

1 pound chicken livers
1 cup chicken broth
½ cup butter
1 small onion, diced
1 tablespoon all-purpose flour
½ cup red wine
Salt and pepper
2 tablespoons fresh parsley, finely chopped

1. Wash chicken livers thoroughly and drain well before using. Bring broth to boil in small pan and let simmer over low heat.

2. Melt butter in another frying pan. Slightly sauté onion; add chicken livers and cook over high heat 3–5 minutes, stirring constantly to avoid browning.

3. Sprinkle flour over top of livers and butter; continue to stir well to form sauce in bottom of pan. Stir constantly to avoid clumping.

4. Slowly add hot broth to pan with livers, stirring constantly. Turn heat to high and slowly add wine; continue to simmer and stir several minutes. Reduce heat to low; cook another 5–10 minutes to thicken sauce.

5. Season with salt and pepper and serve hot with chopped parsley as a garnish over a bed of mashed potatoes.

PER SERVING Calories: 448 | Fat: 38g | Sodium: 811mg | Carbohydrates: 10g | Fiber: 0g | Protein: 16g

Chicken Galantine

You can encase the ground chicken mixture in roasted eggplant instead of using skin. This will add additional flavor to the chicken.

INGREDIENTS | SERVES 6

1 small whole chicken
1 shallot
2 cloves garlic
¼ cup pistachio nuts
8 dates
½ pound ground chicken
1 egg white
1 teaspoon dried oregano
1 teaspoon dried marjoram
Fresh-cracked black pepper, to taste
Kosher salt, to taste

1. Preheat oven to 325°F.

2. Carefully remove all the skin from the chicken by making a slit down the back and loosening the skin with your fingers (keep the skin intact as much as possible); set aside the chicken and the skin. Remove the breast from bone. Chop the shallot and mince the garlic. Chop the nuts and dates.

3. Mix together the ground chicken, egg white, nuts, dates, shallots, garlic, oregano, marjoram, pepper, and salt.

4. Lay out the skin, then lay the breast lengthwise at the center. Spoon the ground chicken mixture on top, and fold over the rest of skin. Place in a loaf pan and bake for 1½ to 2 hours (when the internal temperature of the loaf reaches 170° F, it's done). Let cool, then slice.

PER SERVING Calories: 340 | Fat: 18g | Sodium: 96mg | Carbohydrates: 10g | Fiber: 1.5g | Protein: 33g

Spicy Turkey Breast with Fruit Chutney

*There are several types of pears to choose from, but first try
either Bosc or Anjou (if available) with this recipe.*

INGREDIENTS | SERVES 6

2 jalapeño chili peppers

2 cloves garlic

1 tablespoon olive oil

2 teaspoons all-purpose flour

Fresh-cracked black pepper, to taste

Cooking spray

1½ pounds whole boneless turkey breast

1 shallot

2 pears

1 lemon

1 tablespoon honey

1. Preheat oven to 350°F.

2. Stem, seed, and mince the peppers. Mince the garlic. In a blender, purée the chili peppers, garlic, and oil. Mix together the flour and black pepper.

3. Spray a rack with cooking spray. Dredge the turkey in the flour mixture, then dip it in the pepper mixture, and place on rack. Cover loosely with foil and roast for 1 hour. Remove foil and brown for 10 minutes.

4. While the turkey cooks, prepare the chutney: Finely dice the shallots. Juice the lemon and grate the rind for zest. Dice the pears. Mix together the pears, shallot, lemon juice, zest, and honey.

5. Thinly slice the turkey, and serve with chutney.

PER SERVING Calories: 198 | Fat: 5g | Sodium: 1153mg | Carbohydrates: 20g | Fiber: 3.5g | Protein: 20g

Grilled Duck Breast with Fruit Salsa

Duck breast has the best flavor when cooked rare to medium-rare.
For this recipe, try using Moulard duck breast.

INGREDIENTS | SERVES 6

1 plum
1 peach
1 nectarine
1 red onion
3 sprigs mint
Fresh-cracked black pepper, to taste
1 tablespoon olive oil
1 teaspoon chili powder
1½ pounds boneless duck breast

1. Preheat grill. Dice the plum, peach, nectarine, and onion. Mince the mint. Toss together the fruit, onion, mint, and pepper.

2. Mix together the oil and chili powder. Dip the duck breast in the oil, and cook to desired doneness on grill.

3. Slice duck on the bias and serve with spoonful of salsa.

PER SERVING Calories: 285 | Fat: 15g | Sodium: 96mg | Carbohydrates: 9g | Fiber: 1.5g | Protein: 29g

CHAPTER 15

Meats

Arni Exohiko (Countryside Lamb)
172

Grilled Biftekia Stuffed with Cheese
173

Aubergine Meat Rolls
174

Meatballs in Egg-Lemon Sauce
176

Pork with Leeks and Celery
177

Soutzoukakia (Smyrnaean Meat Rolls with Green Olives)
178

Stifado (Braised Beef with Onions)
179

Braised Lamb Shoulder
180

Pork Chops in Wine
181

Arni Exohiko (Countryside Lamb)

Make sure to cut the parchment paper into pieces large enough to adequately wrap the contents.

INGREDIENTS | **SERVES 4–6**

1½–2 pounds boneless leg of lamb, trimmed of excess fat, cubed

2 tablespoons dried oregano

2 tablespoons fresh rosemary

Salt and pepper

¼ pound spinach

6 large garlic cloves, peeled

6 bay leaves

1 cup grated Greek graviera (or Gruyere) cheese

3 red-skin potatoes, unpeeled, well washed and quartered

1 large onion, peeled and cut into 6 equal wedges

1 large tomato, cut into 6 equal wedges

2 large carrots, peeled and thick sliced

1 large red pepper, cut in half, seeded, and sliced into 6 equal pieces

6 tablespoons extra-virgin olive oil

Wine with Dinner?

It is generally thought that moderate consumption of red wine can be a contributing factor in the overall healthfulness of traditional Mediterranean diets.

1. Preheat oven to 325°F.

2. Place cubed lamb in large bowl and sprinkle generously with half of oregano, half of rosemary, salt, and pepper; make sure to mix meat to ensure an even spread.

3. Cut 6 parchment-paper squares (fold parchment paper into triangles before cutting to ensure each piece is perfectly square); in center of each square make a small bed of spinach. Place ⅙ of lamb cubes (3 cubes) on top of spinach on each parchment square.

4. Put 1 whole garlic clove and 1 bay leaf in center of lamb cubes; sprinkle liberally with the rest of oregano and rosemary. Sprinkle ⅙ of graviera on top of meat on each square.

5. Place 2 potato wedges, 1 onion wedge, 1 tomato slice, ⅙ of carrot slices, and 1 piece of red pepper on top of meat on each square. Sprinkle vegetables lightly with salt and pepper and drizzle 1 tablespoon of olive oil over each pile of ingredients.

6. Pull corners and edges of each parchment square together to fashion a pouch. Twist them together and tie closed tightly with string. Arrange pouches on rimmed baking sheet/pan; bake 2 hours.

7. Remove from oven and allow pouches to stand 5 minutes. Serve each pouch on a dinner plate or shallow bowl.

PER SERVING Calories: 439 | Fat: 25g | Sodium: 702mg | Carbohydrates: 42g | Fiber: 8 g | Protein: 17g

Grilled Biftekia Stuffed with Cheese

Make sure to seal the edges of the biftekia well once you have folded them over in order to avoid having the melted stuffing leaking out into your barbecue.

INGREDIENTS | SERVES 6

2 pounds ground lamb or veal (or a combination of the two)

2 medium-sized onions, grated

2 eggs

1 cup bread crumbs

3 tablespoons fresh parsley, finely chopped

1 tablespoon dried oregano

2 tablespoons dried thyme

1 teaspoon fresh-ground pepper

1 teaspoon salt

1 tablespoon extra-virgin olive oil

1 pound kefalograviera or feta cheese

1. In large bowl, use hands to combine meat, onion, eggs, bread crumbs, parsley, seasonings, and olive oil into a single cohesive mass.

2. Take tennis ball-sized piece of meat mixture; roll between palms to form smooth, compact ball.

3. Spread piece of parchment paper over cutting board; flatten meat ball into thin patty, about ¼" thick or so. Try to ensure a uniform thickness.

4. Place piece of cheese on one side of flattened meat patty. Be sure to leave space around edges of cheese to ensure you can pinch meat closed around cheese. Take up further edge of parchment paper; bring up and toward you to fold meat patty over cheese. Pinch overlapping edges of meat together well; use parchment paper to form patty around cheese. Repeat.

5. Brush or spray outside of each patty with a little olive oil before placing over medium-high heat. Grill about 6–7 minutes on each side, or until done.

PER SERVING Calories: 345 | Fat: 20g | Sodium: 1791mg | Carbohydrates: 24g | Fiber: 4g | Protein: 20g

Aubergine Meat Rolls

Ground beef, pork, or lamb can be substituted for the veal in this dish.

INGREDIENTS | SERVES 4–6

1 large, round eggplant

1 large white onion, finely diced

2 cloves garlic, minced or pressed

½ cup Greek extra-virgin olive oil, divided

1 pound lean ground veal

½ cup white wine (or Retsina)

2 cups strained tomato pulp/juice

1 teaspoon ground cumin

Salt and pepper to taste

Flour for dredging

1 cup shredded or grated Greek graviera cheese (or mild Gruyere)

⅓ cup dried bread crumbs

2 tablespoons finely chopped fresh mint

⅓ cup pine nuts

1 egg

Tomatoes or Lemons

As a general rule in Mediterranean cuisine, when a recipe calls for tomatoes or tomato sauce lemon is not used and vice versa.

1. Preheat oven to 350°F.

2. Wash eggplant thoroughly and remove stalk. Slice thinly along its length; aim for 12 slices. Salt both sides and spread in a flower pattern in colander. Set aside to drain 30 minutes. Remember to flip slices at least once for better drainage.

3. In large frying pan over medium-high heat, sauté onions in ¼ cup olive oil until soft; stir garlic in for 1 minute then add meat and mix well 8–10 minutes to brown it thoroughly. Set aside while you prepare tomato sauce.

4. Add wine, 1 cup tomato juice, cumin, salt, and pepper; stir well to mix completely. Bring to boil and simmer over medium-low heat 30 minutes, stirring occasionally. Once sauce has completely reduced and meat has absorbed the remainder, remove frying pan from heat and set aside to cool.

5. Heat 3 tablespoons olive oil in large fry pan. Lightly flour both sides of eggplant slices; fry in batches until softened. Add olive oil to pan as needed, but do it in a thin stream around entire circumference of pan so it seeps toward center. Shake frying pan back and forth with each batch to keep eggplant slices from sticking to bottom. Once eggplant slices have been lightly fried, spread on paper towels in a pan.

Aubergine Meat Rolls

(*continued*)

6. Retrieve cooled meat mixture. In large mixing bowl, add cheese, bread crumbs, mint, pine nuts, and egg; mix well to combine with meat. (Leave aside a few tablespoonfuls of shredded cheese for use as garnish later.) Pick up eggplant slice; place heaping spoonful of meat mixture in middle of one end. Roll up that end to complete a full end-to-end overlapping roll; use toothpick to pin in place. Be sure not to press center of roll too hard, as you do not want meat to protrude from open sides.

7. Place rolls side by side in close rows in deep-walled pan greased with olive oil. Spoon tomato sauce on top of rolls in single stripe right along middle of rolled slices; sprinkle cheese on top of tomato sauce stripe.

8. Bake 30 minutes. Let stand to cool at least 10 minutes before serving. Garnish with a little more shredded cheese while still warm.

PER SERVING Calories: 424 | Fat: 30g | Sodium: 356mg | Carbohydrates: 14g | Fiber: 3g | Protein: 26g

Meatballs in Egg-Lemon Sauce

Ground beef, pork, or lamb can easily be used as a substitute for the veal in this recipe.

INGREDIENTS | SERVES 6

2 pounds lean ground veal

2 medium onions, finely diced

½ cup dry bread crumbs

1 egg, beaten

¼ cup extra-virgin olive oil

¼ cup fresh mint, finely chopped

¼ cup fresh parsley, finely chopped

1 teaspoon dried oregano

Salt and pepper to taste

4 cups beef or veal stock

2 eggs

Juice of 1 lemon

The Good Old Days

At the start of the 20th century, Greeks consumed less meat than any other European nation. By the start of the 21st century, they were vying with the French for top meat consumers per capita in Europe. A parallel rise in degenerative illnesses has prompted many Greeks to return to traditional eating habits.

1. Preheat oven to 400°F.

2. In large mixing bowl, combine meat, onions, bread crumbs, 1 beaten egg, 2 tablespoons olive oil, mint, parsley, oregano, salt, and pepper; mix together well with hands.

3. Using fingers, take up small pieces of meat mix and fashion into meatballs about size of golf ball. Place in rows in baking dish greased with remaining olive oil. Bake 30–40 minutes, until cooked.

4. In pot, bring stock to boil. Add meatballs; cover and simmer 10 minutes.

5. Beat 2 remaining eggs in mixing bowl; slowly add lemon juice and some of hot stock in slow streams as you beat them to achieve a frothy mix.

6. Pour egg-lemon mix into pot with meatballs. Cover and simmer another 2–3 minutes and serve immediately.

PER SERVING Calories: 493 | Fat: 34g | Sodium: 486mg | Carbohydrates: 9g | Fiber: 0g | Protein: 37g

Pork with Leeks and Celery

Only use the white ends of the leeks and not the green stalks for this dish.

INGREDIENTS | SERVES 4

2 pounds pork shoulder, chopped into cubes

1 onion, finely chopped

½ cup extra-virgin olive oil

½ cup white wine

2 cups water

2 pounds leeks

1 cup finely chopped celery

1 cup tomatoes, diced and sieved (fresh or canned)

1 teaspoon dried oregano

Salt and fresh-ground pepper

Longevity

The oldest olive tree in the world is situated in Vouves, Crete, and is thought to be approximately 3,500 years old.

1. Wash pork well; chop into cubes and set aside to drain.

2. In deep-walled pot, sauté onion in olive oil until slightly soft; add pork and brown thoroughly.

3. Add wine to pot; bring to boil then cover and simmer 15 minutes, stirring regularly. Remove pork; cover to keep warm and set aside.

4. Add water to pan along with leeks and celery; bring to boil and simmer 30 minutes over medium heat.

5. Return pork to pot along with tomatoes, oregano, salt, and pepper; stir well. Bring to boil and continue to simmer until sauce is reduced and thickened, approximately 8–10 minutes. Serve immediately.

PER SERVING Calories: 997 | Fat: 71g | Sodium: 200mg | Carbohydrates: 34g | Fiber: 4.5g | Protein: 56g

Soutzoukakia (Smyrnaean Meat Rolls with Green Olives)

This recipe is originally from the city of Smyrna (Izmir, in modern Turkey), and pairs well with a rice pilaf.

INGREDIENTS | SERVES 4–6

1 pound large green olives, pitted and washed

1 pound lean ground beef or veal

1 pound ground pork

2 eggs, beaten

½ cup dry bread crumbs

1 teaspoon dried oregano

4 cloves garlic, minced or pressed

½ teaspoon ground cumin

Salt and pepper to taste

2–3 heaping tablespoons all-purpose flour

¼ cup extra-virgin olive oil

3 cups diced and sieved tomatoes (fresh or canned)

1. Pit olives with olive pitter; try to keep whole. Wash well and drop in pan of boiling water 15 minutes to remove bitterness. Remove with slotted spoon; rinse once more and set aside to drain.

2. Combine beef and pork and place in bowl; add eggs, bread crumbs, garlic, oregano, cumin, salt, and pepper and mix well.

3. Using hands, take small pieces of meat mixture and roll, forming small sausages. Dredge each in flour before adding to large heated frying pan with olive oil; brown on all sides.

4. When sausages are nicely browned, remove from pan and add tomatoes; bring to boil. Let cook 5 minutes, then return to pan with olives.

5. Bring back to boil; simmer over medium heat 10 minutes, until sauce has thickened and oil has separated. Serve warm.

PER SERVING Calories: 638 | Fat: 46g | Sodium: 1388mg | Carbohydrates: 17g | Fiber: 3g | Protein: 40g

Stifado (Braised Beef with Onions)

If you cannot find pearl onions then use the smallest onions you can find to prepare this dish.

INGREDIENTS | SERVES 4

½ cup extra-virgin olive oil

2 pounds stewing beef, cubed

2 tablespoons tomato paste, diluted in 2 cups of water

2 tablespoons wine vinegar (or a sweet dessert wine like Madeira or Mavrodaphne)

14–16 pearl onions, peeled

6 garlic cloves, peeled

4 spice cloves

1 small cinnamon stick

1 tablespoon dried oregano

Salt and fresh-ground pepper

Stew It Up!

A *stifado* is essentially an onion-based stew with meat. One can use rabbit, chicken, lamb, pork, beef, or veal in this quintessentially Greek dish. *Stifado* can even be made with game.

1. Add olive oil to large pot. Heat to medium-high; add meat and brown well on all sides by stirring continuously so meat does not stick to bottom of pot.

2. Add tomato paste, wine vinegar, onions, garlic, cloves, cinnamon, oregano, salt, and pepper; mix well and turn heat to high. Bring to boil.

3. Cover and turn heat down to medium-low; simmer approximately 1 hour.

4. Serve immediately, accompanied by fresh bread for sauce.

PER SERVING Calories: 776 | Fat: 60g | Sodium: 146mg | Carbohydrates: 2g | Fiber: 0.5g | Protein: 50g

Braised Lamb Shoulder

Serve this dish with rice, plain spaghetti, or fried potatoes.

INGREDIENTS | SERVES 4

1½–2 pounds lamb shoulder

½ cup extra-virgin olive oil

½ cup hot water

2 cups tomatoes, diced and sieved (fresh or canned)

2 bay leaves

4 garlic cloves, peeled and minced

1 cinnamon stick

1 tablespoon dried thyme

Salt and pepper to taste

1. Wash meat well and cut into small pieces; include bones.

2. Heat olive oil in pot; brown meat on all sides.

3. Add water, tomatoes, bay leaves, garlic, cinnamon, thyme, salt, and pepper; cover and bring to boil, then turn heat down to medium-low.

4. Simmer 1½ hours, stirring occasionally.

PER SERVING Calories: 542 | Fat: 45g | Sodium: 203mg | Carbohydrates: 2g | Fiber: 0g | Protein: 31g

Pork Chops in Wine

Though boneless center-cut pork chops can be used in this recipe, it is recommended that you use chops with the bone in for optimum flavor and tenderness.

INGREDIENTS | SERVES 4

4 thick-cut pork chops
½ cup extra-virgin olive oil
1 cup white wine
1 tablespoon dried oregano
Salt and pepper to taste

1. Rinse pork chops well and pat dry with paper towel.

2. Place 2 tablespoons olive oil in frying pan; lightly brown pork chops.

3. Put remaining olive oil in fresh pan and turn heat to medium-high. Cook pork chops 3–4 minutes per side, making sure to turn them over at least once.

4. Add wine; bring to boil. Turn to medium and simmer 10 minutes, turning meat once.

5. Add ½ cup hot water to pan; bring to boil and let simmer until sauce has reduced. Sprinkle with oregano, salt, and pepper and serve immediately.

PER SERVING Calories: 403 | Fat: 37 g | Sodium: 27mg | Carbohydrates: 1g | Fiber: 0g | Protein: 16g

CHAPTER 16

Fish and Seafood

Cod with Raisins
184

Aegean Baked Sole
185

Mastic Shrimp Saganaki
186

Baked Sea Bream with Feta and Tomato
187

Baked Tuna
188

Braised Cuttlefish
189

Stovetop Fish
190

Grilled Sea Bass
191

Grilled Jumbo Shrimp
192

Octopus in Wine
193

Cod with Raisins

In ancient Greece, raisins were used as a seasoning.
They are the only ingredients used to flavor this dish today.

INGREDIENTS | SERVES 4

1½ pounds salted cod, fresh or frozen

3–4 tablespoons extra-virgin olive oil

2 cooking onions, chopped, but not too finely

1 tablespoon tomato paste, diluted in ¾ cup water

¾ cup black raisins

1 cup water

Fresh or Cured

Throughout the Mediterranean, fresh fish that is not for immediate consumption is often salt-cured for easy storage and later use.

1. If using salted cod, make sure to soak in water at least 24 hours, changing water several times to remove salt.

2. Heat olive oil in cooking pot over medium heat. Add onions; and sauté lightly a few minutes. Make sure to stir constantly to avoid browning onion; it should be tender but not burned.

3. Add tomato paste to onions; bring to boil and simmer 10 minutes.

4. Add raisins and continue to cook 3 more minutes.

5. Add water; bring to boil and simmer 30 minutes, until raisins have expanded.

6. Add cod; simmer 15 minutes, until sauce has reduced. Serve with raisin-onion sauce spooned over top.

PER SERVING Calories: 328 | Fat: 12g | Sodium: 147mg | Carbohydrates: 29g | Fiber: 2g | Protein: 30g

Aegean Baked Sole

Turbot, halibut, or flounder can also be used as substitutes for the sole in this recipe.

INGREDIENTS | SERVES 4

8 sole fillets
Salt and pepper to taste
2 lemons
4 tablespoons extra-virgin olive oil
1 teaspoon dried oregano
¼ cup capers
4 tablespoons chopped fresh dill
2 tablespoons chopped fresh green onion (or celery leaves or parsley)

1. Preheat oven to 250°F.

2. Wash fish well under cold water and pat dry with paper towel. Salt and pepper fillets and set aside.

3. Slice 1 lemon into thin slices, then cut slices in half.

4. Pour 2 tablespoons olive oil into baking dish; layer fish and lemon slices alternately.

5. Sprinkle oregano, capers, dill, and onion over fish and lemon slices.

6. Drizzle remaining olive oil and squeeze juice of remaining lemon over everything.

7. Cover and bake 30 minutes.

PER SERVING Calories: 236 | Fat: 3g | Sodium: 455mg | Carbohydrates: 6.5g | Fiber: 3g | Protein: 47g

Mastic Shrimp Saganaki

If you cannot get hold of either mastic resin or mastiha liqueur, then simply use a shot of ouzo. Mastic is one of the ingredients in ouzo. Italian Sambuca liqueur is similar to ouzo.

INGREDIENTS | SERVES 4

2 medium-sized onions, diced

¼ cup extra-virgin olive oil

4 garlic cloves, pressed or finely diced

2 cups diced and sieved tomatoes (fresh or canned)

1 roasted red pepper, minced

½ cup water

Salt and pepper to taste

2 tablespoons mastiha liqueur

¼–½ teaspoon ground mastic resin

20–24 large raw shrimp, shelled with tails on

1 cup crumbled Greek feta (optional)

Fast-Friendly Seafood

According to Greek Orthodox Christian fasting customs, shellfish, octopus, and cuttlefish are considered fast-friendly as they do not contain blood.

1. Sauté onions in olive oil over medium heat until soft and translucent, 3–5 minutes.

2. Add garlic and stir well 30 seconds. Add tomatoes, red pepper, and water; add salt and pepper to taste and stir well to mix. Bring to boil.

3. Reduce heat only slightly and allow sauce to simmer well 8 minutes; do not cover pan.

4. Add mastiha liqueur and mastic resin to sauce; stir well. Continue to simmer another 2 minutes, stirring a couple more times.

5. Quickly add shrimp; give pan a couple shakes to settle shrimp well into sauce. Cook 2 minutes.

6. Using tongs or fork, quickly turn all shrimp over and cook another minute or so.

7. Remove from heat for serving. A cup of crumbled Greek feta can be added to pan just before removing from heat for serving.

PER SERVING Calories: 330 | Fat: 22g | Sodium: 780mg | Carbohydrates: 19g | Fiber: 2g | Protein: 11g

Baked Sea Bream with Feta and Tomato

If you have trouble finding sea bream, this fish is also sometimes referred to as porgy.

INGREDIENTS | SERVES 4

4 small whole sea bream
½ cup extra-virgin olive oil
6 ripe tomatoes, peeled and minced
1 teaspoon dried marjoram
Salt and pepper
½ cup water
½ cup fresh parsley, finely chopped
½ pound Greek feta cheese

1. Preheat oven to 400°F.

2. Wash and clean fish well; set aside to drain.

3. In saucepan, heat olive oil; add tomatoes, marjoram, salt, pepper, and water. Bring to boil; simmer 15 minutes.

4. Place fish side by side in baking dish; pour sauce over top and sprinkle with parsley. Bake 30 minutes.

5. Crumble feta cheese; remove baking dish from oven and sprinkle feta over fish. Return to oven to bake another 5–7 minutes, until cheese starts to melt. Remove and serve immediately.

PER SERVING Calories: 508 | Fat: 41g | Sodium: 711mg | Carbohydrates: 7.5g | Fiber: 1.5g | Protein: 27g

Baked Tuna

Archaeologists have discovered evidence of extensive tuna fishing operations in Argolis, Greece, as early as 6000 B.C.

1. Preheat oven to 400°F.

2. Wash tuna steaks well and set aside.

3. In large frying pan, heat 2 tablespoons olive oil on medium-high. Sauté onion and green pepper until soft.

4. Add garlic, parsley, marjoram, salt, and pepper; stir over heat another minute or so.

5. Add tomatoes and water; bring to boil. Lower heat to medium-low and simmer 15–20 minutes.

6. Place tuna steaks in baking dish along with remaining olive oil, making sure to coat the tuna with the oil; pour sauce over top. Bake uncovered 45 minutes. Serve immediately, spooning some sauce over each portion and garnishing with chopped fresh parsley.

PER SERVING Calories: 301 | Fat: 8.5g | Sodium: 353mg | Carbohydrates: 11g | Fiber: 2g | Protein: 41g

Braised Cuttlefish

The tentacles, eyes, skin, and beak of the cuttlefish need to be removed along with the ink sack and central bony cartilage. Most fish markets will do this for you.

INGREDIENTS | SERVES 4–6

2 pounds cuttlefish, cleaned and cut into strips

⅓ cup extra-virgin olive oil

2 large onions, diced

3 garlic cloves, pressed or finely chopped

1 cup red wine

2 cups minced tomatoes

2 tablespoons fresh parsley, finely chopped

1 teaspoon dried marjoram

1 bay leaf

Salt and pepper to taste

Clever Fish

Since ancient times the cuttlefish has been renowned for its cleverness. Modern studies have concluded that cuttlefish are indeed among the most intelligent of invertebrates.

1. Clean cuttlefish and cut into strips; set aside to drain well. Make sure to pat strips dry with paper towel before using in order to avoid hot oil pops.

2. Heat olive oil in pan; sauté onions until soft.

3. Add garlic and sauté another 30 seconds or so before adding (drained) cuttlefish. Continue to sauté and stir continuously until cuttlefish starts to turn a yellowish color, approximately 6–8 minutes.

4. Add wine and continue to cook another 10 minutes, stirring regularly.

5. Add tomatoes, parsley, marjoram, bay leaf, salt, and pepper; cover and simmer over medium-low approximately 90 minutes, until sauce has thickened and cuttlefish is tender. Add ½–1 cup water to pan should liquid thicken before cuttlefish has softened sufficiently.

6. Serve warm with fresh bread.

PER SERVING Calories: 217 | Fat: 13g | Sodium: 422mg | Carbohydrates: 2g | Fiber: 0g | Protein: 18g

Stovetop Fish

Due to the heat of the summer months in Mediterranean countries, dishes like this are common, as you do not have to use an oven that will add to the heat in the kitchen.

INGREDIENTS | SERVES 4

2 pounds white fish fillets

3 tablespoons extra-virgin olive oil

4–5 cloves garlic, minced

1 pound ripe tomatoes, peeled and minced

6–8 fresh mint leaves, finely chopped

Salt and pepper

1 tablespoon dried oregano

½ cup water

1 small bunch fresh parsley

1. Wash fish fillets and pat with paper towel to dry.

2. Heat olive oil in large frying pan and quickly sauté garlic.

3. Add tomatoes, mint, salt, pepper, and oregano. Bring to boil and let simmer 10 minutes, until thickened.

4. Add water and continue to simmer another 3–4 minutes.

5. Place fish in pan and allow to simmer 15 minutes. Do not stir; simply shake pan gently from time to time to avoid sticking.

6. Garnish with chopped parsley and serve immediately with rice.

PER SERVING Calories: 261 | Fat: 12g | Sodium: 122mg | Carbohydrates: 5.2g | Fiber: 1g | Protein: 33g

Grilled Sea Bass

The secret to successfully grilling sea bass is to not overcook it, so make sure to check the fish on the grill for flakiness and remove it quickly when it is done.

INGREDIENTS | SERVES 4

4 whole sea bass (1½ pounds each), gutted and scaled

Salt and pepper

4 lemons

¼ cup extra-virgin olive oil

1 teaspoon dried oregano

1 cup fresh parsley, finely chopped

1. Wash fish well inside and out. Using sharp knife, cut several diagonal slits on both sides of each fish. Sprinkle with salt and pepper, including inside cavity, and set aside.

2. Squeeze juice from 2 lemons and mix with olive oil and oregano.

3. Slice remaining 2 lemons into thin slices and stuff each fish with chopped parsley and several lemon slices.

4. Brush both sides of each fish liberally with olive oil and lemon mixture and set aside 10 minutes.

5. Heat grill to medium heat; brush grilling rack with oil. Place fish on hot rack and close grill cover.

6. Cook 15 minutes, until fish flakes easily. Brush with remaining olive oil and lemon mixture and serve hot.

PER SERVING Calories: 384 | Fat: 19g | Sodium: 175mg | Carbohydrates: 5g | Fiber: 2g | Protein: 48g

Grilled Jumbo Shrimp

For tips on deveining jumbo shrimp, if you have an Internet connection you can do a search for "deveining shrimp" on YouTube or any other video sharing website.

INGREDIENTS | SERVES 4

2 pounds, jumbo raw shrimp, deveined but unpeeled
¼ cup extra-virgin olive oil
Juice of 1 lemon
4 garlic cloves, minced or pressed
1 tablespoon lemon rind
Salt and pepper
2 tablespoons butter, melted

1. Wash shrimp well under running water and set aside to drain.

2. In a medium-sized mixing bowl, combine the olive oil, lemon juice, garlic, lemon rind, salt, and pepper.

3. Add shrimp to the marinade and toss well then marinate for a couple hours, periodically tossing the shrimp in the sauce.

4. Light the grill, butterfly the shrimp lengthwise just below the head and spread them open. Brush them liberally with the remaining marinade.

5. Rub/spray some olive oil across the cooking surface and grill shrimp over a medium-hot setting with shell side down, for 1 minute. Turn shrimp over and grill lightly browned, about 1 minute. Turn the shrimp over again and brush them liberally with melted butter, and grill for about 1 minute longer. Remove and serve at once.

PER SERVING Calories: 353 | Fat: 23g | Sodium: 311mg | Carbohydrates: 0g | Fiber: 0g | Protein: 34g

Octopus in Wine

When braising the octopus you do not need to use much water, as it will release a good deal of its own liquid into the pan. Also, be sure to remove the beak, eyes, and ink sac before cooking.

INGREDIENTS | SERVES 4

1 large octopus

1 tablespoon white vinegar

½ cup extra-virgin olive oil

3 onions, sliced

4 tomatoes, diced and sieved (fresh or canned)

1 cup white wine

2 bay leaves

1 teaspoon whole peppercorns

Salt and pepper

½ cup drained capers

¼ cup water

1. Place octopus in saucepan with vinegar; cover and simmer over a low heat until soft, approximately 15–20 minutes. Remove and cut into small pieces.

2. Heat olive oil in frying pan and sauté onions until soft.

3. Add tomatoes, wine, bay leaves, peppercorns, salt, and pepper; simmer 15 minutes.

4. Add octopus, capers, and water; simmer until sauce has thickened. Serve hot.

PER SERVING Calories: 388 | Fat: 28g | Sodium: 993mg | Carbohydrates: 12g | Fiber: 2g | Protein: 14g

CHAPTER 17

Desserts

Almond Tangerine Bites
196

Amygdalota (Almond Biscuits)
197

Cypriot Loukoumia
198

Loukoumades (Honey Fritters)
199

Galatopita (Milk Pie)
200

Milopita (Apple Cake)
201

Pasteli (Sesame Brickle)
202

Rizogalo (Rice Pudding)
203

Spiral Baklava
204

Tiganites (Pancakes)
206

Strained Yogurt
207

Stuffed Dried Figs
208

Byzantine Fruit Medley
209

Almond Tangerine Bites

*This Greek almond treat originates from the island of Kerkyra (or Corfu),
one of the Ionian Islands off the west coast of Greece.*

INGREDIENTS | **YIELDS APPROXIMATELY 20–25 PIECES**

2 cups raw almonds

5 tangerines

1 cup brown sugar

Icing sugar

The Greek Nut

The ancient Romans referred to the almond as the "Greek nut" because the almond tree had its origins in Asia Minor (modern-day Turkey).

1. Blanche almonds by boiling them in water; when they start floating to the top they can be removed from the water, drained, and easily peeled. Boil 3 tangerines in generous amount of water 5 minutes to remove bitterness of rind.

2. Squeeze juice from remaining 2 tangerines and set aside; discard skins.

3. Peel 3 boiled tangerines and put skins along with blanched almonds into blender; purée until very finely ground.

4. Remove puréed almond mix from blender; in large bowl, mix with brown sugar.

5. Slowly add tangerine juice while continuing to mix well.

6. Roll small pieces of mixture into walnut-sized balls using palms of hands; set aside on sheet of wax paper to dry.

7. Dust balls lightly with icing sugar before serving.

PER SERVING Calories: 84 | Fat: 4g | Sodium: 4mg | Carbohydrates: 12g | Fiber: 1.5g | Protein: 2g

Amygdalota (Almond Biscuits)

Amygdalota biscuits are a staple product in any Greek bakery and they are wildly popular in Greece.

INGREDIENTS | YIELDS APPROXIMATELY 25–30 PIECES

1 pound blanched almonds
1 tablespoon fine semolina
3 eggs, separated
1½ cups sugar
1 tablespoon orange-blossom water

1. Preheat oven to 350°F.

2. Purée blanched almonds and semolina in food processor until very fine.

3. Beat 2 egg yolks and 1 egg white well with mixer in large bowl; add sugar, almond purée, and orange-blossom water. Mix well with dough hook (stand-mixer) or wooden spoon.

4. In mixing bowl, whip 2 egg whites until nice and stiff with peaks; incorporate thoroughly into almond purée mixture.

5. Take up small pieces of dough and roll into balls between palms. Place balls on cookie sheet and press an almond into center of each, flattening lower hemisphere of biscuit.

6. Bake 20–30 minutes, or until cookies are starting to turn slightly golden. Remove from oven and leave to cool at least 1 hour. Important: To maintain the inner chewiness of these biscuits, it is a good idea to store them in sealed, airtight containers or wrapped in cellophane/plastic.

PER SERVING Calories: 138 | Fat: 8.5g | Sodium: 6.5mg | Carbohydrates: 13g | Fiber: 2g | Protein: 4g

Cypriot Loukoumia

You can use any type of marmalade, jam, or preserved fruit for the filling of these cookies.

INGREDIENTS | YIELDS APPROXIMATELY 20 PIECES

½ cup butter
2 cups flour
1½ cups milk
½ cup sugar
1 egg, beaten
1 teaspoon baking powder
½ cup orange marmalade
1 cup finely chopped almonds
2 tablespoons orange-blossom water
½ teaspoon cinnamon
½ teaspoon nutmeg
Confectioners' sugar

1. Preheat oven to 350°F.

2. Melt butter in pot over medium-high heat. Slowly add flour, stirring constantly with wooden spoon to avoid clumping.

3. Lower heat to medium-low and slowly add milk, making sure to stir continuously as mixture thickens and starts clumping.

4. When all milk has been added, remove from heat and add sugar, egg, and baking powder; mix well until dough is uniformly smooth.

5. Prepare filling by mixing marmalade, almonds, orange-blossom water, cinnamon, and nutmeg.

6. Using rolling pin, spread pieces of dough on floured surface to uniform thickness of a banana peel.

7. Place small amount of filling mixture in center of each disc. Fold each disc in half over filling into a half-moon shape; tightly pinch together edges to ensure a good seal.

8. Place cookies on buttered pan and bake 20 minutes. Let stand 30 minutes. Sprinkle cookies with confectioners' sugar before serving.

PER SERVING Calories: 167 | Fat: 7g | Sodium: 82mg | Carbohydrates: 22g | Fiber: 1g | Protein: 3g

Loukoumades (Honey Fritters)

Many recipes for loukoumades call for a boiled sugar-honey-water syrup bath, but I prefer not to mix sugar with my honey. You can also sprinkle the loukoumades with some crushed walnuts before serving. Loukoumades are best eaten on the same day they are made.

INGREDIENTS | YIELDS APPROXIMATELY 30–40 PIECES

1½ tablespoons active dry yeast
1½–2 cups lukewarm milk or water
4 cups all-purpose flour
½ teaspoon salt
Vegetable oil for deep-frying
1 cup good-quality Greek honey
Cinnamon powder for dusting

Aristaeus

According to Greek mythology, a lesser god by the name of Aristaeus was credited with teaching mankind husbandry and agriculture, including the art of beekeeping for honey.

1. In mixing bowl, dissolve yeast in 1 cup lukewarm milk or water; cover bowl with cloth and let stand 10 minutes to allow yeast to rise.

2. Gently add flour and salt to mixing bowl in stages; continue to mix well.

3. Sparingly add remaining (and/or any additional) lukewarm milk or water while continually mixing. Resulting batter should end up as soft and sticky dough, soft enough to be able to drop from a spoon.

4. Cover mixing bowl with cloth and place in warm spot to rise a couple hours, or until it has doubled in bulk and has bubbles forming on surface.

5. When dough has risen, heat oil in deep pan. You will need a teaspoon and a cup of cold water for this part. Dipping the teaspoon into water before using it to spoon up portions of dough will ensure it does not stick to the spoon.

6. Drop teaspoonfuls of dough directly into hot oil. (Remember to wipe your finger between spoonfuls if you need to use it to get dough off spoon.) Fry each batch of dough balls until they puff up and achieve a golden brown color. Remove from oil with slotted spoon and set on platter lined with paper towels to drain a couple minutes.

7. Place loukoumades on serving platter and drizzle honey to cover. Dust with cinnamon powder and serve immediately.

PER SERVING Calories: 76 | Fat: 0.5g | Sodium: 30mg | Carbohydrates: 17g | Fiber: 0.5g | Protein: 1.5g

Galatopita (Milk Pie)

*The fat content of the milk you use for this recipe is irrelevant, but
I do recommend using 2% or higher for a fuller flavor.*

INGREDIENTS | SERVES 6

5 cups milk

½ cup butter

1 cup sugar

1 cup fine semolina

3 eggs

Ground cinnamon or icing sugar for sprinkling

1. Preheat oven to 350°F.

2. On stovetop, bring milk almost to boil in saucepan. Add butter, sugar, and semolina, making sure to stir continuously until thick crème is formed. Turn off heat and let stand a couple minutes to cool slightly.

3. Beat eggs and add to thickened mixture; whisk well.

4. Butter or oil sides and bottom of pie dish or other high-walled oven pan. Pour in mixture; bake approximately 1 hour, until top has browned. Turn off oven but do not remove pie for another 15 minutes.

5. Once pie is removed from oven, let stand a couple hours. Serve topped with icing sugar or cinnamon. Can also be topped with fruit preserve or jam of your choosing.

PER SERVING Calories: 527 | Fat: 25g | Sodium: 288mg | Carbohydrates: 63g | Fiber: 1g | Protein: 13g

Milopita (Apple Cake)

The Granny Smith variety of apple works best in this cake.

INGREDIENTS | SERVES 6

3 medium-sized apples

1½ cups self-rising flour (regular flour with 1½ teaspoons baking powder will do in a pinch)

Pinch of salt

¾ cup butter

1 cup white sugar

2 eggs, separated

⅓ cup milk

1 tablespoon vanilla extract

1 tablespoon grated lemon rind

¼ cup brown sugar

1 teaspoon ground cinnamon

1. Preheat oven to 350°F.

2. Peel and core apples and slice into sixteenths. Set aside in bowl of water with some lemon juice squeezed into it to keep from browning.

3. Sift flour with salt (and baking powder, if required).

4. Using mixer, cream ½ cup of butter and all of white sugar until smooth. While continually mixing, add egg yolks 1 at a time, alternating with tablespoon of flour to achieve smooth and creamy consistency. Add rest of flour in stages, alternately with milk.

5. Add vanilla and lemon rind; mix until batter is smooth.

6. In separate mixing bowl, whip egg whites into stiff peaks; using spatula, carefully fold into batter.

7. Butter sides of pie dish and pour in batter. Arrange apple slices in perpendicular fashion over top of batter in circular pattern to form an outer ring of apple slices. Fill center of ring with any remaining slices.

8. Melt remaining ¼ cup butter; mix with brown sugar and cinnamon.

9. Pour over apple slices in circular fashion, making sure to distribute evenly in long stream.

10. Bake 60 minutes. Let stand at least a couple hours before serving.

PER SERVING Calories: 540 | Fat: 26g | Sodium: 363mg | Carbohydrates: 74g | Fiber: 2g | Protein: 6g

Pasteli (Sesame Brickle)

You can also toast the sesame seeds and almonds in the oven before using them in this recipe. Simply spread them on a baking sheet and place them in a preheated oven at 350°F for about 5 minutes or so. Make sure not to burn them.

INGREDIENTS | YIELDS APPROXIMATELY 24 PIECES

1½ cups Greek thyme honey

2½ cups sesame seeds

½ cup raw almonds (or pistachios or walnuts)

Orange-blossom water

Pasteli, aka *Itrion*

The combination of honey and sesame seeds to form wafers of chewy wholesome goodness is one Greek food concoction that has been around—quite literally—for ages. In the Archaic age and later in the Classical and Hellenistic periods this confection was known as "itrion." Subsequently, it became known as *pasteli* among the Byzantines and remains a very popular sweet in Modern Greece.

1. In saucepan over medium-low heat, heat honey until it starts to bubble and ball. Add sesame seeds and almonds; mix well. Stir continuously with wooden spoon until rich golden-brown color, about 10 minutes or so.

2. Prepare marble or glass cutting board surface by sprinkling with orange-blossom water and spreading to cover working surface.

3. Pour hot honey-sesame mixture onto working surface; spread with spatula to uniform thickness of ½" or so. Take sufficiently large piece of parchment paper and cover outspread mixture. Use rolling pin to further thin and spread mix into rough rectangle of uniform thickness, about ¼" or so. Remove parchment paper (do not throw it out); square edges with spatula or icing tool and let stand to cool.

4. Equally divide and cut outspread pasteli into full-length rectangles using large sharp knife. Further divide and cut rectangles into squares, then cut squares at 45° angle to achieve triangular pieces.

5. Use metal spatula to remove pasteli triangles from working surface and place in airtight container lined with saved parchment paper. Do not refrigerate, simply store in cupboard or pantry and serve wafers as a snack or dessert.

PER SERVING Calories: 163 | Fat: 8.5g | Sodium: 2.5mg | Carbohydrates: 22g | Fiber: 2g | Protein: 3g

Rizogalo (Rice Pudding)

This rice pudding is particularly good when refrigerated for a couple hours and served on sunny, warm days. The citrus rind adds a whole new dimension of flavor to the dish.

INGREDIENTS | SERVES 6–8

8 cups milk

1 cup Arborio rice

1½ cups sugar

1 teaspoon real vanilla extract

1 tablespoon finely shredded citrus zest (orange, lemon, or lime)

2 egg yolks

¼ cup cold milk

1 tablespoon corn flour (optional)

1 teaspoon ground cinnamon

1. In pot over moderately high heat, bring milk to slight boil. Add rice and stir well until boil returns. Reduce heat to medium-low and gently simmer uncovered 30 minutes. Make sure to stir regularly so milk does not congeal or stick to sides and/or bottom of pot.

2. Add sugar, vanilla, and citrus rind; continue to simmer and occasionally stir another 10 minutes.

3. Beat egg yolks with cold milk; whisk in corn flour and mix well.

4. After 10 minutes in Step 2, pour egg yolk mixture into pot; whisk well to incorporate. Simmer another 3–5 minutes, until thick.

5. Remove from heat. Using ladle, spoon out mixture into bowls. Let stand 1 hour to cool. Sprinkle with cinnamon and garnish with curls of shaved citrus rind.

PER SERVING Calories: 344 | Fat: 10g | Sodium: 126mg | Carbohydrates: 54g | Fiber: 0g | Protein: 9.5g

Spiral Baklava

A 6" springform baking pan or a clay baking vessel of similar dimensions is required to make this pastry.

INGREDIENTS | SERVES 4

½ cup chopped walnuts

1½ cups blanched raw almonds

1 tablespoon finely shredded orange rind

1 teaspoon ground cinnamon

4 sheets phyllo pastry

⅓ cup melted unsalted butter (or vegetable shortening)

½ cup sugar

½ cup water

½ cup Greek thyme honey

Honey as Folk Medicine

A popular Greek folk remedy for sore throats and coughs is to mix equal parts honey and lemon juice and to take a tablespoonful every couple hours as needed.

1. Preheat oven to 350°F.

2. Combine and grind walnuts and blanched almonds until coarsely chopped. Add orange rind and cinnamon; mix well.

3. Spread 1 sheet phyllo on dry work surface in landscape orientation; brush surface completely with melted butter. Add another sheet of phyllo directly over top; brush with butter. Spread ½ ground almond mixture over surface, spreading evenly. Leave 1" gutter of free space all around perimeter of rectangle. Fold 2 short sides of phyllo in toward center about ½" on either side. Brush both side-edge folds with melted butter.

4. Fold over entire length of bottom edge of phyllo about 1" (or to start of almond mix). Carefully roll folded bottom edge tightly up toward top edge. Make sure to brush entire length of roll several times with melted butter as you go, especially the space just before top edge where roll will be completed.

5. When first roll is done, brush exterior with melted butter then liberally brush inside of baking pan with melted butter. Bend roll into circle and line inner periphery of pan with it; the ends will almost but not quite meet. Apply another coat of melted butter to roll then repeat Steps 3–4 with remaining 2 sheets of phyllo and rest of almond mixture.

Spiral Baklava

(*continued*)

6. Carefully (so as not to break it) curl second roll into tighter circle than first; fit within outer circle of rolled phyllo already lining walls of pan. Make sure to leave as little empty space in pan as possible by fitting second roll in a manner that continues outer roll in a tight spiral toward center. Once pan is filled, brush remaining melted butter over top of everything.

7. Bake 30–40 minutes, until pastry takes on uniform golden-brown color.

8. Combine sugar, water, and honey in small saucepan; bring to boil. Turn down heat to medium-low; stir well and let syrup simmer another few minutes until ready. The desired consistency is somewhat thicker than olive oil but not quite as thick as honey on its own.

9. Remove baklava pan from oven and place on plate. Immediately pour hot syrup slowly over top in widening spiral starting from center. Make sure to pour honey mixture over entire pastry. Let stand to cool and for syrup to be absorbed before serving.

PER SERVING Calories: 580 | Fat: 28g | Sodium: 94mg | Carbohydrates: 79g | Fiber: 5.5g | Protein: 11g

Tiganites (Pancakes)

Canadian maple syrup can take the place of the honey normally used in Greek cooking.

INGREDIENTS | **YIELDS 6–8 PIECES**

1 cup all-purpose flour

1 teaspoon baking powder (optional)

½ teaspoon salt

1 egg

1 tablespoon extra-virgin olive oil (or vegetable oil)

1 cup milk

Butter for frying

Greek blossom honey for topping

Some chopped fresh berries and/or walnuts (optional)

1. Combine and sift flour, baking powder, and salt into mixing bowl. (Baking powder is not necessary, but makes a fluffier pancake.)

2. Beat egg in separate mixing bowl. Add olive oil and milk; mix well.

3. Add mixture to bowl with flour; whisk to combine wet and dry ingredients to form smooth batter. If you prefer a thinner pancake, add a little more milk to batter.

4. Heat medium-sized frying pan over medium heat and melt a tablespoonful of butter. (Or use olive oil which is traditionally used instead to fry tiganites.) Use ladle to drop dollop of batter into center of pan so it will spread into a disc as it cooks. When edges of disc start to dry and bubbles appear, flip pancake to cook other side.

5. Serve hot with butter and honey drizzled over top. You can also add fresh berries or chopped walnuts and a sprinkle of cinnamon.

PER SERVING Calories: 107 | Fat: 4g | Sodium: 173mg | Carbohydrates: 14g | Fiber: 0.5g | Protein: 3g

Strained Yogurt

Yogurt of any fat content can be strained.

INGREDIENTS | **SERVES 4**

2 pints store-bought yogurt (any fat content)
½ cup chopped walnuts (optional)
¼ cup Greek thyme honey (optional)

1. Line colander with clean kitchen cloth or cheesecloth; spoon yogurt into it. Place over large bowl and refrigerate. Let stand overnight to drain water content. You will be left with approximately half of the original amount of yogurt.

2. Spoon out small servings of yogurt (about ¼ cup or so), sprinkle with generous amount of chopped walnuts, and drizzle a tablespoon of thyme honey over top of each serving.

3. Garnish with fruits (berries make a nice accompaniment) and serve.

PER SERVING Calories: 312 | Fat: 17g | Sodium: 113mg | Carbohydrates: 32g | Fiber: 1g | Protein: 9.5g

Stuffed Dried Figs

Purchase Kalamata dried string figs if you can find them, as they are larger and sweeter than most other commercially available varieties.

INGREDIENTS | SERVES 4

12 dried figs
24 walnut halves
2 tablespoons thyme honey
2 tablespoons sesame seeds

Need Calcium and Fiber?

Fresh or dried, figs are an excellent source of calcium and fiber, as well as many other nutrients. They are also rich in antioxidants and polyphenols.

1. Snip tough stalk ends off figs. For each fig, slice side and open with fingers.

2. Stuff 2 walnut halves inside each fig and fold closed.

3. Arrange figs on platter. Drizzle with honey and sprinkle with sesame seeds to serve.

PER SERVING Calories: 216 | Fat: 12g | Sodium: 3.5mg | Carbohydrates: 28g | Fiber: 4g | Protein: 4g

Byzantine Fruit Medley

Feel free to experiment with the fruits you use in this recipe.

INGREDIENTS | SERVES 4

2 apples, peeled and cubed
2 pears, peeled and cubed
Seeds from 1 pomegranate
3 mandarins, peeled and sectioned
½ cup red wine
½ cup Greek anthomelo (blossom honey)

1. Prepare fruits and mix together in medium-sized bowl.

2. Bring wine and blossom honey to boil and let roll for a few minutes to burn off most of the alcohol. Allow to cool 20 minutes.

3. Pour over mixed fruit and refrigerate at least 1 hour. Be sure to stir fruit a few times to ensure sauce covers everything. Serve anytime as a snack or dessert.

PER SERVING Calories: 287 | Fat: 0.5g | Sodium: 6mg | Carbohydrates: 74g | Fiber: 6g | Protein: 1

Bonus Recipes: Breakfast and Lunch

BREAKFAST

Breakfast Bruschetta
212

Roasted Potatoes
with Vegetables
213

Frittata
214

Rye-Pumpernickel Strata with
Bleu Cheese
215

Fruit-Stuffed French Toast
216

Polenta
217

Mediterranean Omelet
218

Pastina and Egg
219

Fresh Fruit and Plain Yogurt
220

Stovetop-Poached Fresh Cod
221

Eggs in Crusty Italian Bread
222

Sweetened Brown Rice
223

Creamy Sweet Risotto
224

Israeli Couscous with
Dried-Fruit Chutney
225

Fresh Tuna with Sweet Lemon
Leek Salsa
226

Yogurt Cheese and Fruit
227

Vegetable Pita with Feta Cheese
228

Almond Mascarpone Dumplings
229

Multigrain Toast with
Grilled Vegetables
230

Breakfast Bruschetta

You will notice that it is not unusual for a Mediterranean breakfast dish to be dominated by vegetables.

INGREDIENTS | SERVES 4

½ loaf of Italian or French bread

½ cup extra-virgin olive oil

¼ cup pesto

1 medium tomato

2 egg whites

2 whole eggs

1 roasted red pepper

¼ cup mozzarella cheese

1. Slice the bread into 4¾" lengthwise pieces. Brush 1 side of each with a bit of the oil; toast on grill. When that side is toasted, brush oil on the other side, flip, and toast that side.

2. Place the toasted bread on a sheet pan and spread with pesto. Peel and chop the tomato; combine it with the eggs. Dice the pepper and shred the cheese.

3. Heat the remaining oil in a sauté pan to medium temperature; add the egg mixture and cook omelet style. Cut the omelet and place on the bread; top with cheese and pepper.

Roasted Potatoes with Vegetables

This dish serves double duty as a treat for breakfast or as a side dish at dinner.

INGREDIENTS | SERVES 6

3 Idaho baking potatoes
1 sweet potato
3 carrots
1 yellow onion
½ pound button mushrooms
2 tablespoons olive oil
Fresh-cracked black pepper, to taste
Kosher salt, to taste

1. Preheat oven to 400°F.

2. Large-dice the potatoes and carrots. Large-dice the onion. Trim off any discolored ends from the mushroom stems.

3. In a large bowl, mix together the olive oil, potatoes, onions, carrots, and mushrooms. Place them evenly in a roasting pan, and sprinkle with salt and pepper.

4. Roast the vegetables for 30 to 45 minutes, until tender. Serve warm.

Frittata

This is the Italian version of quiche without a crust. Experiment with different types of vegetables and cheeses.

INGREDIENTS | SERVES 6

1 pound Idaho potatoes
2 each yellow and red peppers
2 Italian green peppers
1 large red onion
½ bunch fresh oregano
3 ounces fontina cheese
2 teaspoons olive oil
Kosher or sea salt
Fresh-cracked black pepper
3 whole eggs
6 egg whites
1 cup plain nonfat yogurt
1 cup skim milk

1. Preheat oven to 375°F.

2. Slice the potatoes into large pieces. Stem, seed, and slice the peppers. Cut the onion into thick slices. Chop the oregano leaves. Grate the fontina.

3. Separately toss the potatoes, peppers, and onion in oil and drain on a rack. Season with salt and black pepper.

4. Roast all the vegetables separately in the oven until partially cooked. Layer all in a baking dish.

5. Whisk together the eggs, egg whites, yogurt, milk, and cheese; pour into the baking dish. Bake until the egg mixture is completely set, approximately 30 to 45 minutes. Sprinkle with chopped oregano and serve.

Rye-Pumpernickel Strata with Bleu Cheese

Savory breakfast is traditional in the Mediterranean. This dish is perfect to serve at brunch as well.

INGREDIENTS | SERVES 6

3 (1½") slices seedless rye bread
3 (1½") slices pumpernickel bread
½ teaspoon extra-virgin olive oil
2 whole eggs
6 egg whites
¼ cup skim milk
¼ cup plain nonfat yogurt
2 ounces bleu cheese
Fresh-cracked black pepper, to taste

1. Preheat oven to 375°F.

2. Tear the bread into large pieces. Grease a 2-quart casserole pan with the oil.

3. In a large mixing bowl, beat the eggs and egg whites; add the milk, yogurt, and cheese. Place the bread pieces in the prepared casserole pan, then pour in the egg mixture. Bake for 40 to 50 minutes, until the mixture is set and the top is golden brown. To serve, cut into squares and season with pepper.

Fruit-Stuffed French Toast

The rich eggy flavor of challah creates the rich profile of this dish.

INGREDIENTS | SERVES 6

½ teaspoon olive oil

3 small to medium loaves challah bread

1 pint seasonal fresh fruit

2 whole eggs

4 egg whites

¼ cup skim milk

1 cup orange juice

¼ cup nonfat plain yogurt

¼ cup confectioners' sugar

1. Preheat oven to 375°F. Grease a baking sheet with the oil.

2. Slice the bread into thick (2½ to 3") slices with a serrated knife at a severe angle to form long bias slices (a medium-large loaf of challah will yield 3 thick bias slices). Cut a slit into the bottom crust to form a pocket.

3. Peel the fruit if necessary, then dice into large pieces and fill the pockets in the bread. Press the pocket closed.

4. In a large mixing bowl, beat the eggs and egg whites, then add the milk. Dip the bread into the egg mixture, letting it fully absorb the mixture. Place the bread on the prepared baking sheet. Bake for 10 minutes on 1 side, flip, and bake 10 minutes more.

5. While the bread is baking, pour the orange juice in small saucepan; boil until reduced by half and the mixture becomes syrupy. Remove the French toast from the oven, and cut in half diagonally. Serve each with dollop of yogurt, a drizzle of juice, and a sprinkling of sugar.

Polenta

Polenta lends itself well to the incorporation of all of your favorite ingredients. Experiment!

INGREDIENTS | **SERVES 6**

1 cup skim milk

2 cups favorite stock

½ cup cornmeal

¼ cup grated cheese (optional)

Fresh-cracked black pepper, to taste

Bring the milk and stock to a boil over medium heat in a saucepan. Slowly whisk in the cornmeal a bit at a time; stir frequently until cooked; approximately 15 minutes until mixture is the consistency of mashed potatoes. Remove from heat, add the cheese, and season with pepper.

Mediterranean Omelet

Omelets in the Mediterranean are light and fluffy; they are not made on a grill.

INGREDIENTS | SERVES 6

2 whole eggs

6 egg whites

¼ cup plain nonfat yogurt

½ teaspoon extra-virgin olive oil

2 ounces pancetta (sliced paper-thin) or lean ham

3 ounces cheese (Swiss or any other), shredded

¼ bunch fresh parsley, chopped

Fresh-cracked black pepper, to taste

Season the Pan

When making omelets, always make sure your pan is properly seasoned. A properly seasoned pan is worth its weight in gold. To season, coat the pan with oil and put it in a warm oven or cover the surface generously with salt and then wipe clean.

1. In medium-size bowl, beat the eggs and egg whites, then whisk in the yogurt. Heat half of the oil to medium temperature in a sauté pan. Quickly sauté the pancetta, then remove and drain on paper towel.

2. Heat the remaining oil to medium temperature in a large sauté pan. Pour in the egg mixture, then sprinkle in the pancetta and cheese. Stir once only. Continuously move the pan over the heat, using a spatula to push the edges inward slightly to allow the egg mixture to pour outward and solidify. When the mixture is mostly solidified, use a spatula to fold it in half.

3. Cover and finish cooking on the stovetop on low heat or uncovered in a 350°F-oven for approximately 5 minutes. Sprinkle with parsley and black pepper and serve.

Pastina and Egg

Pasta for breakfast? Why not—this hearty breakfast is great on a cold morning to fortify you for the day.

INGREDIENTS | SERVES 6

1 whole egg
2 egg whites
3 cups chicken broth (fat removed)
1½ cups pastina
1 ounce fresh Parmesan cheese, grated
Fresh-cracked black pepper, to taste
¼ bunch fresh parsley, chopped

1. Beat the egg and egg whites. Bring the broth to a slow boil in a medium-size saucepot, then add the pastina; stir frequently until almost al dente.

2. Whisk in the eggs, stirring constantly until the eggs are completely cooked and the pasta is al dente. Remove from heat and ladle into bowls. Sprinkle in cheese, pepper, and parsley.

Fresh Fruit and Plain Yogurt

Use fruits that are in season. Mix and match the ripest.

INGREDIENTS | SERVES 6

¼ fresh cantaloupe

¼ fresh honeydew melon

2 fresh kiwi

1 fresh peach

1 fresh plum

½ pint fresh raspberries

6 cups plain nonfat yogurt

6 mint sprigs (top only)

1. Slice the cantaloupe and honeydew paper-thin (use a vegetable peeler if necessary and if the fruit is not overly ripe). Slice the kiwi into ¼" thick circles. Slice the peach and plum into thin wedges. Carefully rinse the raspberries.

2. Spoon the yogurt into serving bowls and arrange the fruits decoratively around each rim. (The cantaloupe and melon can be arranged like a lacy border; the other cut fruit can be fanned and placed atop the yogurt.) Sprinkle the raspberries on top. Garnish with mint.

Stovetop-Poached Fresh Cod

A great example of a savory breakfast that gets in your protein source early in the day. Great for that fresh-caught fish!

INGREDIENTS | **SERVES 6**

3 celery stalks

½ bunch fresh parsley stems

1½ pounds fresh cod (cut into 4-ounce portions)

1 bay leaf

2 cups fish stock

1 tablespoon freshly squeezed lemon juice

Fresh-cracked black pepper, to taste

Kosher salt, to taste

1. Roughly chop the celery and parsley. Place the celery and parsley in the bottom of a sauté pan and arrange the cod pieces on top. Add the bay leaf, stock, and lemon juice, and place over medium-high heat. Cover with parchment paper or a loose-fitting lid.

2. Bring to a simmer and cook covered until the fish flakes, approximately 15 to 20 minutes, depending on the thickness of the fish. Remove from heat and season with pepper and salt. Serve with or without poaching liquid.

Eggs in Crusty Italian Bread

Using crusty Italian bread is so much better than the more familiar version with empty-calorie "white bread."

INGREDIENTS | SERVES 6

6 (2") slices Italian bread
1 teaspoon virgin olive oil
2 red peppers, thinly sliced
½ shallot, minced
6 eggs
Fresh-cracked black pepper, to taste
Kosher salt, to taste

1. Cut out large circles from the center of the bread slices; discard the center pieces and set the hollowed-out bread slices aside. Heat half of the oil to medium in a sauté pan. Sauté the peppers and shallots until tender. Remove from heat and drain on paper towel; keep warm.

2. Heat the remaining oil on medium-high heat in a large sauté pan. Place the bread slices in the pan. Crack 1 egg into the hollowed-out center of each bread slice. When the eggs solidify, flip them together with the bread (being careful to keep the egg in place), and cook to desired doneness.

3. To serve, remove from pan and top with the pepper-shallot mixture. Season with pepper and salt.

Sweetened Brown Rice

This recipe is perfect for a cold winter day, providing a great alternative to cold cereal.

INGREDIENTS | SERVES 6

1½ cups soy milk
1½ cups water
1 cup brown rice
1 tablespoon honey
¼ teaspoon nutmeg
Fresh fruit (optional)

Place all the ingredients except the fresh fruit in a medium-size saucepan; bring the mixture to a slow simmer and cover with a tight-fitting lid. Simmer for 45 to 60 minutes, until the rice is tender and done. Serve in bowls, topped with your favorite fresh fruit.

Creamy Sweet Risotto

Sweet and wonderful. This sweet version of the classic risotto can also be used for a dessert.

INGREDIENTS | SERVES 6

1 teaspoon clarified butter

1 teaspoon olive oil

1 cup Arborio rice

¼ cup white grape juice

2 cups skim milk

⅓ cup shredded coconut

½ cup raisins or dried currants

3 teaspoons honey

1. Heat a large sauté pan to medium temperature, then add the butter and oil. Using a wooden spoon, stir in the rice. Add the juice, stirring until completely incorporated. Add the skim milk ¼ cup at a time, stirring constantly. Make certain that each ¼ cup is fully incorporated before adding the next.

2. When the rice is completely cooked, add the coconut. Serve in bowls or on plates, sprinkled with raisins and drizzled with honey.

Israeli Couscous with Dried-Fruit Chutney

Quick and easy to prepare, this sweet version can also be used as a side dish for a spicy entrée.

INGREDIENTS | SERVES 6

Chutney

¼ cup medium-diced dried dates
¼ cup medium-diced dried figs
¼ cup medium-diced dried currants
¼ cup slivered almonds
¼ cup strawberry jam

Couscous

2¼ cups fresh orange juice
2¼ cups water
4½ cups couscous
1 teaspoon grated orange rind
2 tablespoons nonfat plain yogurt

1. Mix together all the chutney ingredients; set aside.

2. Bring the orange juice and water to a boil in a medium-size pot. Stir in the couscous, then add the orange rind. Remove from heat immediately, cover, and let stand for 5 minutes. Fluff the mixture with a fork.

3. Serve in bowls with a spoonful of chutney and a dollop of yogurt.

Fresh Tuna with Sweet Lemon Leek Salsa

*The tuna can be prepared the night before, refrigerated,
then either reheated or served at room temperature.*

INGREDIENTS | SERVES 6

Tuna

1½ pounds fresh tuna steaks (cut into 4-ounce portions)

¼–½ teaspoon extra-virgin olive oil

Fresh-cracked black pepper, to taste

Kosher salt, to taste

Salsa

1 teaspoon extra-virgin olive oil

3 fresh leeks (light green and white parts only), thinly sliced

1 tablespoon fresh lemon juice

1 tablespoon honey

1. Preheat grill to medium-high temperature.

2. Brush each portion of the tuna with the oil and drain on a rack. Season the tuna with pepper and salt, then place the tuna on the grill; cook for 3 minutes. Shift the tuna steaks on the grill to form an X grill pattern; cook 3 more minutes.

3. Turn the steaks over and grill 3 more minutes, then change position again to create X grill pattern. Cook to desired doneness.

4. For the salsa: Heat the oil in a medium-size sauté pan on medium heat, then add the leeks. When the leeks are wilted, add the lemon juice and honey. Plate each tuna portion with a spoonful of salsa.

Yogurt Cheese and Fruit

This breakfast is worth the extra effort of making the yogurt cheese. If you do not have the time or inclination, use farmer cheese instead.

INGREDIENTS | SERVES 6

1 teaspoon fresh lemon juice
½ cup orange juice
½ cup water
3 cups plain nonfat yogurt
1 fresh golden delicious apple
1 fresh pear
¼ cup honey
¼ cup dried cranberries or raisins

1. Prepare the yogurt cheese the day before by lining a colander or strainer with cheese cloth. Spoon the yogurt into the cheese cloth and place the strainer over a pot or bowl to catch the whey; refrigerate for at least 8 hours before serving.

2. In a large mixing bowl, mix together the juices and water. Cut the apple and pear into wedges, and place the wedges in the juice mixture; let sit for at least 5 minutes. Strain off the liquid.

3. When the yogurt is firm, remove from refrigerator, slice, and place on plates. Arrange the fruit wedges around the yogurt. Drizzle with honey and sprinkle with cranberries just before serving.

Vegetable Pita with Feta Cheese

Let your imagination go wild with seasonal veggies. This simple-to-prepare pita delight is delicious and good for you, too.

INGREDIENTS | SERVES 6

1 eggplant, sliced into ½" pieces, lengthwise

1 zucchini, sliced into ½" pieces, lengthwise

1 yellow squash, sliced

1 red onion, cut into ⅓" rings

1 teaspoon virgin olive oil

Fresh-cracked black pepper, to taste

6 whole-wheat pita bread

3 ounces feta cheese

1. Preheat oven to 375°F.

2. Brush the sliced vegetables with oil and place on a racked baking sheet. Sprinkle with black pepper. Roast until tender. (The vegetables can be prepared the night before [refrigerate]; reheat or bring to room temperature before roasting.)

3. Slice a 3" opening in the pitas to gain access to the pockets. Toast the pitas if desired. Fill the pitas with the cooked vegetables. Add cheese to each and serve.

Almond Mascarpone Dumplings

Mascarpone is Italy's answer to cream cheese, with much more flavor.

INGREDIENTS | SERVES 6

1 cup whole-wheat flour
1 cup all-purpose unbleached flour
¼ cup ground almonds
4 egg whites
3 ounces mascarpone cheese
1 teaspoon extra-virgin olive oil
2 teaspoons apple juice
1 tablespoon butter
¼ cup honey

1. Sift together both types of flour in large bowl. Mix in the almonds. In a separate bowl, cream together the egg whites, cheese, oil, and juice on medium speed with an electric mixer.

2. Combine the flour and egg white mixture with a dough hook on medium speed or by hand until a dough forms.

3. Boil 1 gallon water in medium-size saucepot. Take a spoonful of the dough and use a second spoon to push it into the boiling water. Cook until the dumpling floats to the top, about 5 to 10 minutes. You can cook several dumplings at once, just take care not to crowd the pot. Remove with a slotted spoon and drain on paper towels.

4. Heat a medium-size sauté pan on medium-high heat. Add the butter, then place the dumplings in the pan and cook until light brown. Place on serving plates and drizzle with honey.

Multigrain Toast with Grilled Vegetables

Grilling vegetables brings out the sweet flavor. Use any seasonal vegetables.

INGREDIENTS | SERVES 6

½ eggplant
½ zucchini
½ yellow squash
½ red pepper
½ yellow pepper
½ green pepper
1 teaspoon extra-virgin olive oil
6 multigrain bread slices
3 ounces goat cheese
¼ bunch fresh marjoram
Fresh-cracked black pepper, to taste

1. Slice the eggplant, zucchini, and squash in 3" lengths, ¼" to ½" thick, and cut the peppers in half. Preheat a grill to medium heat. Brush the vegetables with the oil and grill all until fork tender. Cut all the vegetables into a large dice. (Vegetables can be prepared the night before; refrigerate and reheat or bring to room temperature before serving.)

2. Grill the bread until lightly toasted, then remove from heat and top with vegetables. Sprinkle with cheese, chopped marjoram, and black pepper.

LUNCH

Tuna Panini
232

Open-Faced Grilled Cheese
233

Vegetable Pita
234

Wilted Arugula on Flatbread
235

Caesar Sandwich
236

Watercress Sandwiches
237

Greek Pita
238

Curried Chicken on Lavash
239

Almond-Encrusted Salmon on
Toast Points
240

Sesame-Ginger-Encrusted
Tuna Carpaccio
241

Grilled Vegetable Hero
242

Souvlaki with Raita
243

Peanut-Coconut-Grilled
Chicken Sandwich
244

Roasted Garlic Potato Salad
Lettuce Rolls
245

Nut Butter and Honey on
Whole Grain
246

Tuna Panini

This is like making a marinated sandwich!

INGREDIENTS | **SERVES 6**

1 hard-boiled egg

1 red onion

1 medium apple

¼ teaspoon lemon juice

1 cup water

1 pound cooked or canned tuna

¼ cup chopped walnuts

2 tablespoons extra-virgin olive oil

1 tablespoon balsamic vinegar, or to taste

Kosher salt, to taste

Fresh-cracked black pepper

1 small loaf Italian bread

1 head green or red leaf lettuce

1. Medium-dice the egg and onion. Dice the apple and toss it in the lemon juice and water; drain.

2. Mix together the tuna, egg, onion, apple, nuts, oil, and vinegar; season with salt and pepper. Cut the bread in half lengthwise, then layer the lettuce and mound the tuna mixture on top.

3. Wrap the loaf tightly with plastic wrap and refrigerate for 1 hour. Slice into 6 equal portions and serve.

Open-Faced Grilled Cheese

This recipe makes for a delightful lunch when served with a fresh salad.

INGREDIENTS | SERVES 6

1 pear
1 teaspoon lemon juice
1 cup water
6 large slices raisin-pumpernickel bread
1 tablespoon extra-virgin olive oil
6 thick slices Swiss cheese (1 ounce each)
Kosher salt, to taste
Fresh-cracked black pepper, to taste

1. Preheat broiler.

2. Dice the pear and toss it in the lemon juice and water; drain thoroughly.

3. Brush the bread with the oil and toast lightly. Place the cheese on the bread, sprinkle with diced pears, and season with salt and pepper.

4. Place under broiler until the cheese melts and the pears brown slightly, approximately 2 minutes.

Vegetable Pita

Use fresh seasonal vegetables and either roast or grill them for this recipe.

INGREDIENTS | SERVES 6

1 large red onion

1 large head lettuce (any type)

6 large pitas

6 ounces hummus

4½ cups vegetables of your choice

2 tablespoons extra-virgin olive oil

Thinly slice the onion and shred the lettuce. Spread hummus on each pita. Layer with onion, lettuce, and roasted vegetables. Drizzle with olive oil, and serve.

Wilted Arugula on Flatbread

You can use slices of extra-crispy bacon in place of the pancetta.

INGREDIENTS | SERVES 6

1 teaspoon olive oil

2 ounces pancetta

3 cups fresh arugula

12 slices flatbread

Fresh-cracked black pepper

Heat the oil to medium temperature in a medium-size saucepan. Add the pancetta, and brown. Add the arugula, wilt, and immediately mound on the flatbread; add pepper to taste. Serve with Gorgonzola or your favorite cheese.

Caesar Sandwich

You must purchase pasteurized egg yolks to prevent salmonella.

INGREDIENTS | SERVES 6

3 cloves roasted garlic

1 anchovy fillet (optional)

1 ounce pasteurized egg yolk

½ teaspoon dry mustard

Fresh-cracked black pepper

½ cup extra-virgin olive oil

1 large head romaine lettuce

6 slices crusty Italian bread

2 ounces Parmesan cheese, grated

1. Prepare the dressing by mashing together the garlic and anchovy. Add the yolk and seasonings. Whisk in the olive oil.

2. Clean and dry the lettuce, then toss the lettuce with the dressing.

3. Place on bread and sprinkle with Parmesan.

Watercress Sandwiches

This recipe is a slight twist on the classic "watercress tea sandwiches."

INGREDIENTS | SERVES 6

6 slices marble (rye-pumpernickel mix) bread

3 ounces Brie cheese

3 bunches watercress leaves

1. Lightly toast the bread; let cool. Spread each slice with the Brie.

2. Clean and lay out the watercress leaves on 3 slices, then top each with the remaining 3 slices. Cut each sandwich into 6 small pieces. Serve 3 each with soup or salad.

Greek Pita

You must use feta with care; while it adds wonderful flavors, remember it has a salty flavor.

INGREDIENTS | **SERVES 6**

2 European cucumbers
1 large red onion
¼ bunch oregano
2 anchovy fillets (optional)
6 pita bread
3 ounces feta cheese
1 tablespoon olive oil
Fresh-cracked black pepper

1. Peel and dice the cucumber and thinly slice the onion. Chop the oregano. Mash the anchovy fillets.

2. Cut a slit into each pita and stuff with cucumber, onion, oregano, and feta.

3. Drizzle with oil and sprinkle with mashed anchovy and black pepper.

Curried Chicken on Lavash

Lavash is another type of flatbread that originally comes from Armenia.

INGREDIENTS | SERVES 6

Lavash
1 cup whole-wheat flour
¼ cup water
Pinch of iodized salt
1 tablespoon olive oil

Chicken
1 medium-size yellow onion
3 cloves garlic
1 carrot
1 tablespoon olive oil
¾ pound chicken
2 tablespoons curry powder
¼ teaspoon red pepper flakes
Fresh-cracked black pepper
½ cup chicken stock

1. Mix together all the lavash ingredients except the oil with a dough hook or by hand. Heat the oil to medium temperature in a sauté pan. Roll the lavash into 8 1"-thin discs and cook each in the pan for approximately 5 minutes on each side, lightly browning each side.

2. To prepare the chicken, peel and chop the onion, garlic, and carrot. Heat the oil to medium temperature in a saucepan. Sauté the vegetables, then add the chicken, seasoning, and stock. Simmer for 1 hour.

3. Serve the chicken on top of the lavash.

Almond-Encrusted Salmon on Toast Points

Serrano peppers have such a thin skin that you don't need to bother removing it.

INGREDIENTS | SERVES 6

6 flour or corn tortillas
1 serrano pepper
¼ cup almonds
1 teaspoon chili powder
1 pound salmon fillet
¼ cup milk
1 tablespoon olive oil
1 tablespoon extra-virgin olive oil, plus extra for drizzling
Honey

Herb Gardens

If you enjoy Mediterranean cooking, you may want to consider planting an herb garden. This will allow you to have fresh herbs at your fingertips to use in all your Mediterranean recipes.

1. Toast the tortillas under the broiler.

2. Mince the serrano and finely chop the almonds; mix together the serrano, almonds, and chili powder.

3. Clean the salmon in ice water, cut it into 6 portions, then dip it into the milk. Dredge in the almond mix.

4. Heat the olive oil to medium temperature and cook the salmon on each side for approximately 5 minutes, until thoroughly cooked.

5. Serve on tortillas, drizzled with extra-virgin olive oil and honey.

Sesame-Ginger-Encrusted Tuna Carpaccio

Rice cakes make a nice alternative to bread.

INGREDIENTS | SERVES 6

1 tablespoon fresh-minced ginger
3 cloves garlic
½ teaspoon soy sauce
1 tablespoon sesame oil
¼ cup sesame seeds
1 pound fresh tuna steak
1 apple, any type
1 bunch scallions
6 rice cakes

1. Mix together the ginger, garlic, soy, ½ tablespoon sesame oil, and the sesame seeds. Encrust the tuna with the seed mixture.

2. Heat a sauté pan on highest heat; sear the outside of the tuna very quickly. Wrap the tuna in plastic wrap and freeze solid.

3. Remove from plastic wrap and, using a very sharp knife, slice the tuna as thinly as possible. Thinly slice the apple and slice the scallions on an extreme bias.

4. Brush the rice cakes with the rest of the sesame oil, and layer with tuna, apple, and scallions.

Grilled Vegetable Hero

This sandwich is sure to please your vegetarian friends.

INGREDIENTS | SERVES 6

6 club rolls
1 eggplant
1 red pepper
1 Vidalia onion
1 tablespoon extra-virgin olive oil
3 ounces goat cheese (optional)
Fresh-cracked black pepper

1. Preheat oven grill. Slice eggplant, pepper, and onion approximately 1" thick, toss in olive oil, place on grill, and cook al dente.

2. Brush the rolls with oil. Layer the veggies on the rolls. Sprinkle with cheese and pepper, and serve.

Pita, Please

Pita is a great bread to use for sandwiches. The bread opens up into a pocket, which you can stuff with your favorite goodies. For on-the-go convenience, pita is a pleaser. Try it with the sandwich recipes in this chapter.

Souvlaki with Raita

You can serve the lamb rare or medium-rare to suit your preference.

INGREDIENTS | SERVES 6

1 teaspoon olive oil

1 pound diced boneless lamb (fat removed)

Fresh-cracked black pepper, to taste

¼ cup dry red wine

¼ bunch fresh oregano

6 pitas

1 cup raita

1. Heat the oil in a sauté pan on high heat. Season the lamb with pepper. Sear the lamb quickly, then add the wine. Allow the wine to reduce by half.

2. Remove the pan from the heat and toss in the chopped oregano.

3. Place on pitas and serve with raita.

Peanut-Coconut-Grilled Chicken Sandwich

Don't confuse coconut milk with the liquid from a fresh coconut.
Coconut milk is made with water and coconut meat.

INGREDIENTS | SERVES 6

¼ cup peanut butter

½ cup coconut milk

¼ cup chicken stock

1 pound boneless, skinless chicken breasts

6 slices whole-grain bread

½ fresh pineapple

1. Mix together the peanut butter, coconut milk, and stock. Marinate the chicken in this mixture for 4 hours, then remove the chicken and reserve the marinade.

2. Preheat grill.

3. Grill the chicken on each side for approximately 10 minutes.

4. While the chicken is grilling, thoroughly cook the marinade over medium heat in a small saucepan until it is reduced by half.

5. Toast the bread. Slice the chicken on the bias and fan it over the toast. Slice the pineapple and place the slices on top of the chicken.

Roasted Garlic Potato Salad Lettuce Rolls

You can use dried herbs, but be sure to reduce the amount to taste.

INGREDIENTS | **SERVES 6**

6 cooked Idaho potatoes or 12 small red-skinned potatoes

½ bulb roasted garlic

1 yellow onion

¼ cup extra-virgin olive oil

2 tablespoons balsamic vinegar

¼ bunch parsley, chopped

Fresh-cracked black pepper

Kosher salt

1 head large-leaf lettuce

Chop the potatoes and mash them with the garlic. Mix together all the ingredients except the lettuce. Adjust seasoning to taste. Place the potato salad on lettuce leaves, then roll up.

Nut Butter and Honey on Whole Grain

Walnuts and almonds work great in this recipe, although any of your favorite nuts is fine to use.

INGREDIENTS	SERVES 6

2 cups nuts (shelled)

6 tablespoons honey

12 slices whole-grain bread (toast if desired)

Purée the nuts until a smooth paste forms; spread onto bread and drizzle with honey.

APPENDIX B

Glossary of Terms

Aerobic Activity

Brisk activity that requires the heart and lungs to work harder to meet the body's need for oxygen. Aerobic activity burns more calories than anaerobic and is good for the cardiovascular system.

Antibacterials

Compounds that destroy or prevent the growth of bacteria, they can kill both harmful and good bacteria.

Antioxidants

Substances or nutrients in food that can slow or prevent oxidation in the body. Plants foods, especially those that are darkly colored or strongly flavored, provide a good source of antioxidants.

Bulgur

Whole wheat kernels that have been parboiled, dried, and crushed. Bulgur is used in pilaf and tabbouli.

Cannellini Bean

White Italian bean that is similar to a navy bean.

Carotenoids

Plant compounds that provide the dark orange, yellow, or red color of many fruits and vegetables. Carotenoids act as antioxidants and can be converted into vitamin A in the body.

Chickpeas

Chickpeas are also known as garbanzo beans and are common in the Mediterranean, West Asia, and India. Chickpeas are good in salads but are most commonly found in hummus and falafel.

Clafoutis

A popular French dessert made from cherries and flan baked together.

Complex Carbohydrates

Chains of three or more simple sugars linked together. There are two types of complex carbohydrates, starches and cellulose. Complex carbohydrates are digested more slowly than simple sugars and are found in vegetables, grains, nuts, seeds, and beans.

Couscous

Couscous is made by rolling and shaping semolina wheat and then coating this with wheat flour. Couscous is commonly used as a side dish or in place of rice or pasta. Israeli couscous is a larger round ball and is more similar to pasta.

Cruciferous

Cruciferous vegetables come from the Brassica family of vegetables. The cruciferous name, in Latin *Crucifer*, reflects the four sections of the plant that appear in the shape of a cross. They are sulfur-containing vegetables, which is why they all have a stronger taste.

Ellagic Acid

A phytochemical found in raspberries, strawberries, cranberries, walnuts, pecans, pomegranates, and other plant foods. Ellagic acid acts as an antioxidant and may help reduce the risk of several forms of cancer.

Fava Beans

An Italian bean that is sometimes called a broad bean. Fava beans are enjoyed plain, in casseroles, or stews.

Flavonoids

A group of phytonutrients found in a wide variety of fruits, vegetables, and tea. Flavonoids act as antioxidants, help with brain function, and may keep the immune system healthy.

Glutathione

A naturally occurring, sulfur containing antioxidant. Cruciferous vegetables are rich in glutathione.

Homocysteine

Homocysteine is an amino acid found in the blood. Too much homocysteine is associated with an increased risk of heart disease. Folic acid, found in green, leafy vegetables and fortified grains, can help keep homocysteine levels low.

Inflammation

Inflammation is a normal reaction of the body to foreign bodies or matter. Inflammation helps the body protect itself while healing occurs. Inflammation that goes on all the time, called chronic inflammation, is not a healthy process and is the cause of damage to the body leading to aging and disease. Studies show diet plays a role in triggering and eliminating inflammation but the how it does it, as well as the why it does it are points that aren't clear.

Insoluble Fiber

Insoluble fiber is a group of three fibers that act together to aid regularity. Insoluble fibers do not dissolve in water but do hold on to water, helping to move waste products through the intestine. They may help protect against cancer. Common fibers are wheat, corn, flax, and many vegetables.

Inulin

One of three probiotics found in grains, onions, fruits, garlic, honey, artichokes, and a few other vegetables. Inulin can help lower blood cholesterol and promotes a healthier environment in the intestine.

Isothiocyanates

Antioxidant found in cruciferous vegetables that also helps detoxify harmful compounds in the body and can help boost antioxidant capability of cells. Found in sulphur containing foods like broccoli, cabbage, cauliflower, turnips, and kale.

Legume

Pod, such as a bean, that splits in two. The side the seed is attached to is used as food. Common legumes are black beans, navy beans, kidney beans, split peas, and lentils.

Lignin

A type of insoluble fiber that combines with other fibers to give plants their structure. Lignin and other insoluble fibers are found in greatest concentrations in grains like wheat and corn, along with beans.

Lutein

A member of the carotenoid family it helps with vision and may reduce the incidence of macular degeneration and some forms of cancer. The best sources of lutein are green vegetables and egg yolks.

Lycopene

A member of the carotenoid family it helps reduce the risk of prostate cancer and may reduce the risk of heart disease. The best sources of lycopene are red fruits and vegetables like tomatoes, pink grapefruit, and watermelon.

Metabolic Syndrome

A trio of health conditions including high blood pressure, high blood lipid levels, and high blood sugar levels. The combination of all three of these conditions leads to a significantly increased risk for heart disease.

Millet

A small, round grain most commonly used in Europe, Asia, and Africa. It has a mild flavor and it can be used in casseroles or cooked like rice.

Monounsaturated Fats

Types of fat that, along with polyunsaturated fats, help lower blood cholesterol when used in place of saturated fats. Monounsaturated fats are found in oils, nuts, seeds, and fatty fish.

Oleuropein

The chemical found in the olive tree and the olive stem that provides some of the health benefits associated with olive oil.

Oligosaccharide

Simple sugar phytonutrients that act in the body as prebiotics. Common oligosaccharides are shallots, onions, garlic, asparagus, and wheat.

Omega–3 Fatty Acids

Essential fats needed by the body but the body is not able to make these fats. Omega 3's must be provided by the diet with fatty fish, flaxseeds, walnuts, and canola and soybean oils providing the best sources.

Oxidation

Oxidation is a chemical process that causes a change in cells, resulting in free radicals. Free radicals are compounds that then enter cells and can cause damage to the cells. Free radicals as a result of oxidation are the triggers for aging and damage to cells and tissues.

Phytic Acid

A natural plant antioxidant found in cereal grains, seeds, and beans. Phytic acid can bind with iron and calcium decreasing the amount that is absorbed but it may also prevent some forms of cancer and it appears to help control blood sugar levels.

Phytochemicals

A term often used in place of phytonutrients as a way to convey that these compounds are not essential to life as opposed to the meaning of the word nutrient.

Phytonutrients

Plant compounds that provide health benefits beyond those normally provided by the vitamins, minerals, proteins, carbohydrates, and fat in food. Phytonutrients are not essential for life.

Polenta

An Italian grain dish made from yellow or white cornmeal.

Polyphenols

Compounds found in a wide variety of plants. Polyphenols are grouped into flavonoids and nonflavonoids. Common polyphenols are berries, tea, wine, and soybeans.

Polyunsaturated Fats

Fats that are chemically unstable and that are liquid at room temperature. Polyunsaturated fats are found mainly in corn, safflower, soybean, and sunflower oils. Polyunsaturated fats can help lower blood cholesterol when used in place of saturated fats.

Prebiotics

Nondigestible compounds in food that help normal, healthy bacteria grow in your colon. Prebiotics aid in digestion and help prevent bloating and gas.

Probiotics

Live microorganisms that are similar to healthy bacteria in the intestine and when consumed they act as healthy bacteria promoting overall health. Common probiotics are yogurt, fermented milk products like kefir, miso, and tempeh.

Quinoa

A grain that is native to South America and is often referred to as the "Mother of All Grains." Quinoa is a complete protein making it a good choice for vegetarians. It cooks like rice and can be used in recipes that call for rice.

Registered Dietitian

A credentialed professional who fulfilled specific requirements, including earning at least a bachelor's degree, completed a supervised practice program, and passed a registration examination.

Resistance Training

Training that causes muscles to contract against an external resistance with the intent of increasing strength, muscle mass, and endurance. Common resistance tools are weights, dumbbells, and exercise bands.

Resveratrol

A phytonutrient found in the skin and seeds of grapes. It functions as an antioxidant helping to promote heart health and may also help keep blood platelets from sticking together to prevent blood clots.

Saturated Fats

Fats that are chemically stable making them solid at room temperature. Common saturated fats are meat, poultry, butter, whole milk, coconut, palm, and palm kernels oils. Saturated fats can increase blood cholesterol.

Soluble Fiber

Soluble fiber dissolves in water to form a gel-like compound making it a good fiber to help lower cholesterol. Soluble fiber is found in high amounts in beans, barley, flaxseeds, oats, oranges, and other fruits and vegetables.

Sulfides

Sulfides are a group of phytonutrients found in vegetables and fruits. Sulfides are also referred to as thiols and common sulfides are garlic, onion, leeks, scallions, and cruciferous vegetables.

Tannins

Compounds found in grape skin, seeds, and stems; they are the source of the antioxidants found in wine.

Tocopherols

A group of closely related fat-soluble alcohols that act like vitamin E. They are found in nuts, oils, wheat germ, and seeds.

APPENDIX C

Resources

American Cancer Society

1-800-ACS-2345

www.cancer.org

The American Cancer Society is a nationwide, community-based voluntary health organization dedicated to eliminating cancer as a major health problem.

American Dietetic Association

1-800-877-1600

www.eatright.org

The world's largest organization of food and nutrition professionals, ADA is committed to improving the nation's health and advancing the profession of dietetics through research, education, and advocacy.

American Heart Association

1-800-AHA-USA1

www.heart.org

The American Heart Association is a nonprofit organization dedicated to building healthier lives, free of cardiovascular diseases and stroke. Tips for healthy living, latest news about heart disease, and ways to recognize the symptoms of a heart attack or stroke are included on their site.

National Cancer Institute

1-800-4CANCER

www.cancer.gov

The National Cancer Institute coordinates the National Cancer Program, which conducts and supports research, training, health information dissemination, and other programs with respect to the cause, diagnosis, prevention, and treatment of cancer, rehabilitation from cancer, and the continuing care of cancer patients and the families of cancer patients.

Oldways

1-617-421-5500

www.oldwayspt.org

Oldways is a nonprofit organization founded in 1990 to promote healthy eating and drinking. Oldways was instrumental in the development of the Mediterranean diet pyramid that shows the importance of the right food choices and the pleasures of the table.

The Food Information Council

1-202-296-6540

www.foodinsight.org

A public education foundation dedicated to the mission of effectively communicating science-based information on health, food safety, and nutrition for the public good.

The United States Department of Agriculture

1-202-720-2791

www.usda.gov

Branch of the U.S. government charged with providing news and information on food, agriculture, and nutrition.

Whole Grains Council

1-617-421-5500

www.wholegrainscouncil.org

The Whole Grains Council is a nonprofit consumer advocacy group working to increase consumption of whole grains for better health.

Farmers' Markets by State

Here is a selection of Farmer's Markets by state. For a complete listing and to search by zip code, visit *http://apps.ams.usda.gov/farmersmarkets*.

ALASKA

Anchorage Downtown Market & Festival
3rd Avenue
Anchorage, Alaska 99501
http://www.anchoragemarkets.com

Anchorage Farmers Market
1420 Cordova Street
Anchorage, Alaska 99645
www.anchoragefarmersmarket.org

Central Kenai Peninsula Farmers Market
Intersection of E. Corral Avenue
& Soldotna
Soldotna, Alaska 99669
www.alaskaartguild.com

Haines Farmer Market
Located in Payson's Pavilion in the Fair
Grounds
Haines, Alaska 99827

Highway's End Farmers' Market
Corner of Alaska Highway and
Richardson Highway
Delta Junction, Alaska 99737

Juneau Farmers Market
Juneau Arts and Culture Center
Juneau, Alaska 99801

Kenai's Saturday Market
Kenai Visitor & Cultural Center
Kenai, Alaska 99611
www.visitkenai.com

Northway Mall Wednesday Market
3101 Pennland Blvd.
Anchorage, Alaska 99510
www.anchoragemarkets.com

Palmer Friday Fling
Pavillion across from Visitor's Center
Palmer, Alaska 99645

Sitka Farmers Market
235 Katlian Street
Sitka, Alaska 99835
www.sitkalocalfoodsnetwork.org

Soldotna Wednesday Market
Soldotna Creek Park, behind
Don Jose's
Soldotna, Alaska 99669

South Anchorage Farmers Market I
Subway Sports Centre/Cellular One
Sports Centre
Anchorage, Alaska 99501
*http://www.southanchoragefarmers
market.com*

South Anchorage Farmers Market II
Behind Dimond Mall, in front of Dimond
Hotel
Anchorage, Alaska 99501
*http://www.southanchoragefarmers
market.com*

Tanana Valley Farmers Market
College Road and Caribou Way
Fairbanks, Alaska 99708
http://www.tvfmarket.com

Wasilla Farmers Market
Behind Wasilla Public Library
Wasilla, Alaska 99654
http://home.gci.net/%7ewasillaknikhistory/

ALABAMA

Alexander City Downtown Market
Broad Street
Alexander City, Alabama 35010
http://www.mainstreetac.org

Anniston Downtown Farmers Market
14th & Gurnee

Anniston, Alabama 36201
www.spiritofanniston.org

Calera Farmers Market
9758 Hwy 25
Calera, Alabama 35040
www.calerafarmersmarket.com

City of Albertville Farmers Market
Main Street downtown
Albertville, Alabama 35950
www.cityofalbertville.com

East Chase Farmers Market
7274 East Chase Parkway
Montgomery, Alabama 36117
www.theshoppesateastchase.com

East Lake Farmers Market
7753 First Avenue, South
Birmingham, Alabama 35206
www.peerinc.org

Festhalle Market Platz
209 1st Ave. NE
Cullman, Alabama 35056
www.cullmancity.org

Homegrown Alabama Farmers Market
812 5th Avenue
Tuscaloosa, Alabama 35401
www.homegrownalabama.org

Jack o Lantern Farm Market
430 Garage Rd.
Muscle Shoals, Alabama 35661
www.jackolanternfarm.com

**Jefferson County Truck
Growers Association**
344 Finley Ave., West
Birmingham, Alabama 35204
http://www.alabamafarmersmarket.org

Madison City Farmers Market
1282 Hughes Road
Madison, Alabama 35758
*http://www.MadisonCityFarmers
Market.com*

Pepper Place Saturday Market
2829 2nd Avenue, South
Birmingham, Alabama 35233
http://www.pepperplace.com

Pioneer Farmers Market
Oak & Academy
Troy, Alabama 36081
www.troyfarmersmarket.com

Valleydale Farmers Market
4601 Valleydale Rd.
Birmingham, Alabama 35242
www.valleydalefarmersmarket.com

ARKANSAS

ASN Local Food Club
509 Scott St.
Little Rock, Arkansas 72201
www.littlerock.locallygrown.net

ASU Regional Farmers Market
3407 S. Carway Rd. Ste 7
Jonesboro, Arkansas 72404
*http://agri.astate.edu/Farmersmarket
/farmersmarket.html*

Bella Vista Farmers Market
1451 Bella Vista Way
Bella Vista, Arkansas 72714
http://market.cbmcci.com/

Bentonville Farmers Market
412 S. Main Street

Bentonville, Arkansas 72712
www.downtownbentonville.org

Boone County Farmers Market
Courthouse Square in Harrison
Harrison, Arkansas 72602
http://www.mainstreetharrison.org

**Botanical Gardens of the Ozarks
Farmers Market**
4703 N Crossover Rd.
Fayetteville, Arkansas 72764
www.fayettevillefarmersmarket.org

**Certified Arkansas Farmers Market
Argenta**
520 Main St.
North Little Rock, Arkansas 72114
http://www.arkansasfood.net

**Certified Arkansas Farmers Market
Searcy**
124 E. Woodruff
Searcy, Arkansas 72143
http://www.arkansasfood.net

Downtown Fayetteville Farmers Market
4703 N. Crossover Road
Fayetteville, Arkansas 72764
*http://www.downtownfayettevilee
market.com*

Downtown Fort Smith Farmers Market
Located at 2nd & Garrison parking lot
Fort Smith, Arkansas 72901
www.GoDowntownFS.com

Eureks Springs Farmers Market
10 Woolridge
Eureka Springs, Arkansas 72632
http://www.naturallyarkansas.org

Gentry Farmers' Market
500 East Main Street
Gentry, Arkansas 72734
www.gentrymarket.com

Pope County Farmers Market
Russellville Depot

Russellville, Arkansas 72811
www.popecountyfarmersmarket.com

Randolf County Farmers Market
Highway 67 S
Pocahontas, Arkansas 72455
www.randolphchamber.com

ARIZONA

Avalon Organic Gardens Farm Stand
29 Tubac Plaza Gazebo
Tubac, Arizona 85646
http://avalongardens.org/

Bisbee Farmers Market
Vista Park
Bisbee, Arizona 85603
http://www.bisbeefarmersmarket.org

Cave Creek Farmers & Crafts Market
6900 E Cave Creek Road
Cave Creek, Arizona
www.arizonafarmersmarkets.com

**Community Food Bank
Farmers' Market**
3003 S. Country Club Road
Tucson, Arizona 85713
www.communityfoodbank.com

Concho Farmers Market
Corner of Highway 61 and 180A
Concho, Arizona 85924
http://www.conchofarmersmarket.org

Downtown Glendale Farmers Market
5734 W. Glendale Ave. (Mad Hatters parking lot)
Glendale, Arizona
www.arizonafarmersmarkets.com

Downtown Phoenix Public Market
721 N. Central
Phoenix, Arizona 85028
www.phoenixpublicmarket.com

Elgin Farmers Market
Kief-Joshua Vineyards, 370 Elgin Road

Elgin, Arizona 85611
www.kj-vineyards.com

Flagstaff Community Market
211 W. Aspen
Flagstaff, Arizona 86001
www.flagstaffmarket.com

Market in Downtown Yuma
Downtown Main Street
Yuma, Arizona 85365
http://www.yumafoodbank.org

Payson Farmer's Market
816 S Beeline Hwy
Payson, Arizona 85541
www.PaysonFarmersMarket.info

Prescott Farmers Market
1100 E. Sheldon Street
Prescott, Arizona 86301
http://www.prescottfarmersmarket.org/

Rincon Valley Farmers & Artisans Market
12500 E. Old Spanish Trail
Tucson, Arizona 85747
www.rvfm.org

Roadrunner Park Farmers' Market
3502 E. Cactus Rd
Phoenix, Arizona 85032

CALIFORNIA

Anaheim Thursday Farmers Market
Center St. Promenade & Lemon St.
Anaheim, California 92805
http://www.downtownanaheim.com

Berkeley Farmers' Market - Saturday
Center Street & Martin Luther
King Jr., Way
Berkeley, California 94702
http://www.ecologycenter.org/bfm

Pacific Grove Certified Farmers' Market
Along Lighthouse Ave.
Pacific Grove, California 93950

www.everyonesharvest.org

Pasadena Victory Park CFM
2925 North Sierra Madre Blvd
Pasadena, California 91104
www.pasadenafarmersmarket.org

Placerville Farmers Market
Main St. & Cedar Ravine
Placerville, California 95667
www.eldoradofarmersmarkets.com

Sacramento Florin Certified Farmers' Market
Florin Road and 65th Street
Sacramento, California 95814
http://www.california-grown.com

San Diego Little Italy Mercato
Date Street
San Diego, California 92101
www.littleitalymercato.com

San Francisco Ferry Plaza Farmers Market
Embarcadero & Market Streets
San Francisco, California 94102
http://www.cuesa.org

Vista Farmers Market
300 block South Melrose Drive
Vista, California 92084
www.vistafarmersmarket.com/

Walnut Creek Certified Farmers Market
North Locust
Walnut Creek, California 94596
http://www.cccfm.org

Wednesday Santa Monica Farmers Market
Arizona @ 2nd Street
Santa Monica, California 90401
www.farmersmarket.smgov.net

West Hollywood Thursday Farmers Market
647 North San Vicente Blvd.

West Hollywood, California 90069
http://www.cafarmersmarkets.org

Westside CFM
Corner of Western Drive and Mission St.
Santa Cruz, California 95060
http://www.santacruzfarmers market.org

Westwood Farmers Market
11011 Constitution Ave
Los Angeles, California 90073
www.westwoodfarmersmarket.com

COLORADO

Boulder Farmers' Market
1708 13th Street
Boulder, Colorado 80302
www.boulderfarmers.org

Canon City Farmers' Market
6th and Macon
Canon City, Colorado 81212
www.canoncityfarmersmarket.com

Cherry Creek Fresh Market
3000 East First Avenue
Denver, Colorado 80206
http://www.coloradofreshmarkets.com/

Colorado Farm and Art Market (Saturday Market)
The Margarita at Pine Creek
Restaurant, 7350 Pine Creek Road
Colorado Springs, Colorado 80919
www.farmandartmarket.com

Durango Farmers Market
259 West 8th Street
Durango, Colorado 81301
www.durangofarmersmarket.org

Glenwood's Downtown Market
Centennial Park
Glenwood Springs, Colorado 81601
http://glenwoodmarket.com

Golden Farmers Market
10th Avenue & Illinois Street
Golden, Colorado 80401
www.goldencochamber.org

Greeley Farmers Market at the Depot
902 7th Avenue
Greeley, Colorado 80631
http://www.greeleygov.com/fm

Larimer County Farmers' Market
200 W. Oak Street
Fort Collins, Colorado 80521
www.larimercountyfarmersmarket.org

Mancos Farmer's Market
178 E. Frontage Rd.
Mancos, Colorado 81328
www.mancoscolorado.com

South Fork Farmers Market
Junction Routes 160 & 149
South Fork, Colorado 81154
www.sffarmersmarket.org

The Evergreen Farmers Market
1200 Sugarbush Drive
Evergreen, Colorado 80401
www.coloradooutdoormarkets.com

The Minturn Market
Historic Downtown Minturn
Minturn, Colorado 81645
http://www.minturnmarket.org

Woodland Park Farmers' Market
Center Street & Henrietta
Woodland Park, Colorado 80866
www.woodlandparkfarmersmarket.com

CONNECTICUT

Bozrah Farmers Market
Maples Farm Park, 45 Bozrah Street
Bozrah, Connecticut 06334
www.bozrahfarmersmarket.org

City Farmers' Market Edgewood Park
Whalley Ave. and West Rock Ave.

New Haven, Connecticut 06515
http://www.cityseed.org

Collinsville Farmers Market
4 Market Street
Collinsville, Connecticut 06019
www.collinsvillefarmersmarket.org

Coventry Regional Farmers' Market
2299 South St
Coventry, Connecticut 06238
www.coventryfarmersmarket.com

Hartford Regional Market
I-91, Exit 27, 101 Reserve Road
Hartford, Connecticut 06114
www.ctgrown.gov

Lebanon Farmers Market
579 Exeter Road
Lebanon, Connecticut 06249
www.lebanontownhall.org

Norfolk Farmers' Market
Center of Town, Rte. 44
Norfolk, Connecticut
www.norfolkfarmersmarket.org

Old Saybrook Farmers Market
210 Main Street, Cinema Plaza
Old Saybrook, Connecticut 06475
www.oldsaybrookfarmersmarket.com

Plainfield Farmers Market
482 Norwich Road (Route 12)
Plainfield, Connecticut 06354
www.nectfaremrsmarket.org

Putnam Farmers Market
18 Kennedy Drive
Putnam, Connecticut 06260
www.nectfaremrsmarket.org

Sandy Hook Organic Farmers Market
5 Washington Avenue, Sandy
Hook Center
Sandy Hook, Connecticut 06482
*www.sandyhookorganicfarmers
market.org*

**Stamford - Bartlett Arboretum &
Gardens Farmers' Market**
Bartlett Arboretum & Gardens, 151
Brookdale Road
Stamford, Connecticut 06901
*www.bartlettarboretum.org
/newsevents/farmersmarket2009/*

Storrs Farmers Market
Mansfield Town Hall Parking Lot
Storrs, Connecticut 06268
www.storrsfarmers.org

Suffield Farmers Market
Town Green, North Main and
High Streets
Suffield, Connecticut 06078
http://www.suffieldtownhall.com

DISTRICT OF COLUMBIA

14&U Farmers' Market
1400 U Street NW
Washington, District of Columbia 20009
www.marketsandmore.info

Broad Branch Farmers Market
Lafayette Elementary School
Washington, District of Columbia 20015
http://www.redbudfarm.com

Dupont Circle FRESHFARM Market
1500 20th Street, NW
Washington, District of Columbia 20036
www.freshfarmmarkets.org

**Eastern Market Outdoor
Farmers Market**
306 7th Street SE
Washington, District of Columbia 20002
http://www.easternmarketdc.com/

Glover Park-Burleith Farmers' Market
1819 35th St. NW
Washington, District of Columbia 20007
www.dcgreens.org

Palisades Farmers Market
48th Place NW at MacArthur Blvd
Washington, District of Columbia 20007
*http://www.palisadesfarmers
market.com/*

**US Dept of Health & Human Services
FRESHFARM Market**
200 Independence Avenue, SW
Washington, District of Columbia 20201
www.freshfarmmarkets.org

USDA Farmers Market
Corner 12th St. & Independence Ave.
Washington, District of Columbia 20250
*http://www.ams.usda.gov/farmers
markets*

Ward 8 Farmers Market
500 Alabama Ave. SE
Washington, District of Columbia 20032
www.ward8farmersmarket.com

DELAWARE

Bethany Beach Farmers Market
Garfield Parkway at
Pennsylvania Avenue
Bethany Beach, Delaware 19930
www.bethanybeachfarmersmarket.com

Camp FRESH Farmers Market
501 W. 14th Street
Wilmington, Delaware 19801
*http://www.christianacare.org
/campfresh*

Carousel Park Farmers Market
Carousel Park Equestrian Center
Wilmington, Delaware 19808

Co-op Farmers Market
280 E. Main Street
Newark, Delaware 19711
*www.newarknaturalfoods.coop
/farmersmarket*

**Delaware State University
Farmers Market**
Southwest Corner of Rt 13 and
College Rd on Delaware State
University Property
Dover, Delaware 19901

Georgetown Farmers' Market
22518 Lewes Georgetown Highway
Georgetown, Delaware 19947-5533

Historic Lewes Farmers Market
Corner of Third and
Shipcarpenter Streets
Lewes, Delaware 19958
www.historiclewesfarmersmarket.org

L.I.N.A. Farmers Market
8th and Bancroft Parkway
Wilmington, Delaware 19805

Milford Farmers Market
North Walnut Street at Riverwalk Park
Milford, Delaware 19963
http://www.downtownmilford.org

Rehoboth Beach Farmers Market
Grove Park
Rehoboth Beach, Delaware 19971
www.rbfarmersmarket.com

Western Sussex Farmers' Market
310 Virginia Avenue
Seaford, Delaware 19973

FLORIDA

Alachua County Farmers' Market
5920 NW 13th Street
Gainesville, Florida 32653
www.441market.com

Beaches Green Market
Jarboe Park, Intersection of A1A and
Florida Blvd.
Neptune Beach, Florida 32266
www.BeachesLocalFoodNetwork.org

Boca Raton Green Market
Royal Palm Place south parking lot
Boca Raton, Florida 33432

Brevard County Farmers Market
2500 Parkway Drive
Melbourne, Florida 32935
*http://brevardcountyfarmersmarket
.com*

Cape Coral Chamber Farmers Market
SE 10th Pl. & SE 47th Terr
Cape Coral, Florida 33904
www.capecoralfarmersmarket.com

Coral Gables Farmers Market
405 Biltmore Way
Coral Gables, Florida 33134
www.coralgables.com

Delray Green Market
29 SE 4th Avenue
Delray Beach, Florida 33444
www.delraycra.org

**Downtown Farmers Market of Fort
Pierce, Inc.**
On Melody Lane
Ft. Pierce, Florida 32950
www.ftpiercefarmersmarket.com

Farmer's Market Oceanside
2999 Ocean Drive
Vero Beach, Florida 32963
www.farmersmarketoceanside.com

Flagler Beach Farmers Market
111 S. Central Avenue
Flagler Beach, Florida 32136
*http://www.flaglerbeachfarmers
market.com*

High Springs Farmer's Market
James Paul Park, Historic Downtown
High Springs
High Springs, Florida 32643
www.farmersmarket.highsprings.com

Jackson Memorial Foundation Green Market
1611 NW 12th Avenue
Miami, Florida 33136
www.themarketcompany.org

Jacksonville Farmers Market
1810 West Beaver Street
Jacksonville, Florida 32209
www.JaxFarmersMarket.com

Palafox Market
Martin Luther King Jr. Plaza, Palafox St.
(between Chase & Wright Sts.)
Pensacola, Florida 32502
www.PalafoxMarket.com

GEORGIA

Athens Farmers Market
705 Sunset Dr.
Athens, Georgia 30601
www.athensfarmersmarket.net

Battlefield Farmers Market
10052 Hwy 27 N
Rock Spring, Georgia 30739
www.battlefieldfmkt.org

Cotton Mill Farmers Market
401 Rome St.
Carrollton, Georgia 30117
www.cottonmillfarmersmarket.org

Downtown Gainesville Farmers Market
Main and Spring Streets on the Historic
Downtown Square
Gainesville, Georgia 30503
http://www.hallfarmers.org

Marietta Square Farmers Market
Church Street at Hansell Street
Marietta, Georgia 30060
www.mariettasquarefarmers market.com

Morningside Farmers Market
1393 N. Highland Ave

Atlanta, Georgia 30306
www.morningsidemarket.com

North Georgia Locally Grown
290 South Main St.
Clayton, Georgia 30525
www.northeastgeorgia.locally grown.net

Peachtree Road Farmers Market
2744 Peachtree Rd
Atlanta, Georgia 30305
www.peachtreeroadfarmers market.com

Savannah State Farmers Market
701 U.S. Highway 80-West
Savannah, Georgia 31408

Suwanee Farmers Market
370 Highway 23
Suwanee, Georgia 30024
www.suwanee.com

Union County Farmers Market
Old Smokey Road
Blairsville, Georgia 30512
www.ucfarmersmarket.com

HAWAII

City Hall Parking Lot Deck (People's Open Market)
Alapai & Beretania Street
Honolulu, Hawaii 96813
http://www.co.honolulu.hi.us/parks /programs/pom

Get Fresh Maui
Honopiilani HWY
Maui, Hawaii 96761
http://www.getfreshmaui.com

Hanalei Saturday Farmers Market
Downtown Hanalei
Hanalei, Hawaii 96714
http://www.halehalawai.org /market.htm

Hilo's Farmers Market
Corner of Kamehameha Ave. &
Mamo St.
Hilo, Hawaii 96720
http://www.hilofarmersmarket.com

Honolulu Farmers Market
Blaisdell Concert Hall Lawn
777 Ward Avenue
Honolulu, Hawaii 96814
www.hfbf.org

Makeke O Maunalua Farmers Market
511 Lunalilo Home Road
Hawaii Kai, Hawaii 96825
www.makekeomaunaluafarmers market.com

IOWA

Ames Downtown Farmers Market
Main Street Station 526 Main Street
Ames, Iowa 50010
www.amesfarmersmarket.com

Boone Farmers Market Association
1815 S Story St.
Boone, Iowa 50036
www.boonefarmersmarket.com

Cedar Rapids Downtown Farmers Market
Greene Square Park, 3rd & 4th Ave SE
Cedar Rapids, Iowa 52401
www.downtowncr.org

Des Moines Downtown Farmers Market
Court Avenue between First and
Fifth Streets
Des Moines, Iowa 50309
http://www.desmoinesfarmers market.com/

Downtown Waterloo Farmers Market
420 Jefferson Street
Waterloo, Iowa 50701
www.mainstreetwaterloo.org

Dubuque Farmers Market
Iowa Street between 11th &
13th Streets
Dubuque, Iowa 52001
www.dubuquemainstreet.org

**Farmers Market at Living
History Farms**
Living History Farms, 2600 111th Street
Urbandale, Iowa 50322
*www.livinghistoryfarms.org/
farmersmarket.html*

Freight House Farmers Market
421 West River Drive
Davenport, Iowa 52801
www.freighthousefarmersmarket.com

Hiawatha Farmer's Market
701 Emmons St.
Hiawatha, Iowa 52233
www.hiawatha-iowa.com

Iowa City Farmers Market
East Washington Street
Iowa City, Iowa 52240
www.icgov.org

Marion Farmers Market
East End Shopping Center,
2275 7th Avenue
Marion, Iowa 52302
www.cityofmarion.org

Oskaloosa Farmers Market I
East side of Town Square
Oskaloosa, Iowa 52577
*http://www.hawkeye-re.com/farmer
smarket/index.htm*

Sheldon Farmers Market
Pamida parking lot on Highway 18
Sheldon, Iowa 51201
www.sheldoniowa.com

Sioux City Farmers Market
201 Pearl St
Sioux City, Iowa 51101
www.siouxcityfarmersmarket.com

IDAHO

Bonners Ferry Farmers Market
6373 Bonner St
Bonners Ferry, Idaho 83805
*http://www.bonnersferryfarmers
market.org*

Capital City Public Market I
Downtown Boise - 8th St. between Ban-
nock & Main
Boise, Idaho 83701
http://www.capitalcitypublicmarket.com

Emmett Farmers Market
Blaser Park - North Washington Avenue
Emmett, Idaho 83617
www.EmmettFarmersMarket.com

Farmers' Market at Sandpoint
Farmin Park, 3rd & Oak Street
Sandpoint, Idaho 83864
*http://www.sandpointfarmersmarket.
com*

Grangeville Farmers Market
Heritage Sq., Main Street
Grangeville, Idaho 83703
www.grangevillefarmersmarket.org

Idaho Falls Farmers' Market
501 West Broadway
Idaho Falls, Idaho 83402
http://idahofallsfarmersmarket.org/

Kootenai County Farmers Market I
Corner of Hwy. 95 & Prairie Ave.
Hayden, Idaho 83835
*http://www.kootenaicountyfarmers
market.com*

Kuna Farmers Market
323 Avenue E
Kuna, Idaho 83643
http://www.kunafarmersmarket.com

Lewiston Farmers' Market
525 D Street

Lewiston, Idaho 83501
*www.beautifuldowntownlewiston.org
/farmersmarket*

Meridian Farmers' Market and Bazaar
3400 N. Eagle Rd. (Lowe's Parking Lot)
Meridian, Idaho 83646
*http://www.meridianfarmersmarket
.com*

**Moscow Food Co-op Tuesday
Growers Market**
121 E. 5th Street
Moscow, Idaho 83843
www.moscowfood.coop

Nampa Farmers' Market
12 South 12th Avenue
Nampa, Idaho 83687
http://www.nampafarmersmarket.com

Rathdrum Farmers Market
City Park off Hwy 53
Rathdrum, Idaho 83858
www.rathdrumfarmersmarket.org

ILLINOIS

3 French Hens French Country Market
Canal Port, W. Illinois Ave.
Morris, Illinois 60450
*www.3frenchhensmarket.blogspot
.com*

61st Street Farmers Market
6100 S. Blackstone Ave.
Chicago, Illinois 60637
www.experimentalstation.org

Andersonville Farmers Market
1500 W. Berwyn Ave.
Chicago, Illinois 60640
http://www.andersonville.org

Aurora Farmers Market West
1901 N. Galina
Aurora, Illinois 60506
http://www.aurora-il.org

Bolingbrook Farmers Market
Brouton & Janes
Bolingbrook, Illinois 60443
www.merrillsmarkets.com

Brookfield Farmers Market
8820 Brookfield Avenue
Brookfield, Illinois 60513
www.brookfieldchamber.net

Chicago's Green City Market
Between 1750 N. Clark &
Stockton Drive
Chicago, Illinois 60614
www.chicagegreencitymarket.org

Downers Grove Farmers Market
Main Street Metro Station
Downers Grove, Illinois 60516
www.indianboundaryymca.org

**Downtown Bloomington
Farmers Market**
N. Main St. at E. Jefferson St.
Bloomington, Illinois 61701
*http://www.downtownbloomington
.org*

Evanston's Farmers Market
University at Oak Ave.
Evanston, Illinois 60201
http://www.cityofevanston.org

**Farmers Market on Historic North
1st Street**
North 1st Street
Champaign, Illinois 61820
*http://thefarmersmarketonhistoricn1st
.blogspot.com/*

Frankfort Country Farmers Market
Downtown at Breidert Green Oak & Kansas St.
Frankfort, Illinois 60423
www.frankfortcountrymarket.org

Urbana's Market at the Square
400 South Vine Street

Urbana, Illinois 61801
www.city.urbana.il.us/market

Village of Skokie Farmer's Market
5127 Oakton
Skokie, Illinois 60077
www.skokie.org

INDIANA

Binford Farmers Market
5060 East 62nd Street
Indianapolis, Indiana 46220
www.BinfordFarmersMarket.com

**Bloomington Community
Farmers' Market**
401 North Morton St.
Bloomington, Indiana 47404
*www.bloomington.in.gov/farmers
market*

Carmel Farmers Market
One Civic Square
Carmel, Indiana 46032
www.carmelfarmersmarket.com

**Community Farmers' Market of
Owen County**
60 S. Main St.
Spencer, Indiana 47460
www.farmersmarketowencounty.com

Crown Point Farmers Market
South Main Street
Crown Point, Indiana 46307
www.crownpoint.in.gov

Goshen Farmer's Market
212 W. Washington St.
Goshen, Indiana 46526
www.goshenfarmersmarket.org

**Greensburg/Decatur County
Farmers' Market**
150 Courthouse Square
Greensburg, Indiana 47240
www.downtowngreensburg.com

**Historic West Main Street
Farmers Market**
1936 West Main Street
Fort Wayne, Indiana 46808

Lafayette Farmers Market at Purdue
Sheetz and Wood Streets
West Lafayette, Indiana 47906
www.lafayettefarmersmarket.com

New Albany Farmers Market
Corner of Bank and Market Street
New Albany, Indiana 47150
www.newalbanyfarmersmarket.com

Orange County HomeGrown Valley Farmers Market
Hwy. 56
French Lick, Indiana 47432
*http://www.orangecountyhome
grown.org*

Shelby County Farmers Market
Public Square
Shelbyville, Indiana 46176
www.mainstreetshelbyville.org

**The Original Farmers' Market at
Indianapolis City**
222 E. Market Street
Indianapolis, Indiana 46204
http://www.indycm.com

KANSAS

Capitol Midweek Farmers' Market
1000 SW Jackson St.
Topeka, Kansas 66612
*www.kdheks.gov/bhp/farmers
_market*

Clay Center Farmers' Market
1282 21st Road
Clay Center, Kansas 67432
*www.ClayCenterfarmersmarket
.blogspot.com*

Delano Community Farmers Market
200 S. Walnut
Delano, Kansas 67213
www.historicdelano.com/market

Downtown Lawrence Farmers Market (Saturday)
824 New Hampshire Ave.
Lawrence, Kansas 66044
http://www.lawrencefarmers market.com/

Downtown Topeka Farmers Market
10th & Topeka Blvd.
Topeka, Kansas 66618
http://www.downtowntopekafarmers market.com

Kansas Grown Farmers Market
21st & Ridge Road
Witchita, Kansas 67203
www.kansasgrownmarket.com

Lawrence Farmers Market
824 New Hampshire
Lawrence, Kansas 66044
www.lawrencefarmersmarket.com

Merriam Farmers Market
5740 Merriam Drive
Merriam, Kansas 66203
http://www.merriam.org/park/ Marketplace

Old Town Farmers Market I
1st Street & Mosley
Wichita, Kansas 67202
http://www.oldtownfarmersmarket .com

Reno County Farmers Market
115 West 2nd Ave
Hutchinson, Kansas 67501
http://www.renocountyfarmers market.org

Spring Hill Farmers Market
300 S. Webster St.

Spring Hill, Kansas 66083
www.springhillmarket.org

Walnut Valley Farmers' Market
300 Main
Winfield, Kansas 67156
www.walnutvalleyfarmersmarket.com

KENTUCKY

Boone County Farmers Market
1961 Burlington Pike
Burlington, Kentucky 41005
www.boonecountyfarmersmarket.org

Bounty of the Barrens Farmers' Market
301 West Main Street
Glasgow, Kentucky 42141
www.barrencountybounty.com

Downtown Saturday Market
201 S 4th Street
Murray, Kentucky 42071
www.murraymainstreet.org

Hardin County Farmers' Market
200 Peterson Drive
Elizabethtown, Kentucky 42701
www.thehardincountyfarmers market.com

Jeffersontown Farmers Market
10434 Watterson Trail
Jeffersontown, Kentucky 40299
www.jeffersontownky.com

La Grange Farmers' Market & Artisans
100 W. Main Street
La Grange, Kentucky 40031
www.discoverlagrange.org

Mercer County Farmers' Market
900 S College St
Harrodsburg, Kentucky 40330
http://ces.ca.uky.edu/mercer/ FarmersMarket

Norton Commons Farmers Market
9420 Norton Commons Boulevard
Prospect, Kentucky 40059
http://www.nortoncommons.com /farmers.asp

The Lexington Farmers' Market
In front of Goodyear Tire and
Slone's Market
Lexington, Kentucky
www.lexingtonfarmersmarket.com

LOUISIANA

Amerisafe Downtown Pavilion & Farmers Market
120 North Washington Av
DeRidder, Louisiana 70634
www.cityofderidder.org

Cane River Green Market
Downtown Riverbank
Natchitoches, Louisiana 71457
www.canerivergreenmarket.com

Crescent City Farmers Market
200 Broadway
New Orleans, Louisiana 70118
www.crescentcityfarmersmarket.org

German Coast Farmers Market (West Bank)
12715 Highway 90
Luling, Louisiana 70070
http://www.germancoastfarmers market.org

Gretna Farmers Market
739 Third Street - Downtown
Gretna, Louisiana 70053
http://www.gretnala.com

Lafayette's Hub City Farmer's Market
427 Heymann Blvd
Lafayette, Louisiana 70503
www.lafayettehubcitymarket.com

Mandeville Trailhead Community Farmers' Market
675 Lafitte St.
Mandeville, Louisiana 70448
http://www.mandevilletrailhead.com

Marksville Farmers' Market
Historic Courthouse Square
Marksville, Louisiana 71351
http://www.slowfoodavoyelles
.blogspot.com

Red Stick Farmers Market Saturday
501 Main Street
Baton Rouge, Louisiana 70802
www.breada.org

Ruston Farmers Market
Downtown Ruston, public parking lot
east of Monroe Street
Ruston, Louisiana 71270
http://www.rustonfarmersmarket.org

Westwego Farmers & Fisheries Market
484 Sala Ave
Westwego, Louisiana 70094
www.cityofwestwego.com

MASSACHUSETTS

Acton-Boxborough Farmers Market
1 Pearl St
Acton, Massachusetts 01720
www.abfarmersmarket.org

Allston Farmers Market
175 N. Harvard St.
Allston, Massachusetts 02134
www.dining.harvard.edu/flp/ag
_market.html

Amherst Farmers' Market
Spring Street Parking Lot
Amherst Center, Massachusetts 01002
www.amherstfarmersmarket.com

Arlington Farmers Market
20 Russell St

Arlington, Massachusetts 02474
http://www.farmersmarketarlington
.org/

Boston Public Market - South Station
Dewey Square, across from
South Station
Boston, Massachusetts 02111
www.bostonpublicmaket.org

Braintree Farmers Market
One JFK Memorial Drive
Braintree, Massachusetts 02184
www.sustainablebraintree.org/food

Carlisle Farmer's Market
343 Bedford Road - Rt 225
Carlisle, Massachusetts 01741
http://www.carlislefarmersmarket.org/

City Hall Plaza Farmers Market
Boston City Hall Plaza (Government
Center, along Cambridge Street)
Boston, Massachusetts 02108
www.massfarmersmarkets.org

Dedham Farmers Market
Corner of Eastern Ave and High St
Dedham, Massachusetts 02026
www.dedhamfarmersmarket.org

Plymouth Farmers Market
Stephen's Field, 132R Sandwich Street,
Rte 3A
Plymouth, Massachusetts 02360
www.plymouthfarmersmarket.org

Quincy Farmers' Market
Chestnut Street/Hancock Parking Lot.
Quincy, Massachusetts 02169
www.quincyfarmersmarket.com

Springfield Farmers Market at the X
In Forest Park Cyr Arena parking lot
Springfield, Massachusetts 01108
www.thefarmersmarketatthex.com

The Sandwich Farmers Market
Route 6A Village Green

Sandwich, Massachusetts 02563
www.sandwichfarmersmarket.com

Tuesday Market
Behind Thornes Marketplace, off Old
South St.
Northampton, Massachusetts 01060
www.northamptontuesdaymarket.com

MARYLAND

American Market at National Harbor
Waterfront St. & Fleet St.
National Harbor, Maryland
http://www.americanmarketnh.com

Annapolis FRESHFARM Market
Compromise Street
Annapolis, Maryland 21401
www.freshfarmmarkets.org

Bel Air Farmers Market
Mary Risteau Building
Bel Air, Maryland
http://www.belairfarmersmarket.com

Boordy Vineyards-Good Life Thursdays
12820 Long Green Pike
Hydes, Maryland 21082
www.boordy.com

Calvert County Farmers Market
98 South Solomons Island Rd.
Prince Frederick, Maryland 20678
http://www.calvertcountrymarket.com

Catonsville Farmers Market
106 Bloomsbury Avenue
Catonsville, Maryland 21228
www.catonsvillefarmersmarket.com

Greenbelt Farmers Market
25 Crescent Rod
Greenbelt, Maryland 20770
http://www.greenbeltfarmersmarket.org

Mount Rainier Farmers Market
One Municipal Place

Mount Rainier, Maryland 20912
www.mountrainierfarmersmarket.com

Mountain Fresh Farmers Market
East Oak Street at South 2nd Street
Oakland, Maryland 21550
www.MountainFresh.org

Olney Farmers and Artists Market
2805 Olney-Sandy Spring Road
Olney, Maryland 20832
www.olneyfarmersmarket.org

Pikesville Farmers Market
In front of the MD State Police
Headquarters
Pikesville, Maryland 21208
http://www.pikesvillechamber.org

Silver Spring FRESHFARM Market
900 Ellsworth Drive
Silver Spring, Maryland 20910
www.freshfarmmarkets.org

Takoma Park Farmers' Market
At Laurel St. and Carroll Avenue
Takoma Park, Maryland 20912
www.takomaparkmarket.com

MAINE

Belgrade Lakes Farmers' Market
Main Street
Belgrade Lakes, Maine 04918
www.belgradelakesfarmersmarket.org

Brewer Farmers Market
Brewer Auditorium on Wilson Street
Brewer, Maine 04412
www.brewerfarmersmarket.org

Bridgton Farmers Market
Depot Street in front of
Community Center
Bridgton, Maine 04009
http://bridgtonfarmersmarket.com/

Castine Farmers' Market
1 School St.

Castine, Maine 04420
http://castinefarmersmarket.org/

**Damariscotta Farmers' Market -
Friday Market**
109-110 Belvedere Rd.
Damariscotta, Maine 04543
*http://www.damariscottafarmers
market.org/*

Gardiner Farmers Market
The Commons
Gardiner, Maine 04345
www.gardinerfarmersmarket.org

Gateway Farmers Market
1 Stonewall Lane
York, Maine 03909
www.gatewayfarmersmarket.com

Kennebunk Farmers' Market
Municipal Parking Lot Rt 1 and
Grove St
Kennebunk, Maine 04043
*http://www.kennebunkfarmers
market.org*

North Berwick Farmers' Market
21 Main Street
North Berwick, Maine 03906
www.northberwickfarmersmarket.org

Orono Farmers Market
Steam Plant Parking Lot on
College Ave
Orono, Maine 04473
http://www.oronofarmersmarket.org

Skowhegan Farmers Market
13 High St.
Skowhegan, Maine 04976
www.skowheganfarmersmarket.com

Wells Farmers' Market
Rt 109
Wells, Maine 04090
www.wellsfarmersmarket.org

MICHIGAN

Ann Arbor Farmers Market
315 Detroit St
Ann Arbor, Michigan 48104
www.a2gov.org/market

Auburn Hills Farmers Market
3308 Auburn Rd
Auburn Hills, Michigan 48326
www.auburnhills.org/farmersmarket

Birmigham Farmers Market
660 North Old Woodward
Birmigham, Michigan 48009
www.birmighafarmersmarker.org

Boyne City Farmers Market
Veterans Park, Lake Street
Boyne City, Michigan 49712
www.boynecityfarmersmarket.com

Canton Farmers Market
500 N. Ridge Road
Canton, Michigan 48187
www.cantonfun.org

City of Grand Blanc Farmers Market
On Grand Boulevard
Grand Blanc, Michigan 48439
http://www.cityofgrandblanc.com

City of Otsego Farmers Market
112 Kalamazoo Street/M-89
Otsego, Michigan 49078
www.otsegochamber.org

Downtown Petoskey Farmers' Market
Near corner of Howard &
Michigan Streets
Petoskey, Michigan 49770
*www.petoskey.com/chamber
/farmers-market_120/*

Downtown Rochester Farmers' Market
Corner of E. Third & Water
Rochester, Michigan 48307
www.DowntownRochesterMI.com

Downtown Ypsilanti Farmers' Market
Ferris St between Hamilton and Adams
Ypsilanti, Michigan 48197
www.growinghope.net/programs
/market

Eastern Market Detroit
2934 Russell Street
Detroit, Michigan 48207
www.detroiteasternmarket.com

Howell Farmers Market
123 E. Washington St.
Howell, Michigan 48843
www.howell.org

Kalamazoo Farmers Market
1200 Bank St
Kalamazoo, Michigan 49007
http://www.kalamazoocity.org
/portal/government.php?page_id=203

Lansing City Market
325 City Market Drive
Lansing, Michigan 48912
www.lansingcitymarket.com

Northville Farmers' Market
W. 7 Mile Rd & Center Street
Northville, Michigan 48167
www.northville.org/events/
farmersmarket

MINNESOTA

Bemidji Area Farmers Market
200 Paul Bunyan Drive South
Bemidji, Minnesota 56601
www.bemidjifarmersmarket.com

Bloomington Farmers Market
1800 W. Old Shakopee Road
Bloomington, Minnesota 55431
www.ci.bloomington.mn.us/market

Centennial Lakes Farmers Market
7499 France Avenue
Edina, Minnesota 55435
www.CentennialLakesPark.com

City of Plymouth Farmers Market
3600 Plymouth Blvd
Plymouth, Minnesota 55447
www.plymouthmn.gov

Duluth Farmer's Market
14th Ave. E. and 3rd St.
Duluth, Minnesota 55803
www.duluthfarmersmarket.com

Eagan Market Fest
1501 Central Parkway
Eagan, Minnesota 5512
www.cityofeagan.com/marketfest

Grand Rapids Farmers Market
104 NW 4th St
Grand Rapids, Minnesota 55744
http://www.grfarmersmarket.org/

Kingfield Farmers Market
4310 Nicollet Ave. S.
Minneapolis, Minnesota 55409
www.kingfieldfarmersmarket.org

Lakes Area Farmers Market
600 Washington Avenue
Detroit Lakes, Minnesota 56501
http://www.lakesareafarmersmarket
.com

Maple Grove Farmers Market
12951 Weaver Lake Road
Maple Grove, Minnesota 55369
www.maplegrovefarmersmarket.com

Mill City Farmers Market
704 2nd Street S
Minneapolis, Minnesota 55401
www.millcityfarmersmarket.org

Minneapolis Farmers Market
I-94, Exit 230 East
Minneapolis, Minnesota 55405
http://www.mplsfarmersmarket.com

Red Wing Farmers Market
Bush and 4th Street, in front of
City Hall
Red Wing, Minnesota 55066
www.redwingfarmersmarket.org

St. Paul Downtown Farmers Market
290 East Fifth St.
St. Paul, Minnesota 55101
http://www.stpaulfarmersmarket.com

MISSOURI

BADSEED Funky Friday Night
Farmers Market
1909 McGee, Downtown
Kansas City, Missouri 64108
www.badseedfarm.com

Blue Springs Farmers Market
11th and Main
Blue Springs, Missouri
www.bluespringsfarmersmarket.com

Boone County Farmers Market
1005 W. Worley St
Columbia, Missouri 65203
www.boonecountyfarmers.com

Brookfield Farmers Market
Tormey Park on the 200 block of South
Main Street
Brookfield, Missouri 64628
www.brookfieldmochamber.com
/farmersmarket.htm

Byrne's Mill Farmers' Market
Byrnes Mill Park, between High Ridge
Blvd & House Springs
Byrne's Mill, Missouri 63051
http://www.byrnesmill.org/farmers
market

C-Street Market
321 East Commercial
Springfield, Missouri 65803
www.itsalldowntown.com/cstreet

Cass County Farmers' Market
2601 Cantrell Rd, outside Mill Walk Mall
in Harrisonville MO
Adrian, Missouri 64720
http://www.cassfarmers.com

Columbia Farmers Market
1701 West Ash
Columbia, Missouri 65201
www.columbiafarmersmarket.org

**Downtown Lee's Summit
Farmers Market**
113 SE Douglas Street
Lee's Summit, Missouri 64063
www.downtownls.org

Eastland Farmers Market
1835 E. Saint Louis Street
Springfield, Missouri 65802

Fair Grove Farmers' Market
Hwy 125 & Main Street
Fair Grove, Missouri 65648
www.fairgrovefarmersmarket.com

Ferguson Farmers' Market
20 S. Florissant Rd.
Ferguson, Missouri 63135
www.fergusonfarmersmarket.com

Greater Polk County Farmers Market
105 W Locust
Bolivar, Missouri 65613
*http;//.www.greaterpolkcountyfarmers
market.blogspot.net*

The Clayton Farmer's Market
8282 Forsyth Blvd.
St. Louis, Missouri 63105
http://claytonfarmersmarket.com/

MISSISSIPPI

Bay Saint Louis Main Street Market
Corner of Second and Main Streets
Bay Saint Louis, Mississippi 39520
www.realfoodgulfcoast.org

Charles R. Hedgewood Farmers Market
Underneath the I-110 overpass and Howard Avenue
Biloxi, Mississippi 39530
http://biloxi.ms.us/pr/

Crystal Springs Farmers Market
West Railroad Avenue
Crystal Springs, Mississippi 39059
*http://www2.msstate.edu/~ricks/csto
mato/tomfest.html*

Hernando Farmers Market
2335 Highway 51 South
Hernando, Mississippi 38632
www.hernandomarket.com

Long Beach Real Food Market
126 Jeff Davis Avenue
Long Beach, Mississippi 39560
www.realfoodgulfcoast.org

Mississippi Farmers Market
929 High Street
Jackson, Mississippi 39202
http://www.msfarmersmarket.com

Ocean Springs Fresh Market
1000 Washington Ave.
Ocean Springs, Mississippi 39564
www.oceanspringsfreshmarket.com

Picayune Farmers Market
Downtown Picayune
Picayune, Mississippi 39466
http://www.picayunemainstreet.com

Taylor Farmers' Market
1 Town Square Lane
Taylor, Mississippi 38673
http://pleinairtaylor.com/farmers.html

Tupelo Farmers Market
South Springs St. at the Railroad
Tupelo, Mississippi 38804
http://www.tupelomianstreet.com

Vicksburg Farmers Market
Corner of Grove & Levee Streets, at Catfish Row Art Park
Vicksburg, Mississippi 39180
www.vicksburgfarmersmarket.org

MONTANA

Big Sky Farmers Market
Fire Pit Park, Big Sky Town Center
Big Sky, Montana 59716
www.bigskytowncenter.com

Bogert Farmers' Market
Bogert Park, S. Church Ave.
Bozeman, Montana 59715
http://www.bogertfarmersmarket.com

Butte Farmers Market
Uptown Butte
Butte, Montana 59701
http://mainstreetbutte.org/fmarket.htm

Clark Fork River Market
125 Bank Street
Missoula, Montana 59802
http://www.clarkforkrivermarket.com

Great Falls Original Farmers Market
Downtown (Civic Center Park)
Great Falls, Montana 59403
*http://www.mainstreetgreatfalls.com
/farmersmarket.html*

Hamilton Farmers Market Cooperative
Corner of South 3rd and Bedford Sts.
Hamilton, Montana 59840
www.hamiltonfarmersmarket.webs.com

**Laurel Chamber of Commerce
Farmers Market**
110 1st Ave. N
Laurel, Montana 59044
www.laurelmontana.org

Livingston Farmers Market
Miles Park, 215 River Drive next to
Civic Center

Livingston, Montana 59047
http://www.westernsustainability
exchange.org

Miles City Farmers Market
Riverside Park; West end of Main St.
Miles City, Montana 59301
http://www.mcfarmersmarket.com

Stanford Farmers Market
Central Avenue
Stanford, Montana 59479
http://www.stanfordfarmersmarket.com

Thompson Falls Market
West Lot of the Falls Motel, Lincoln
Street & Maiden Lane
Thompson Falls, Montana 59873
www.ThompsonFallsMarket.com

Whitefish Downtown Farmers Market
Central and Railway
Whitefish, Montana 59937
http://www.whitefishfarmersmarket.org

Yellowstone Valley Farmers Market
Heart of N. 29th & 2nd Ave. N.
Billings, Montana 59104
http://yvfarmersmarket.googlepages
.com/home

NORTH CAROLINA

Asheville City Market
161 South Charlotte St.
Asheville, North Carolina 28801
http://www.asapconnections.org
/citymarket.html

Black Mountain Tailgate Market
130 Montreat Road
Black Mountain, North Carolina 28711
www.blackmountaintailgatemarket
.org

Carrboro Farmers' Market
301 W. Main St. on the
Town Commons

Carrboro, North Carolina 27510
www.carrborofarmersmarket.com

Charlotte Regional Farmers Market
1801 Yorkmont Road
Charlotte, North Carolina 28266
www.ncdamarkets.org

Downtown City Market
6th & Cherry Streets
Winston Salem, North Carolina 27109
http:/www.dsfair.com

Downtown Waterfront Market
113 South Water St. ·
Elizabeth City, North Carolina 27909
www.downtownwaterfrontmarket
.com

Durham Farmers' Market
501 Foster Street
Durham, North Carolina 27701
www.durhamfarmersmarket.com

Eno River Farmers Market
E. Margaret Lane
Hillsborough, North Carolina 27278
www.enoriverfarmersmarket.com

Farmers Market at Poplar Grove
10200 US Hwy 17
Wilmington, North Carolina 28411
http://www.poplargrove.com

Greensboro Farmers' Curb Market
501 Yanceyville Street
Greensboro, North Carolina 27405
www.greensboro-nc.gov/farmers
market

Haywood's Historic Farmers Market
250 Pigeon Street
Waynesville, North Carolina 28786
www.haywoodfarmersmarket.com

Southern Village Farmers Market
Market Street in Southern Village
Chapel Hill, North Carolina 27517
http://www.carrborofarmersmarket.com

State Farmers Market
1201 Agriculture Street
Raleigh, North Carolina 27603
http://www.ncdamarkets.org

Western Wake Farmers' Market, Inc.
1225 Morrisville Carpenter Rd
Cary, North Carolina 27519
www.westernwakefarmersmarket.org

NORTH DAKOTA

Bottineau Farmers Market/Chamber
Central School on Main St.
Bottineau, North Dakota 58318
http://www.bottineau.com

Capitol Farmers Market II
2625 State St.
Bismarck, North Dakota 58505

Devils Lake Community Market
Roosevelt Park, Devils Lake
Devils Lake, North Dakota 58380
http://www.devilslakecommunity
market.netfirms.com

Downtown Festival Market
2nd Ave. N & Broadway, on the
US Bank
Fargo, North Dakota

Langdon Area Farmers Market
City Park
Langdon, North Dakota 58249
http://www.cityoflangdon.com

Lewis & Clark Farmers Market
By Sinex & Washburn
Washburn, North Dakota 58530
http://www.skylineranchorganicproduce
.com

North Prairie Farmers Market - Minot
300 block of Broadway
Minot, North Dakota 58701
www.northprairiefarmersmarket.com

Rugby Chamber Farmers Market
Junction Hwy. 2 & 3
Rugby, North Dakota 58368
http://www.rugbynorthdakota.com

Sakakewea Farmers Market of Hazen
Hayzen All Seasons Arena parking lot
Hazen, North Dakota 58547
*http://www.skylineranchorganic
produce.com*

NEBRASKA

Chadron Farmers Market
Courthouse lawn, 400 Main St.
Chadron, Nebraska 69337
http://www.chadron.com

Community CROPS Farmers' Market
2600 Potter Street
Lincoln, Nebraska 68503
*http://www.communitycrops.org
/market*

Cortland Farmers Market
4th & Main Street, 1 block west of Highway 77
Cortland, Nebraska 68331
http://www.cortlandne.com

Lincoln Haymarket Farmers Market
7th & P Street
Lincoln, Nebraska 68505
http://www.lincolnhaymarket.org

Main Street Beatrice Farmers Market
Hwy 77 between High & Ella St.
Beatrice, Nebraska 68310
http://www.mainstreetbeatrice.com

**Main Street Downtown
Farmers Market**
John C. Fremont Park, corner of 8th
& Main St.
Freemont, Nebraska 68026
http://www.mainstreetfremont.org

Nebraska City Farmers Market
Central Ave. between 9th & 10th St.
Nebraska City, Nebraska 68410
http://www.NebraskaCity.com

Old Cheney Road Farmers' Market
5500 Old Cheney Road
Lincoln, Nebraska 68516
*www.oldcheneyroadfarmersmarket
.com*

St. James Marketplace
89039 570 Ave
St. James, Nebraska 68792
http://www.stjamesmarketplace.com

Stromsburg Farmers Market
Downtown Square
Stromsburg, Nebraska 68666
http://www.stromsburgnebraska.com

Village Pointe Farmers Market
17002 Burke Street
Omaha, Nebraska 68118
www.VoteRealFood.com

York Farmers Market
6th St. in front of County Courthouse
York, Nebraska 68467
http://www.yorkchamber.org

NEW HAMPSHIRE

Bedford Farmers Market
Wallace Rd
Bedford, New Hampshire 03110
www.bedfordfarmersmarket.org

City Hall Plaza Farmers Market
229 Main St.
Nashua, New Hampshire 03060
www.downtownnashua.org

Claremont Farmers Market
Broad Street Park
Claremont, New Hampshire 03743
www.claremontfarmersmarket.com

Hanover Area Farmers Market
The Green
Hanover, New Hampshire 03755
www.hanoverfarmersmarket.org

Lebanon Farmers Market
Colburn Park
Lebanon, New Hampshire 03766
www.lebanonfarmersmarket.org

Lisbon Farmers Market
No. Main Street (Route 302)
Lisbon, New Hampshire 03585
www.lisbonmainstreet.org

Main Street Bridge Farmers Market
53-75 Main St.
Nashua, New Hampshire 03060
www.downtownnashua.org

Milford Farmers Market
185 Elm St, Rte 101A Granite
Town Plaza
Milford, New Hampshire 03055
www.milfordnhfarmersmarket.com

New Durham Farmers Market
From Route 11, just off Depot Rd., next to
Post Office, on the lawn
New Durham, New Hampshire 03855
http://newdurhamfarmersmarket.com

Newport Farmers' Market
North Main St.
Newport, New Hampshire 03773
www.NewportNHmarket.org

Seacoast Farmers Market - Dover
181 Silver St.
Dover, New Hampshire 03820
www.seacoastgrowers.org

Seacoast Farmers Market - Portsmouth
1 Junkins Ave.
Portsmouth, New Hampshire 03801
www.seacoastgrowers.org

Wakefield Farmers Market
Wakefield Rd. & Rte. 16

Wakefield, New Hampshire 03872
http://www.wakefieldmarketplace
.homestead.com

Wilmot Farmers Market
Town Green
Wilmot, New Hampshire 03287
www.wilmotfarmrsmarket.com

NEW JERSEY

Atlantic City Farmers' Market
Atlantic Avenue between North & South
Carolina Avenue
Atlantic City, New Jersey 08401
www.acsid.com

Burlington County Farmers Market
500 Centerton Rd.
Moorestown, New Jersey 08505
www.burlcoagcenter.com

Caldwell Farmers Market
Municpal Lot between Smull
and Personette (behind the Caldwell
Cinema
Caldwell, New Jersey
www.caldwellfarmersmarket.org

Chatham Borough Farmers' Market
Fairmount Avenue and Railroad
Plaza South
Chatham, New Jersey 07928
www.ChathamBoroughFarmers
Market.org

Collingswood Farmers Market
Between Collings & Irvin Aves. along
High Speed Line
Collingswood, New Jersey 08108
http://www.collingswoodmarket.com

Common Greens Farmers Market
Between Broad & Park Place
Newark, New Jersey 07102
http://www.downtownnewark.com

Galleria Red Bank Farmers Market
2 Bridge Ave
Red Bank, New Jersey 07701
www.thegalleriaredbank.com

Haddonfield Farmers Market
Parking lot behind Haddonfield
Presbyterian Church
Haddonfield, New Jersey 08033
http://www.haddonfieldfarmers
market.org

Hammonton Farmer's Market
Front Street
Hammonton, New Jersey 08037
www.hammontonfarmersmarket.com

Rutgers Gardens Farmers Market
112 Ryders Ln.
New Brunswick, New Jersey 08901
http://rutgersgardens.rutgers.edu
/farmmarket.htm

Tenafly Farmers' Market
Lot N Washington Ave
Tenafly, New Jersey 07670
www.tenaflyfarmersmarket.com

Trenton Farmers Market
960 Spruce St.
Trenton, New Jersey 08648

West Milford Farmers' Market
1911 Union Valley Road
West Milford, New Jersey 07421
www.wmfarmersmarket.org

**West Windsor Community
Farmers Market**
Vaughn Drive, Southbound side of Princeton Junction train station, off Alexander Road.
West Windsor, New Jersey 08550
http://www.westwindsorfarmersmarket.
com

NEW MEXICO

Albuquerque Downtown Growers' Market
Central Ave NW
Albuquerque, New Mexico 87102
www.downtownabq.com

Dixon Farmers Market
Town Center in front of library
Dixon, New Mexico 87527
http://www.dixonmarket.com

Espanola Farmers Market
1005 N. Railroad Avenue
Espanola, New Mexico 87532
www.espanolafarmersmarket.blogspot
.com

Farmington Farmers Market
Animas Park off Browning Parkway
Farmington, New Mexico 87401

Los Ranchos Growers Market
City Hall, 6718 Rio Grande Blvd. NW
Los Ranchos, New Mexico 87114

Santa Fe Farmers' Market
1607 Paseo de Peralta
Santa Fe, New Mexico 87501
www.santafefarmersmarket.com

Shiprock Farmers' Market
North Hwy 64
Shiprock, New Mexico 87420

Sunland Park Farmers Market
Ardovino's Desert Crossing &
Ardovino Dr.
Sunland Park, New Mexico 88063
http://www.ardovinos.com

NEW YORK

Angelica Farmers' Market
Angelica Park Circle
Angelica, New York 14709
http://www.localharvest.org
/farmers-markets/M23451

Bernadette Martin
1 West Chester Street
Long Beach, New York 11561
www.kennedyplazafarmersmarket
.com

Brighton Farmers' Market
1150 Winton Road South
Rochester, New York 14618
www.brightonfarmersmarket.org

Callicoon Farmers Market
Callicoon Creek Park, Audrey
Dorrer Rd.
Callicoon, New York 12723
www.sullivancountyfarmersmarket
.org

Canandaigua Farmers Market
Corner of Mill and Beaman Sts.
Canandaigua, New York 14424
www.canandaiguafarmersmarket.com

Central Avenue Farmers Market
339 Central Ave.
Albany, New York 12206
www.centralavenuefarmersmarket
.com

Clinton Farmers Market
Village Green
Clinton, New York 13323
www.clintonnychamber.org

Delmar Saturday Farmers Market
332 Kenwood Ave.
Delmar, New York 12054
www.delmarmarket.org

East New York Farmers Market
613 New Lots Ave
Brooklyn, New York 11207
www.eastnewyorkfarms.org

**The New York Botanical Garden
Farmers Market**
Mosholu Pkwy. Gate at Kazimiroff Blvd.
(in garden)

New York, New York
www.cenyc.org

Troy Waterfront Farmers Market
Front Street
Troy, New York 12180
www.troymarket.org

Trumansburg Farmers Market
Village Park, Rts 96 & 227
Trumansburg, New York 14886
www.trumansburg-ny.gov.com

Westhampton Beach Farmers Market
85 Mill Road
Westhampton Beach, New York 11978
www.westhamptonbeachfarmers
market.com

Woodstock Farm Festival
Maple Lane
Woodstock, New York 12498
www.woodstockfarmfestival.com

NEVADA

3rd & Curry St. Farmers Market
3rd & Curry St.
Carson City, Nevada 89703
www.carsonfarmersmarket.com

Alamo Farmers Market
Buckhorn Ranch Road
Alamo, Nevada 89001
www.NevadaGrown.com

Downtown Henderson Farmers Market
In front of City Hall
Henderson, Nevada 89103
http://www.hendersonfarmersmarket
.com

**Elko Downtown Business Association
Farmer's Market**
5th and Commercial
Elko, Nevada 89801
www.elkodowntown.org

Ely Farmers Market
Ely Renaissance Village
Ely, Nevada 89301
www.elyrenaissance.com

**Las Vegas Farmers Market at Bruce
Trent Park**
1600 N. Ramport
Las Vegas, Nevada 89134
http://www.lasvegasfarmersmarket.com

Minden Farmers Market
Downtown at Esmeralda Ave.
Minden, Nevada 89423
http://www.nevadagrown.com

Reno Booth St. Farmers Market
Booth St. at California Ave.
Reno, Nevada 89502
http://www.farmersmarkets.intuit
websites.com

Sparks Hometowne Farmers Market
Victorian Ave. downtown
Sparks, Nevada 89431
http://www.sparksrec.com

Tonopah Farmers Market
Hwy 95, Main St. at Pocket Park
Tonopah, Nevada 89049
http://www.localharvest.org/
farmers-markets/M19984

Winnemucca Farmers Market
Next to Community Garden
Winnemucca, Nevada 89445
http://www.nevadagrown.com

OHIO

Alliance Farmers' Market
Corner of E. Main St. & Mechanic Ave.
(no #)
Alliance, Ohio 44601
www.alliancefarmersmarket.com

Anderson Farmers' Market
7832 Five Mile Road

Anderson Township, Ohio 45230
http://www.andersonfarmersmarket.org

Canal Winchester Farmers Market
36 South High Street
Canal Winchester, Ohio 43110
www.thecwfm.com

Chillicothe Farmers' Market
275 Western Ave
Chillicothe, Ohio 45601
www.chillicothefarmersmarket.org

Countryside Farmers' Market at Howe Meadow
4040 Riverview Road
Peninsula, Ohio 44264
www.cvcountryside.org

Dublin Farmers' Market
81 West Bridge Street
Dublin, Ohio 43017
www.dublinfarmersmarket.com

Findlay Market
1801 Race St.
Cincinnati, Ohio 45202
www.findlaymarket.org

Geauga Fresh Farmers' Market
Rt. 306 and Bell Rd.
South Russell, Ohio 44022
www.geaugafarmersmarket.com

The Great Sidney Farmers Market
101 S. Ohio Avenue - Floor 2
Sidney, Ohio 45365
www.downtownsidney.com

North Union Farmers Market in Chagrin Falls
North Franklin Street
Chagrin Falls, Ohio 44022
www.northunionfarmersmarket.org

Oxford Farmers Market Uptown
High and Main Street

Oxford, Ohio 45056
www.oxfordfarmersmarket.com

PNC 2nd Street Market
600 E. 2nd Street
Dayton, Ohio 45402
www.metroparks.org

Powell Farmers Market
47 Hall Street
Powell, Ohio 43065
www.visitpowell.com

Toledo Farmers Market
525 Market Street
Toledo, Ohio 43602
www.toledofarmersmarket.org

Tremont Farmers' Market
Lincoln Park, at W14 St and Howard Ave
Cleveland, Ohio 44113
www.tremontfarmersmarket.com

OKLAHOMA

Bartlesville Farmers Market
217 Southeast Adams Boulevard
Bartlesville, Oklahoma 74003
http://www.hotmarket.org

Cherry Street Farmers Market
15th Street between Rockford and Quaker
Tulsa, Oklahoma 74120
www.cherrystreetfarmersmarket.com

Coweta Farmers Market
Northwest corner of Avenue B & Cypress
Coweta, Oklahoma 74429
http://www.downtowncushing.com

Downtown Tulsa Farmers Market
Third and Boston
Tulsa, Oklahoma 74101
www.localharvest.org

Eastern Oklahoma County Farmers Market
2001 North Harper St.
Choctaw, Oklahoma 73020
http://www.choctawcity.org

Edmond Farmers Market
First Street, between Boulevard & Littler
Edmond, Oklahoma 73083
http://www.edmondok.com

Haskell County Farmers Market
104 Northeast 6th St.
Stigler, Oklahoma 74462
http://www.stiglerchamber.org

Jenks Farmers Market
West Main Street
Jenks, Oklahoma 74037
www.localharvest.org

Lawton Farmers Market
920 S Sheridan Rd
Lawton, Oklahoma 73501
www.swokgrowers.org

Mayes County Farmers Market
Mayes County Courthouse
Pryor, Oklahoma 74361
www.pryorchamber.com

Mid Del Farmers' Market
7209 SE 29th
Midwest City, Oklahoma 73049
www.mdfma.org

Norman Farmers Market
615 East Robinson St.
Norman, Oklahoma 73071
http://www.clevelandcountyfair.org

Nowata County Farmers Market
612 E Roxy/Nowata County Fairgrounds
Nowata, Oklahoma 74048
www.nowataoklahoma.wordpress.com

OSU-OKC Farmers' Market
400 N Portland Ave

Oklahoma City, Oklahoma 73107
www.osuokc.edu/farmersmarket

Ponca City Farmers Market
14th Strret and Lake Road
Ponca City, Oklahoma 74601
www.poncacityfarmersmarket.com

OREGON

2nd Street Public Market
2003 2nd Street
Tillamook, Oregon 97141
www.secondstreetpublicmarket.com

Albany Farmers' Market
4th Avenue & Ellsworth Street
Albany, Oregon 97321
http://www.locallygrown.org

Beaverton Farmers Market
Hall Blvd.
Beaverton, Oregon 97075
*http://www.beavertonfarmersmarket
.com*

Buckman Portland Farmers Market
SE Salmon & 20th between SE Belmont
& Hawthorne
Portland, Oregon 97214
*http://www.portlandfarmersmarket
.org*

Cedar Mill Sunset Farmers Market
13565 NW Cornell Rd
Portland, Oregon 97229
http://www.cmfmarket.org

Corvallis Farmers Market - Saturday
1st & Jackson (North end of Riverfront)
Corvallis, Oregon 97330
http://www.locallygrown.org

Forest Grove Farmers Market
Main Street (between 21st & Pacific)
Forest Grove, Oregon 97116
www.adelantemujeres.org

Grants Pass Growers Market
Corner of 4th & F St.
Grants Pass, Oregon 97528
http://www.growersmarket.org

**Hillsboro Farmers' Market at
Tanasbourne**
19440 NW Cornell Rd
Hillsboro, Oregon 97124
www.hillsboromarkets.org

Hood River Saturday Market
5th and Columbia
Hood River, Oregon 97031
www.hrsaturdaymarket.com

Rogue Valley Growers & Crafters Market
1701 S. Pacific Hwy
Medford, Oregon 97501
www.rvgrowersmarket.com

Salem Saturday Market
500 block of Summer Street NE
Salem, Oregon 97301
www.salemsaturdaymarket.com

Scappoose Farmers' Market
E. 2nd St., ½ block south of E.
Columbia Ave.
Scappoose, Oregon 97056
www.scappoosefarmermarket.com

Umpqua Valley Farmers Market
2082 Diamond Lake Blvd.
Roseburg, Oregon 97470
http://www.UVFarmersMarket.com

PENNSYLVANIA

**Allentown Fairgrounds
Farmers Market**
1825 Chew Street
Allentown, Pennsylvania 18104
www.fairgroundsfarmersmkt.com

Bird-in-Hand Farmers Market
2710 Old Philadelphia Pike

Bird-in-Hand, Pennsylvania 17505
www.BirdInHandFarmersMarket.com

Cecil B. Moore
Cecil B. Moore Ave. (btwn. Broad St.
and Park Walk)
Philadelphia, Pennsylvania
www.headhousemarket.org

Central Market York
34 W. Philadelphia St.
York, Pennsylvania 17401
www.centralmarketyork.com

Creekside Co-Op and Farmers' Market
Corner of High School Road and
Montgomery Ave.
Elkins Park, Pennsylvania 19027
www.creekside.coop

Eastern Market
308 East King Street
Lancaster, Pennsylvania 17602
www.historiceasternmarket.org

Easton Farmers' Market
30 Centre Square
Easton, Pennsylvania 18042
www.EastonFarmersMarket.com

Ellwood City Farmers' Market
Beaver Ave. Municipal Parking Lot
Ellwood City, Pennsylvania 16117
www.ellwoodcityfarmersmarket.com

Green Dragon Farmers Market
955 N. State St.
Ephrata, Pennsylvania 17522
www.greendragonmarket.com

Lancaster Central Market
23 N. Market St.
Lancaster, Pennsylvania 17603
www.centralmarketlancaster.com

Main Street Farmers Market, Inc.
139 South Main Street
Washington, Pennsylvania 15301
www.mfsm.org

Pittsburgh Public Market
2100 Smallman Street
Pittsburgh, Pennsylvania 15222
www.pittsburghpublicmarket.org

Reading Terminal Market
51 North 12th Street
Philadelphia, Pennsylvania 19107
www.readingterminalmarket.org

Saturday's Market
3751 East Harriburg Pike
Middletown, Pennsylvania 17057
www.SaturdaysMarket.com

RHODE ISLAND

Aquidneck Growers Saturday
Newport Vineyards and Winery
Middletown, Rhode Island 02840
*http://www.farmfreshri.org/find
/farmersmarkets.php*

Brown University Farmers Market
111 George St
Providence, Rhode Island 02906
*http://www.farmfresh.org/food/farm
ersmarkets_details.php?market=5*

Burrillville Farmers Market
135 Main Street
Harrisville, Rhode Island 02830
www.burrillvillefarmersmarket.org

Downtown Providence Farmers' Market
Kennedy Plaza and Burnside Park
Providence, Rhode Island 02906
*http://www.farmfreshri.org/find
/farmersmarkets.php*

**Fisherman's Memorial Park
Farmers Market**
Fisherman's Memorial State Park
Narragansett, Rhode Island 02879
*http://www.farmfreshri.org/find
/farmersmarkets.php*

Goddard Park Farmers Market
Goddard State Park
East Greenwich, Rhode Island 02886
*http://www.state.ri.us/dem/topics
/agricult.htm*

Johnston Farmers Market
Johnston Memorial Park
Johnston, Rhode Island 02919
www.rigrown.ri.gov

Pawtuxet Village Farmers Market
Rhodes on the Pawtuxet Parking Lot
Cranston, Rhode Island 02905
*http://www.farmfreshri.org/find
/farmersmarkets.php*

Richmond Farmers' Market
5 Richmond Townhouse Rd
Richmond, Rhode Island 02898
www.richmondrifarmersmarket.com

Wintertime Farmers Market
1005 Main St.
Pawtucket, Rhode Island 02860
www.farmfreshri.org

SOUTH CAROLINA

All-Local Farmers Market
711 Whaley St
Columbia, South Carolina 29205
www.stateplate.org

Beaufort Downtown Farmers Market
950 Bay Street (Freedom Park)
Beaufort, South Carolina 29902
www.downtownbeaufort.com

Carolina First Saturday Market
Downtown Greenville
Greenville, South Carolina 29603
http://www.saturdaymarketlive.com

Charleston Farmers Market
Marion Square, King &
Calhoun Streets

Charleston, South Carolina 29401
www.charlestonarts.sc

Downtown Conway Farmers Market
217 Laurel Street
Conway, South Carolina 29526
www.conwayfarmersmarket.org

Easley Farmers Market
205 N. 1st St
Easley, South Carolina 29640
www.easleyfarmersmarket.com

Farmers Market of Bluffton
40 Calhoun Street
Bluffton, South Carolina 29910
www.farmersmarketbluffton.com

Habersham Farmers Market
13 Market
Beaufort, South Carolina 29906
*http://www.habershamfarmersmarket
.com*

Hub City Farmers' Market
298 Magnolia St.
Spartanburg, South Carolina 29306
www.hubcityfm.org

Main Street Marketplace
Corner of Hampton Street &
Main Street
Columbia, South Carolina 29201
http://www.citycentercolumbia.sc

Mount Pleasant Farmers Market
645 Coleman Boulevard
Mount Pleasant, South Carolina 29464
*http://www.townofmountpleasant
.com/index.cfm?section=11&page=6*

Pee Dee State Farmers Market
2513 West Lucas Street
Florence, South Carolina 29501
www.pdfarmersmarket.sc.gov

Pendleton Farmers Market
On the Village Green

Pendleton, South Carolina 29670
www.pendletonfarmersmarket.org

Sandhill Farmers Market
900 Clemson Road
Columbia, South Carolina 29229
www.clemson.edu/sandhill

SOUTH DAKOTA

Aberdeen Farmers Market
2nd Ave., S.E. & S. Lincoln Street
Aberdeen, South Dakota 57401
*http://www.dakotaflavor.com
/category.asp?catid=12*

Black Hills Farmers Market
West Omaha Park
Rapid City, South Dakota 57701
*http://www.dakotaflavor.com
/category.asp?catid=12*

Brookings Farmers Market
603 Main St.
Brookings, South Dakota 57006
www.brookingsfarmersmarket.com

Custer Farmers Market
Corner of Crook and N 7th Street.
Custer City, South Dakota 57730
www.custerfarmersmarket.com

Farmers Market
115 West Highway 14
Spearfish, South Dakota 57783
*http://www.spearfishfarmersmarket
.com*

Huron Farmers Market
3rd Street S.W., SD State Fairgrounds
Huron, South Dakota 57350
*http://www.dakotaflavor.com
/category.asp?catid=12*

Letcher Farmers Market
Letcher Park
Letcher, South Dakota 57359
http://www.letchersd.com/

Sturgis Main Street Farmer's Market
1110 Main Street
Sturgis, South Dakota 57785
www.sturgisfarmersmarket.com

Uptown Farmers Market
East Camp Ave.
Watertown, South Dakota 57201
http://www.uptownwatertown.com

Vermillion Area Farmers Market
515 High Street
Vermillion, South Dakota 57069
http://vafm.wordpress.com

TENNESSEE

**Agricenter International
Farmers Market**
Walnut Grove Road
Memphis, Tennessee 38120
www.agricenter.org

Appalachian Farmers' Market
Intersection of Fair Street and
Lakeview Drive
Gray, Tennessee 37615
http://www.appfarmersmarket.com

Chattanooga Market
1829 Carter Street
Chattanooga, Tennessee 37401
www.chattanoogamarket.com

**Cooper-Young Community
Farmers Market**
1000 S. Cooper Street
Memphis, Tennessee 38104
www.cycfarmersmarket.org

Downtown Greenville Farmers Market
College Street
Greenville, Tennessee 37745
http://www.ruralresources.net

Farmers' Market at the Garden
750 Cherry Road
Memphis, Tennessee 38117

www.memphisbotanicgarden.com

Franklin Farmers Market
230 Franklin Road
Franklin, Tennessee 37064
www.franklinfarmersmarket.org

Knoxville FARM Market
3457 Kingston Pike
Knoxville, Tennessee 37919
http://www.easttnfarmmarkets.org

Nashville Farmers Market
900 Rosa L. Parks Blvd
Nashville, Tennessee 37208
http://nashvillefarmersmarket.org

The Market Square Farmers' Market
1 Market Square
Knoxville, Tennessee 39702
*http://www.marketsquarefarmersmar
ket.org*

White County Farmers Market
Metcalf Park
Sparta, Tennessee 38583
http://www.utextension.utk.edu/white

TEXAS

Apple Country Farmers Market
1922 Avenue A
Lubbock, Texas 79404
www.applecountryorchard.com

Austin Farmers Market Association I
422 W. Guadalupe
Austin, Texas 78701
http://www.austinfarmersmarket.org

Barton Creek Farmers Market
2901 Capital of Texas Hwy South, Barton
Creek Square Mall
Austin, Texas 7874
www.sunsetvalleyfarmersmarket.org

Beaumont Farmers Market
801 Pearl Street

Beaumont, Texas 77701
http://www.beaumonttxfarmersmarket.
org/

Brazos Valley Farmers Market
201 North Texas Avenue
Bryan, Texas 77803
www.brazosvalleyfarmersmarket.com

Coppell Farmers Market
455 W Bethel Rd
Coppell, Texas 75019
www.coppellfarmersmarket.org

Dallas Farmers Market
1010 S. Pearl Expressway
Dallas, Texas 75201
www.dallasfarmersmarket.org

Downtown Farmers Market I
600 W. Rosedale
Fort Worth, Texas 76141

El Paso Farmers Market
6375 Montana
El Paso, Texas 79902

Four Seasons Markets at Addison
5100 Belt Line Rd
Dallas, Texas 75254
http://www.fourseasonsmarkets.com

Pearl Farmers Market
200 E. Grayson Street
San Antonio, Texas 78215
www.pearlfarmersmarket.com

Rice University Farmers Market
Rice University, 6100 Main
Houston, Texas 77005
http://farmersmarket.rice.edu

San Marcos/New Braunfeis Farmers Market Assoc. I
104 Edward Gary and 104 C.M. Allan Parkway
San Marcos, Texas 78666
www.sanmarcosfarmersmarket.com

Wimberley Farmers Market
Lions Club Parking Lot #1 on FM 2325
Wimberley, Texas 78676
http://www.wimberley.
org/d/2089343_12663.htm

UTAH

Ashley Valley Farmers Market
200 East Main (Old Dinosaur Gardens)
Vernal, Utah 84078
http://avfarmersmarket.webs.com/

Benson Mill Harvest Days
325 State Road #138
Stansbury Park, Utah 84074
http://bensonmill.org

Cache Valley Gardeners' Market
100 South 200 West
Logan, Utah 84321
www.gardenersmarket.org

Downtown Clearfield Farmers Market
140 East Center Street (approximately)
Clearfield, Utah 84015
www.clearfieldcity.org

Downtown Farmers Market
Historic Pioneer Park (300 S. 300 W.)
Salt Lake City, Utah 84111
www.slcfarmersmarket.org

Downtown Farmers Market at Ancestor Square
1 W. St. George Blvd.
St. George, Utah 84770
www.ancestorsquare.com

Heber Valley Farmers Market and Concert in the Park
City Park 250 South Main
Heber City, Utah 84032

Historic 25th Street Farmers & Art Market
301 25th Street, Ogden, UT. 84401
Ogden, Utah 84403
www.OgdenFarmersMarket.com

Park City Farmers Market
Canyons Ski Resort
Park City Utah, Utah 84098
www.parkcityfarmersmarket.com

Park Silly Sunday Market
Main Street
Park City, Utah 84060
www.parksilly.org

People's Market
1000 S 900 W
Salt Lake City, Utah 84104
www.slcpeoplesmarket.org

Provo's Farmers Market
500 West 100 South
Provo, Utah 84601
www.provosfarmersmarket.blogspot
.com

South Jordan Farmers Market
South Jordan Towne Center Drive (1600 W. & Redwood Rd.)
South Jordan, Utah 84095
www.sjc.utah.gov

Zion Canyon Farmers Market
1212 Zion Park Blvd.
Springdale, Utah 84767
http://zionharvest.org/

VIRGINIA

Abingdon Farmers Market
Latture Field Parking Lot
Abingdon, Virginia 24212
www.abingtonfarmersmarket.com

Alexandria Farmers Market
301 King St., Market Square
Alexandria, Virginia 22314
http://alexandriava.gov/market
/farmersmarket.html

Arlington County Farmers Market
North 14th St. & North Courthouse Rd.

Arlington, Virginia 22210
http://www.arlingtonfarmersmarket
.com

Blacksburg Farmers Market
Corner of Roanoke Street and
Draper Road
Blacksburg, Virginia 24063
www.bbfarmersmarket.org

Byrd House Market
224 S. Cherry Street
Richmond, Virginia 23220
http://byrdhousemarket.blogspot.com

Charlottesville City Market
Next to 200 W Water St
Charlottesville, Virginia 22902
www.charlottesvillecitymarket.com

Chesapeake Farmers Market
900 Greenbrier Parkway-Chesapeake
City Park
Chesapeake, Virginia 23320
http://www.chesapeake.va.us/services
/depart/agricul/farmers-market/index
.shtml

Clarke County Farmers Market
Town parking lot, S. Church St.
Berryville, Virginia 22611
http://www.clarkecountyfarmers
market.com

Crystal City FRESHFARM Market
2000 Crystal Drive
Crystal City, Virginia 22202
www.freshfarmmarkets.org

Dale City Farmers Market
Center Plaza, Dale Blvd.
Dale City, Virginia 22193
http://www.pwcparks.org

Farmers in the Park
1301 Chesapeake St
Charlottesville, Virginia 22902
www.charlottesville.org/parksandrec

Five Points Community Farm Market
2500 Church Street
Norfolk, Virginia 23504
http://www.5PtsFarmMarket.org

The Farmers Market @ St. Stephen's
6000 Grove Avenue
Richmond, Virginia 23226
http://www.saintstephensrichmond
.net/farmersmarket

Williamsburg Farmers Market
402 W Duke of Gloucester Street
Williamsburg, Virginia 23185
www.williamsburgfarmersmarket.com

VERMONT

Bellows Falls Farmers Markert
Waypoint Center
Bellows Falls, Vermont 05101
http://www.bffarmersmarket.com/

Brattleboro Area Farmers' Market
Gibson-Aiken Center, Main St. & Rt. 9
past Creamery Covered Bridge
Brattleboro, Vermont 05302
www.brattleborofarmersmarket.com/

Bristol Farmers Market
Village Green
Bristol, Vermont 05443
www.bristolfarmersmarket.org

Burlington Downton Farmers Market
College Street and City Hall Park
Burlington, Vermont 05402
www.burlingtonfarmersmarket.org

Chester Farmers Market
Zachary's Pizza House on Rte 103
& Rte 11
Chester, Vermont 05143
www.chesterfarmersmarket.ning.com

Dorset Farmers' Market
H.N. Williams General Store, Rt. 30

Dorset, Vermont 05251
www.dorsetfarmersmarket.com

Five Corners Farmers Market
Lincoln Place
Essex Junction, Vermont 05452
www.5cornersfarmersmarket.com

Hartland Farmers Market
Hartland Public Library, Rt 5
Hartland, Vermont 05048
www.hartlandfarmersmarket.org

Ludlow Farmers Market Inc.
53 Main Street
Ludlow, Vermont 05149
www.ludlowfarmersmarket.org

Middlebury Farmers Market
137 Maple Street
Middlebury, Vermont 05733
www.middleburyfarmersmarket.org

Poultney Farmers Market
Main Street
Poultney, Vermont 05735
www.vtfarmersmarket.org

Shelburne Farmers Market
Shelburne Parade Ground, Church St.
Shelburne, Vermont 05482
http://www.sbpavt.org/farmers
_market.php

Stowe Farmers Market
Rte. 108
Stowe, Vermont 05672
www.stowevtfarmersmarket.com

Waitsfield Farmers Market
Mad River Green, Rte. 100
Waitsfield, Vermont 05673
www.waitsfieldfarmersmarket.com

WASHINGTON

Anacortes Farmers Market
611 R Avenue

Anacortes, Washington 98221
www.anacortesfarmersmarket.org

Auburn International Farmers Market
23 A Street SW
Auburn, Washington 98001
www.auburnfarmersmarket.org/

Bainbridge Island Farmers' Market
Town Square at City Hall
Bainbridge Island, Washington 98110
www.bainbridgefarmersmarket.com

Ballard Farmers Market
5300 Ballard Ave NW
Seattle, Washington 98107
*www.ballardfarmermarket.wordpress
.com*

Bellevue Farmers Market - Saturday
10610 NE 8th Street
Bellevue, Washington 98004
www.bellevuefarmersmarket.org

Bellingham Farmers Market - Downtown
1100 Railroad Ave.
Bellingham, Washington 98225
www.bellinghamfarmers.org

Bothell Farmers Market
23718 Bothell Everett Highway
Bothell, Washington 98021
*www.countryvillagebothell.com
/farmersmarket*

Broadway Sunday Farmers Market
East side of Broadway at East
Thomas St.
Seattle, Washington 98112
http://www.seattlefarmersmarkets.org

Burien Farmers Market
5th Place SW & Southwest 152nd St.
Burien, Washington 98166
http://www.discoverburien.com

Gig Harbor Farmers Market
3500 Hunt St. NW

Gig Harbor, Washington 98349
*http://www.gigharborfarmersmarket
.com*

Kingston Farmers Market
Central Avenue & Washingto Blvd
Kingston, Washington 98346
www.kingstonfarmersmarket.com

Liberty Lake Farmers' Market
1421 N. Meadowwood Lane
Liberty Lake, Washington 99019
www.spokanemarkets.org

Maple Valley Farmers' Market
25700 Maple Valley Hwy. SE
Maple Valley, Washington 98038
www.maplevalleyfarmersmarket

Pike Place Market
Pike Place
Seattle, Washington 98101
www.pikeplacemarket.org

WISCONSIN

7 Mile Fair
2720 W. 7 Mile Road
Caledonia, Wisconsin 53108
www.7milefair.com

Appleton Downtown Farm Market
100 College Avenue
Appleton, Wisconsin 54911
www.appletondowntown.org

Brookfield Farmers Market
2000 North Calhoun Road
Brookfield, Wisconsin 53005
www.brookfieldfarmersmarket.com

Dane County Farmers Market I
Capitol Square, Downtown
Madison, Wisconsin 53701
www.dcfm.org

Dawn Kleinknecht
777 Carmichael Road

Hudson, Wisconsin 54016
*www.hudsonfarmersmarket
carmichael.com*

Downtown Beloit Farmer's Market
300 block of State Street and 400 block
of East Grand Avenue
Beloit, Wisconsin 53511
www.downtownbeloit.com

Downtown Burlington Farmers Market
Wehmoff Square
Burlington, Wisconsin 53105
http://www.burlington-wi.gov

East Side Green Market
1901 E. North Ave.
Milwaukee, Wisconsin 53207
www.theeastside.org

Farmers Market on Broadway
Broadway Street
Green Bay, Wisconsin 54303
www.farmersmarketonbroadway.com

Janesville Farmers Market
100 & 200 Blocks of Main Street
Janesville, Wisconsin 53545
www.janesvillefarmersmarket.com

Kenosha Harbor Market
200 56th Street
Kenosha, Wisconsin 53140
www.kenoshaharbormarketplace.com

Menomonee Falls Farmers Market
On Main Street just West of
Appleton Avenue
Menomonee Falls, Wisconsin 53051
*http://www.menomoneefalls
downtown.com*

Mineral Point Market
Water Tower Park
Mineral Point, Wisconsin 53565
www.mineralpointmarket.com

Oshkosh Saturday Farmers Market
215 Church Avenue

Oshkosh, Wisconsin 54901
www.oshkoshsaturdayfarmersmarket
.com

WEST VIRGINIA

**Barbour County Community
Garden Market**
309 S. Main Street
Philippi, West Virginia 26416
www.heartandhandhouse.org

Inwood Farmers Market
178 Pilgrim St.
Inwood, West Virginia 25428

Jefferson County Farmers Market
Beside Old Charles Town Library
Charles Town, West Virginia
www.jeffersonfarms.org/

Monroe Farm Market
Rt 3 East and Pump Street
Union, West Virginia 24983
http://www.monroefarmmarket.org

Morgantown Farmers Market
Corner of Spruce St. & Fayette St.
Morgantown, West Virginia 26501
www.morgantownfarmers.org/

Romney Farmers Market
Route 50, Bank of Romney
Community Center
Romney, West Virginia 26757
www.romneyfarmersmarket.com

**South Morgantown Community
Farmers Market**
1966 Grafton Rd
Morgantown, West Virginia 26508
www.smcfarmersmarket.org

Summersville Tailgate Market, Inc
Broad Street, across from Dairy Queen
Summersville, West Virginia 26651
*www.wvfarmers.org/memberpages
/summersvilletailgatemarket.html*

Terra Alta Farmers Market
Terra Alta Community Park
Terr Alta, West Virginia 26764
*www.wvfarmers.org/memberpages
/gardenfreshfarmersmarket.html*

Upshur County Farmers Market
Madison Street
Buckhannon, West Virginia 26201
*www.localharvest.org/farmers-markets/
M860*

Wheeling Farmers Market I
1221 National Rd
Wheeling, West Virginia 26003
*www.wvfarmers.org/memberpages
/wheelingfarmersmarket.html*

WYOMING

Buffalo Main Street Market
3 S. Main St.
Buffalo, Wyoming 82834
www.buffalowyo.com

**Downtown Casper Community
Farmers Market**
400 E Collins Dr
Casper, Wyoming 82601
*www.cprdowntownfarmersmarket
.com*

Farmers Market on the Town Square
100 West Broadway
Jackson, Wyoming 83001
www.jacksonholefarmersmarket.org

Jackalope Square Farmers Market
130 S. 3rd
Douglas, Wyoming 82633
www.mainstreetdouglas.org

Lovell Farmers Market
262 East Main Street, Wueen Bee
Garden Parking Lot
Lovell, Wyoming 82431
www.lovellinc.org/farmersmarket.html

Pinedale Farmers Market
Tyler Street at Pine Street
Pinedale, Wyoming 82941
www.pinedalefarmersmarket.com

Rawlins Downtown Farmers Market
400 W Front Street
Rawlins, Wyoming 82301
www.rawlinsmainstreet.org

Sheridan Farmers Market
Alger Street at Whitneys Commons
Sheridan, Wyoming 82801

Star Valley Farmers' Market
981 North Main Street (Highway 89)
Thayne, Wyoming 83127
www.starvalleyfarmersmarket.org

Wyoming Fresh Market
N Yellowstone Road, next to Great
Harvest
Cheyenne, Wyoming 82001

Standard U.S./Metric Measurement Conversions

VOLUME CONVERSIONS

U.S. Volume Measure	Metric Equivalent
⅛ teaspoon	0.5 milliliters
¼ teaspoon	1 milliliters
½ teaspoon	2 milliliters
1 teaspoon	5 milliliters
½ tablespoon	7 milliliters
1 tablespoon (3 teaspoons)	15 milliliters
2 tablespoons (1 fluid ounce)	30 milliliters
¼ cup (4 tablespoons)	60 milliliters
⅓ cup	90 milliliters
½ cup (4 fluid ounces)	125 milliliters
⅔ cup	160 milliliters
¾ cup (6 fluid ounces)	180 milliliters
1 cup (16 tablespoons)	250 milliliters
1 pint (2 cups)	500 milliliters
1 quart (4 cups)	1 liter (about)

WEIGHT CONVERSIONS

U.S. Weight Measure	Metric Equivalent
½ ounce	15 grams
1 ounce	30 grams
2 ounces	60 grams
3 ounces	85 grams
¼ pound (4 ounces)	115 grams
½ pound (8 ounces)	225 grams
¾ pound (12 ounces)	340 grams
1 pound (16 ounces)	454 grams

OVEN TEMPERATURE CONVERSIONS

Degrees Fahrenheit	Degrees Celsius
200 degrees F	100 degrees C
250 degrees F	120 degrees C
275 degrees F	140 degrees C
300 degrees F	150 degrees C
325 degrees F	160 degrees C
350 degrees F	180 degrees C
375 degrees F	190 degrees C
400 degrees F	200 degrees C
425 degrees F	220 degrees C
450 degrees F	230 degrees C

BAKING PAN SIZES

American	Metric
8 x 1½ inch round baking pan	20 x 4 cm cake tin
9 x 1½ inch round baking pan	23 x 3.5 cm cake tin
1 x 7 x 1½ inch baking pan	28 x 18 x 4 cm baking tin
113 x 9 x 2 inch baking pan	30 x 20 x 5 cm baking tin
2 quart rectangular baking dish	30 x 20 x 3 cm baking tin
15 x 10 x 2 inch baking pan	30 x 25 x 2 cm baking tin (Swiss roll tin)
9 inch pie plate	22 x 4 or 23 x 4 cm pie plate
7 or 8 inch springform pan	18 or 20 cm springform or loose bottom cake tin
9 x 5 x 3 inch loaf pan	23 x 13 x 7 cm or 2 lb narrow loaf or pate tin
1½ quart casserole	1.5 litre casserole
2 quart casserole	2 litre casserole

Index

Note: Page numbers in **bold** indicate recipe category lists.

Activity and exercise, 10–12, 60–62
  daily recommendations, 10–11, 60–61
  getting started/fitting it in, 11, 12, 61
  hydration requirements during, 64
  importance of, 10, 60
  muscle-strengthening programs, 11–12, 61, 62
  raising goals, 62
  workout meals and, 63–64
Aegean Baked Sole, 185
Aegean Tyropita (No-Pastry Cheese Pie), 126
Aging, reversing effects of, 75–78, 139
Agriculture in Mediterranean countries, 2–3
Almond-Encrusted Salmon on Toast Points, 240
Almonds. See Nuts and seeds
Amaranth Salad, 104
Amygdalota (Almond Biscuits), 197
Antioxidants, 15, 21–22, 27, 30, 36, 39–40, 53, 70–71, 108, 208
Appetizers, **89**–101
  Baked Feta Cheese, 97
  Cheese Saganaki, 93
  Dolmades (Stuffed Grape Leaves), 100
  Feta and Roasted Red Pepper Piquante, 91
  Feta Fritters, 92
  Garlic Feta Spread, 101
  Gigantes Tiganiti (Pan-Fried Giant Beans), 94
  Kalamarakia (Pan-Fried Calamari Rings), 95
  Scorthalia, 90
  Sfougato (Aegean Omelette), 98
  Tomato Fritters, 99
  Village-Style Zucchini Fritters, 96

Apple Cake (Milopita), 201
Arakas (Stewed Green Peas), 158
Aristaeus, 199
Arni Exohiko (Countryside Lamb), 172
Aubergine Meat Rolls, 174–75
Avgolemono (Egg-Lemon Soup), 133. See also Bakaliaros Avgolemono (Cod Egg-Lemon Soup)

Bakaliaros Avgolemono (Cod Egg-Lemon Soup), 134
Baked Chickpeas (Revithia Sto Fourno), 153
Baked Feta Cheese, 97
Baked Giant Butter Beans, 156
Baked Sea Bream with Feta and Tomato, 187
Baked Tuna, 188
Baked Vegetable Medley (Briami), 155
Baklava, Spiral, 204–5
Beans and legumes, **147**
  about: boosting intake of, 40; chickpea as gift of Poseidon, 113; legumes defined, 34; Mediterranean diet and, 8, 94; nutrients in, 9, 39–40; phytonutrients in, 39–40; recommended daily intake of, 38–39; reducing gas from, 37–38; serving sizes, 39
  Arakas (Stewed Green Peas), 158
  Baked Giant Butter Beans, 156
  Black-Eyed Peas and Swiss Chard, 160
  Chickpea Rissoles, 157
  Fakkes (Lentil Soup), 131
  Fasolada (White Bean Soup), 128
  Fassolakia Moraïtika (Peloponnesian Braised Green Beans), 152
  Gigantes Tiganiti (Pan-Fried Giant Beans), 94
  Revithia Sto Fourno (Baked Chickpeas), 153
  Revithosoupa (Chickpea Soup), 129

Santorini (Favas), 116
Béchamel Sauce, 111
Beef. See Meats
Beets
  about: selecting, 82
  Beets with Yogurt, 159
Benefits of Mediterranean diet, 67–78. See also Science of Mediterranean diet
  balanced, healthy nutrition, 15–16, 17–18, 55
  cancer reduction, 15, 72–73
  on diabetes, 73–75
  family involvement, 19, 88
  fighting disease and ailments, 68–70
  heart health, 14–17, 22
  nervous system disorders and, 77–78
  preventing/reducing oxidation, 22, 31, 75–76
  reversing aging effects, 75–78, 139
  skin health, 70–71
  studies validating. See Science of Mediterranean diet
  of wine, 7, 22–23
Bougatsa (Minced Meat Pies), 124
Braised Beef with Onions (Stifado), 179
Braised Cuttlefish, 189
Braised Lamb Shoulder, 180
Breads and sandwiches
  about: pita, 242
  Breakfast Bruschetta, 212
  Caesar Sandwich, 236
  Grilled Vegetable Hero, 242
  Multigrain Toast with Grilled Vegetables, 230
  Nut Butter and Honey on Whole Grain, 246
  Open-Faced Grilled Cheese, 233
  Peanut-Coconut-Grilled Chicken Sandwich, 244
  Rye-Pumpernickel Strata with Bleu Cheese, 215
  Tuna Panini, 232

Breads and sandwiches—*continued*
    Vegetable Pita, 234
    Vegetable Pita with Feta Cheese, 228
    Watercress Sandwiches, 237
    Wilted Arugula on Flatbread, 235
Breakfast recipes, **211**–30
    Almond Mascarpone Dumplings, 229
    Breakfast Bruschetta, 212
    Creamy Sweet Risotto, 224
    Eggs in Crusty Italian Bread, 222
    Fresh Fruit and Plain Yogurt, 220
    Fresh Tuna with Sweet Lemon Leek Salsa, 226
    Frittata, 214
    Fruit-Stuffed French Toast, 216
    Israeli Couscous with Dried-Fruit Chutney, 225
    Mediterranean Omelet, 218
    Multigrain Toast with Grilled Vegetables, 230
    Pastina and Egg, 219
    Polenta, 217
    Roasted Potatoes and Vegetables, 213
    Rye-Pumpernickel Strata with Bleu Cheese, 215
    Stovetop-Poached Fresh Cod, 221
    Sweetened Brown Rice, 223
    Vegetable Pita with Feta Cheese, 228
    Yogurt Cheese and Fruit, 227
Bulgur Medley (Grandma's Pligouri), 137
Butter Beans, Giant, Baked, 156
B vitamins, 10, 16
Byzantine Fruit Medley, 209

Cabbage
    about: selecting, 82
    Lahanosalata (Cabbage Salad), 107
Caesar Sandwich, 236
Cancer reduction, 15, 72–73
Carbohydrates, 9
Cheese. *See* Dairy
Chicken. *See* Poultry
Chickpeas. *See* Beans and legumes

Cholesterol
    activity and, 60, 62
    monounsaturated fats and, 9, 40, 76, 134
    recommended daily intake of, 46
    reduction of bad, increase of good, 14–15, 22, 27
    saturated fats and, 44, 47–48
Chutney
    Dried-Fruit Chutney, 225
    Fruit Chutney, 168
Citrus
    about: history of lemons, 162; lemon juice as antioxidant, 108; lemons and tomatoes, 174
    Egg-Lemon Sauce, 176
    Lemon Mustard Sauce, 118
    Patates Lemonates (Lemon Potatoes), 148
    Roast Lemon Chicken, 162
    Sweet Lemon Leek Salsa, 226
Cod. *See* Fish and Seafood
Cooks and poets, 153
Countryside Lamb (Arni Exohiko), 172
Couscous, Israeli, with Dried-Fruit Chutney, 225
Creamy Sweet Risotto, 224
Cretan Dakos (Rusk Salad), 105
Cucumbers
    about: selecting, 82
    Greek Pita, 238
Curried Chicken on Lavash, 239
Cuttlefish, Braised, 189
Cypriot Loukoumia, 198
Cypriot Orzo Yiouvetsi, 141

Dairy
    about: adjusting intake of, 51–52; as complements to other dishes, 49; fat-free choices and added sugars, 50; feta cheese, 105, 145; history of yogurt, 115; lactose intolerance and, 49; Mediterranean diet and, 8, 49–52; nutrients in, 51; recommended daily intake of, 50; serving sizes, 50; shopping

tips, 83; smaller portions, 49–50; types of cheeses, 49; yogurt lore, 163
    Aegean Tyropita (No-Pastry Cheese Pie), 126
    Baked Feta Cheese, 97
    Cheese Saganaki, 93
    Feta and Roasted Red Pepper Piquante, 91
    Feta Fritters, 92
    Fresh Fruit and Plain Yogurt, 220
    Galatopita (Milk Pie), 200
    Garlic Feta Spread, 101
    Grilled Halloumi Salad, 112
    Open-Faced Grilled Cheese, 233
    Spanakotyropita (Spinach and Cheese Pie), 125
    Strained Yogurt, 207
    Tzatziki (Yogurt-Garlic Sauce), 115
    Yogurt Cheese and Fruit, 227
Dandelion Greens, 119
Desserts, **195**–209
    about: sweets and Mediterranean diet, 54–55
    Almond Tangerine Bites, 196
    Amygdalota (Almond Biscuits), 197
    Byzantine Fruit Medley, 209
    Cypriot Loukoumia, 198
    Galatopita (Milk Pie), 200
    Loukoumades (Honey Fritters), 199
    Milopita (Apple Cake), 201
    Pasteli (Sesame Brickle), 202
    Rizogalo (Rice Pudding), 203
    Spiral Baklava, 204–5
    Strained Yogurt, 207
    Stuffed Dried Figs, 208
    Tiganites (Pancakes), 206
Diabetes, impact on, 73–75
Dolmades (Stuffed Grape Leaves), 100
Domatorizo (Tomato Rice), 136
Duck Breast with Fruit Salsa, Grilled, 169

Eggplant
    about: extensive use of, 154

Briami (Baked Vegetable Medley), 155

Grilled Eggplant Salad, 106

Grilled Vegetable Hero, 242

Imam Bayildi (Fainting Cleric), 149, 157

Melitzanes Yiahni (Braised Eggplant), 154

Melitzanosalata (Eggplant Dip), 113

Multigrain Toast with Grilled Vegetables, 230

Vegetable Pita with Feta Cheese, 228

Eggs

about: adjusting intake of, 48–49; Mediterranean diet and, 46–49; nutrients in, 48; recommended intake of, 47–48; seasoning pan for omelets, 218; which came first, chickens or, 165

Avgolemono (Egg-Lemon Soup), 133

Bakaliaros Avgolemono (Cod Egg-Lemon Soup), 134

Breakfast Bruschetta, 212

Egg-Lemon Sauce, 176

Eggs in Crusty Italian Bread, 222

Frittata, 214

Fruit-Stuffed French Toast, 216

Mediterranean Omelet, 218

Pastina and Egg, 219

Rye-Pumpernickel Strata with Bleu Cheese, 215

Sfougato (Aegean Omelette), 98

Exercise. See Activity and exercise

Fainting Cleric (Imam Bayildi), 149, 157

Fakkes (Lentil Soup), 131

Farmer's markets by state, 261–88

Fassolakia Moraïtika (Peloponnesian Braised Green Beans), 152

Fast-friendly seafood, 186

Fats

monounsaturated, 9, 40, 45, 76

omega-3 fatty acids, 3, 9, 41, 45–46, 84

overconsumption of, diet effectiveness and, 17–18

recommended daily intake of, 18

reduction of cholesterol and, 14–15

saturated, 14–15, 16, 44, 45, 46, 47–48, 51

studies on heart health and consumption of, 14–17

weight loss and. See Weight loss

Feta and Roasted Red Pepper Piquante, 91

Feta Fritters, 92

Fiber and whole grains, 26–28. See also Grains and pasta

Figs, Stuffed Dried, 208

Fish and Seafood, **183**–93

about: boosting intake of, 46; buying, 83, 84; cuttlefish, 189; environmental considerations of, 44; fast-friendly, 186; fresh, choosing, 83; fresh or cured fish, 184; nutrients in, 9, 44, 45–46; popular varieties of, 44; recommended intake of, 44–45

Aegean Baked Sole, 185

Almond-Encrusted Salmon on Toast Points, 240

Bakaliaros Avgolemono (Cod Egg-Lemon Soup), 134

Baked Sea Bream with Feta and Tomato, 187

Baked Tuna, 188

Braised Cuttlefish, 189

Cod with Raisins, 184

Fresh Tuna with Sweet Lemon Leek Salsa, 226

Grilled Jumbo Shrimp, 192

Grilled Sea Bass, 191

Kakavia (Fish Soup), 130

Kalamarakia (Pan-Fried Calamari Rings), 95

Mastic Shrimp Saganaki, 186

Octopus in Wine, 193

Sesame-Ginger-Encrusted Tuna Carpaccio, 241

Stovetop Fish, 190

Stovetop-Poached Fresh Cod, 221

Taramosalata/Tarama (Fish Roe Salad), 109

Tuna Panini, 232

Flavonoids, 21

Folate (folic acid), 16, 28

Food safety, 80

French Toast, Fruit-Stuffed, 216

Fresh Fruit and Plain Yogurt, 220

Fresh Tuna with Sweet Lemon Leek Salsa, 226

Frittata, 214

Fruit. See also specific fruit

about: benefits of, 32; boosting intake of, 36–37; canned, 84; importance of, 32–33, 36; judging/buying, 82–83; nutrients in, 35–36; phytonutrients in, 32–33, 35–36; recommended daily intake of, 18, 33; serving sizes, 33

Byzantine Fruit Medley, 209

Dried-Fruit Chutney, 225

Fresh Fruit and Plain Yogurt, 220

Fruit Chutney, 168

Fruit-Stuffed French Toast, 216

Yogurt Cheese and Fruit, 227

Frying foods, 149

Galatopita (Milk Pie), 200

Garlic

about: health benefits of, 156

Garlic Feta Spread, 101

Gemista (Stuffed Peppers and Zucchini), 150–51

Gigantes Tiganiti (Pan-Fried Giant Beans), 94

Glossary of terms, 247–56

Gluten intolerance, 30

Grains and pasta, 28–32, **135**–45

about: boosting intake of, 31–32; fiber and whole grains, 26–

Grains and pasta—*continued*
28; folate added to, 28; gluten intolerance and, 30; of Mediterra
nean diet, 8; nutrients from, 28, 30;
phytonutrients in, 28, 31; plan-
ning meals and, 85–86; recom-
mended daily intake of, 29–30,
84; serving sizes, 29; types of,
28, 29
Chicken with Egg Noodles and Wal-
nuts, 164
Creamy Sweet Risotto, 224
Cretan Dakos (Rusk Salad), 105
Cypriot Orzo Yiouvetsi, 141
Dolmades (Stuffed Grape Leaves),
100
Domatorizo (Tomato Rice), 136
Grandma's Pligouri (Bulgur Med-
ley), 137
Israeli Couscous with Dried-Fruit
Chutney, 225
Makaronada (Spaghetti with Meat
Sauce), 140
Pastitsio, 142–43
Pilafi (Rice Pilaf), 144
Prassorizo (Leeks and Rice), 138
Rizogalo (Rice Pudding), 203
Sam's Greek Rigatoni, 145
Spanakorizo (Spinach Rice), 139
Sweetened Brown Rice, 223
Grandma's Pligouri (Bulgur Medley),
137
Grapes
about: as gift of Dionysus, 113
Dolmades (Stuffed Grape Leaves),
100
Greek Pita, 238
Greek Salad, 110
Green beans, in Fassolakia Moraïtika
(Peloponnesian Braised Green
Beans), 152
Greens
about: selecting, 82
Black-Eyed Peas and Swiss Chard,
82
Dandelion Greens, 119

Grilled Banana Pepper Salad, 117
Grilled Biftekia Stuffed with Cheese,
173
Grilled Duck Breast with Fruit Salsa,
169
Grilled Eggplant Salad, 106
Grilled Halloumi Salad, 112
Grilled Jumbo Shrimp, 192
Grilled Sea Bass, 191
Grocery shopping, 80–83, 159. *See also*
Farmer's markets by state

Heart health, 14–17, 22. *See also* Science of Mediterranean diet
Herbs and spices
availability of, 52
benefits of, 53
boosting intake of, 53–54
dill seed stimulants, 107
by foods to flavor, 54
herb gardens, 240
historical perspective, 148
list of, 52–53
phytonutrients in, 53
Holiday meals, 87–88
Honey
about: as folk medicine, 204; history of sesame and, 202; itrion
and, 202; origin of bee-keeping
and, 199
Honey Fritters (Loukoumades), 199
Nut Butter and Honey on Whole
Grain, 246
Pasteli (Sesame Brickle), 202
Spiral Baklava, 204–5
Hydration requirements, 6, 64

Imam Bayildi (Fainting Cleric), 149, 157
Israeli Couscous with Dried-Fruit Chutney, 225

Kakavia (Fish Soup), 130
Kalamarakia (Pan-Fried Calamari
Rings), 95
Keys, Dr. Ancel, 14–15, 57

Labels, reading and understanding,
81–82
Ladolemono (Olive Oil and Lemon
Sauce), 108
Lahanosalata (Cabbage Salad), 107
Lamb. *See* Meats
Leeks
Prassopita (Leek Pie), 122
Prassorizo (Leeks and Rice), 138
Sweet Lemon Leek Salsa, 226
Legumes. *See* Beans and legumes
Lemon. *See* Citrus
Lentils. *See* Beans and legumes
Lifestyle, 6–7, 19
Loukoumades (Honey Fritters), 199
Lunch recipes, **231**–46
Almond-Encrusted Salmon on Toast
Points, 240
Caesar Sandwich, 236
Curried Chicken on Lavash, 239
Greek Pita, 238
Grilled Vegetable Hero, 242
Nut Butter and Honey on Whole
Grain, 246
Open-Faced Grilled Cheese, 233
Peanut-Coconut-Grilled Chicken
Sandwich, 244
Roasted Garlic Potato Salad Lettuce
Rolls, 245
Sesame-Ginger-Encrusted Tuna Car-
paccio, 241
Souvlaki with Raita, 243
Tuna Panini, 232
Vegetable Pita, 234
Watercress Sandwiches, 237
Wilted Arugula on Flatbread, 235
Lyon Diet Heart Study, 14–17

Makaronada (Spaghetti with Meat
Sauce), 140
Mastic Shrimp Saganaki, 186
Meal planning, 79–88
family involvement, 88
food safety and, 80

grocery shopping and, 80–83, 159. *See also* Farmer's markets by state

holiday meals, 87–88

picky eaters and, 86–87

portion guide, 81

stocking pantry and, 83–84

weeknight meals, 85–86

Meats, **171**–81

about: adjusting intake of, 48–49; Greek diet and, 176; Mediterranean diet and, 46–49; nutrients in, 48; recommended intake of, 47

Arni Exohiko (Countryside Lamb), 172

Aubergine Meat Rolls, 174–75

Bougatsa (Minced Meat Pies), 124

Braised Lamb Shoulder, 180

Cypriot Orzo Yiouvetsi, 141

Grilled Biftekia Stuffed with Cheese, 173

Makaronada (Spaghetti with Meat Sauce), 140

Meatballs in Egg-Lemon Sauce, 176

Pastitsio, 142–43

Pork Chops in Wine, 181

Pork with Leeks and Celery, 177

Soutzoukakia (Smyrnaean Meat Rolls with Green Olives), 178

Souvlaki with Raita, 243

Stifado (Braised Beef with Onions), 179

Mediterranean diet

activity, exercise and, 10–12

adoption of, 69–70

balancing, 55

benefits of. *See* Benefits of Mediterranean diet

dairy foods and, 8, 49–52. *See also* Dairy

eating environment and, 129

fish and seafood in, 44–46. *See also* Fish and Seafood

meat, poultry, eggs in, 46–49. *See also* Eggs; Meats; Poultry

Mediterranean agriculture and, 2–3

Mediterranean people changing from, 112

nutrients from, 9–10. *See also* specific main ingredients; *specific nutrients*

overview of foods, 8–9

pace of eating and, 10

popularity of, 3

religious influence on, 155

sweets and, 54–55. *See also* Desserts

using effectively, 20

what it is, 2

when it doesn't work, 17–19

who should use it, 19

why it works, 14–17. *See also* Science of Mediterranean diet

Mediterranean diet pyramid, 3–7

about: overview of, 3–5

compared to US pyramid, 5–6

hydration requirements and, 6

illustrated, 4

lifestyle aspects of, 6–7, 19

non-food aspects of, 6–7

structure of, 5

tips for using, 6

wine as part of, 7

Mediterranean foods. *See also* Mediterranean diet pyramid; *specific foods*

Mediterranean Omelet, 218

Melitzanes Yiahni (Braised Eggplant), 154

Melitzanosalata (Eggplant Dip), 113

Menus. *See* Meal planning

Metabolic syndrome, 74–75

Milk Pie (Galatopita), 200

Milopita (Apple Cake), 201

Minced Meat Pies (Bougatsa), 124

Multigrain Toast with Grilled Vegetables, 230

Nervous system disorders, 77–78

Nonflavonoids, 21–22

North Karelia Study, 16

Nutrients, 9–10. *See also specific main ingredients*; *specific nutrients*

Nuts and seeds

about: almonds, 196; boosting intake of, 40; "Greek nut," 196; nutrients in, 39–40; omega-3 fatty acids in, 3; phytonutrients in, 37, 39–40; recommended daily intake of, 38–39; serving sizes, 39

Almond Mascarpone Dumplings, 229

Almond Tangerine Bites, 196

Amygdalota (Almond Biscuits), 197

Cypriot Loukoumia, 198

Nut Butter and Honey on Whole Grain, 246

Octopus in Wine, 193

Olive oil, 40–41, 91

about: frying with, 149; as gift of Athena, 113; monounsaturated fats and, 40, 134; nutrients/phytonutrients in, 41; oldest olive tree and, 177; overview of, 40; phytonutrients in, 41; recommended daily intake of, 41; switching to, 41

Ladolemono (Olive Oil and Lemon Sauce), 108

Onions

about: health benefits of, 156

Vegetable Pita, 234

Open-air markets, 159

Open-Faced Grilled Cheese, 233

Oxidation, preventing, 22, 31, 75–76

Pancakes (Tiganites), 206

Pan-Fried Calamari Rings (Kalamarakia), 95

Pantry, stocking, 83–84

Parsley Spread, 114

Parsnips, in Briami (Baked Vegetable Medley), 155

Pasta. *See* Grains and pasta

Pasteli (Sesame Brickle), 202

Pastina and Egg, 219

Pastitsio, 142–43
Patates Lemonates (Lemon Potatoes), 148
Patatopita (Potato Pie), 123
Peanut-Coconut-Grilled Chicken Sandwich, 244
Peas. See Beans and legumes
Peloponnesian Braised Green Beans (Fassolakia Moraïtika), 152
Peppers
    about: history of, 123; selecting, 82
    Feta and Roasted Red Pepper Piquante, 91
    Gemista (Stuffed Peppers and Zucchini), 150–51
    Grilled Banana Pepper Salad, 117
    Grilled Vegetable Hero, 242
    Multigrain Toast with Grilled Vegetables, 230
Phytonutrients
    in beans, nuts, and seeds, 37, 39–40
    in fruits and vegetables, 32–33, 35–36, 82
    in grains, 28, 31
    in herbs and spices, 53
    in olive oil, 41
    what they are, 10, 27
    whole foods and, 26
    in wine, 21–22
Pies, 121–26
    Aegean Tyropita (No-Pastry Cheese Pie), 126
    Bougatsa (Minced Meat Pies), 124
    Patatopita (Potato Pie), 123
    Prassopita (Leek Pie), 122
    Spanakotyropita (Spinach and Cheese Pie), 125
Pilafi (Rice Pilaf), 144
Plant-based foods. See also Phytonutrients
    whole foods, 26–28
Poets and cooks, 153
Polenta, 217
Pork. See Meats
Portion guide, 81
Potassium, 9
Potatoes

about: history of, 123
Briami (Baked Vegetable Medley), 155
Feta Fritters, 92
Patates Lemonates (Lemon Potatoes), 148
Patatopita (Potato Pie), 123
Roasted Garlic Potato Salad Lettuce Rolls, 245
Roasted Potatoes and Vegetables, 213
Scorthalia, 90
Village-Style Zucchini Fritters, 96
Poultry, 161–69
    about: adjusting intake of, 48–49; leaving skin on, 48; Mediterranean diet and, 46–49; nutrients in, 48; recommended intake of, 47
    Chicken Galantine, 167
    Chicken Livers in Red Wine, 166
    Chicken with Egg Noodles and Walnuts, 164
    Chicken with Yogurt, 163
    Curried Chicken on Lavash, 239
    Grilled Duck Breast with Fruit Salsa, 169
    Peanut-Coconut-Grilled Chicken Sandwich, 244
    Roast Lemon Chicken, 162
    Spicy Turkey Breast with Fruit Chutney, 168
    Stuffed Grilled Chicken Breasts, 165
Prassopita (Leek Pie), 122
Prassorizo (Leeks and Rice), 138
Proteins. See also Eggs; Fish and Seafood; Meats; Poultry
    balancing Mediterranean diet and, 55
    from beans and legumes, 37–38
    importance of, 20
    from nuts and seeds, 38
    weight loss and, 58–59

Resources, 257–59
Revithia Sto Fourno (Baked Chickpeas), 153

Revithosoupa (Chickpea Soup), 129
Rice. See Grains and pasta
Rizogalo (Rice Pudding), 203
Roasted Garlic Potato Salad Lettuce Rolls, 245
Roasted Potatoes and Vegetables, 213
Roast Lemon Chicken, 162
Rusk Salad (Cretan Dakos), 105
Rye-Pumpernickel Strata with Bleu Cheese, 215

Salad dressings and sauces, **103**
    Balsamic Vinaigrette, 120
    Béchamel Sauce, 111
    Fruit Salsa, 169
    Ladolemono (Olive Oil and Lemon Sauce), 108
    Lemon Mustard Sauce, 118
    Melitzanosalata (Eggplant Dip), 113
    Parsley Spread, 114
    Sweet Lemon Leek Salsa, 226
    Tzatziki (Yogurt-Garlic Sauce), 115
Salads, **103**–20
    Amaranth Salad, 104
    Cretan Dakos (Rusk Salad), 105
    Dandelion Greens, 119
    Grilled Banana Pepper Salad, 117
    Grilled Eggplant Salad, 106
    Grilled Halloumi Salad, 112
    Lahanosalata (Cabbage Salad), 107
    Santorini (Favas), 116
    Sliced Tomato Salad with Feta and Balsamic Vinaigrette, 120
    Taramosalata/Tarama (Fish Roe Salad), 109
    Village Greek Salad, 110
Sandwiches. See Breads and sandwiches
Santorini (Favas), 116
Sauces. See Salad dressings and sauces
Science of Mediterranean diet. See also Benefits of Mediterranean diet
    Dr. Ancel Keys and, 14–15, 57
    evidence consolidated, 16–17
    initial studies, 14–15
    Lyon Diet Heart Study, 15–16
    North Karelia Study, 16

weight loss and, 59–60
when diet doesn't work, 17–19
why it works, 14–17
Scorthalia, 90
Sesame Brickle (Pasteli), 202
Sesame-Ginger-Encrusted Tuna Carpaccio, 241
Sfougato (Aegean Omelette), 98
Shrimp. *See* Fish and Seafood
Skin health, 70–71
Sliced Tomato Salad with Feta and Balsamic Vinaigrette, 120
Smyrnaean Meat Rolls with Green Olives (Soutzoukakia), 178
Sole, Aegean Baked, 185
Soups and stews, **127**–34
    about: as main meal, 133; planning meals and, 85; stifado, 179
    Avgolemono (Egg-Lemon Soup), 133
    Bakaliaros Avgolemono (Cod Egg-Lemon Soup), 134
    Fakkes (Lentil Soup), 131
    Fasolada (White Bean Soup), 128
    Kakavia (Fish Soup), 130
    Revithosoupa (Chickpea Soup), 129
    Stifado (Braised Beef with Onions), 179
    Tahini Soup, 132
Soutzoukakia (Smyrnaean Meat Rolls with Green Olives), 178
Souvlaki with Raita, 243
Spaghetti with Meat Sauce (Makaronada), 140
Spanakorizo (Spinach Rice), 139
Spanakotyropita (Spinach and Cheese Pie), 125
Spicy Turkey Breast with Fruit Chutney, 168
Spinach
    Spanakorizo (Spinach Rice), 139
    Spanakotyropita (Spinach and Cheese Pie), 125
Squash
    Briami (Baked Vegetable Medley), 155
    Gemista (Stuffed Peppers and Zucchini), 150–51

Multigrain Toast with Grilled Vegetables, 230
Vegetable Pita with Feta Cheese, 228
Village-Style Zucchini Fritters, 96
Stewed Green Peas (Arakas), 158
Stifado (Braised Beef with Onions), 179
Stovetop Fish, 190
Stovetop-Poached Fresh Cod, 221
Strained Yogurt, 207
Stuffed Dried Figs, 208
Stuffed Grape Leaves (Dolmades), 100
Stuffed Grilled Chicken Breasts, 165
Stuffed Peppers and Zucchini (Gemista), 150–51
Sweetened Brown Rice, 223
Sweet Lemon Leek Salsa, 226

Tahini Soup, 132
Taramosalata/Tarama (Fish Roe Salad), 109
Tiganites (Pancakes), 206
Tomatoes
    about: history of, 123; lemons and, 174
    Domatorizo (Tomato Rice), 136
    Sliced Tomato Salad with Feta and Balsamic Vinaigrette, 120
    Tomato Fritters, 99
Tuna. *See* Fish and Seafood
Turkey Breast, Spicy, with Fruit Chutney, 168
Tyropita, Aegean (No-Pastry Cheese Pie), 126
Tzatziki (Yogurt-Garlic Sauce), 115

Vegetables, **147**–60. *See also specific vegetables*
    about: benefits of, 32–33; boosting intake of, 36–37; canned, 84; cruciferous, 36; importance of, 32–33, 36; judging/buying, 82–83; as main meal, 138; Mediterranean diet and, 8; nutrients in, 35–36; phytonutrients in, 32–33, 35–36, 82; planning meals and, 85–86; recommended daily intake of, 18, 33–34; serving sizes, 34

Briami (Baked Vegetable Medley), 155
Multigrain Toast with Grilled Vegetables, 230
Vegetable Pita, 234
Vegetable Pita with Feta Cheese, 228
Village Greek Salad, 110
Village-Style Zucchini Fritters, 96
Vitamins and minerals, 9, 10

Watercress Sandwiches, 237
Weight loss, 57–66
    about: overview of, 57–58
    activity and, 60–62. *See also* Activity and exercise
    calories per pound and, 59
    eating balanced meals and, 62–64
    fat intake and, 17–18, 58–59
    keeping weight off, 64–66
    overconsumption in general and, 18
    science of, 58–60
    special treats and, 66
    studies on, 59–60
    when diet doesn't work, 17–19
    workout meals and, 64
White Bean Soup (Fasolada), 128
Whole grains. *See* Fiber and whole grains
Wilted Arugula on Flatbread, 235
Wine, 21–23
    benefits of, 7, 22–23, 172
    calories from, 23
    flavonoids, nonflavonoids in, 21–22
    moderation in consuming, 7
    as part of Mediterranean diet pyramid, 7
    phytonutrients in, 21–22
    recommended daily intake of, 22
    red vs. white, 21

Yogurt. *See* Dairy

Zucchini. *See* Squash

We Have
EVERYTHING
on Anything!

With more than 19 million copies sold, the Everything® series has become one of America's favorite resources for solving problems, learning new skills, and organizing lives. Our brand is not only recognizable—it's also welcomed.

The series is a hand-in-hand partner for people who are ready to tackle new subjects—like you!

For more information on the Everything® series, please visit *www.adamsmedia.com*

The Everything® list spans a wide range of subjects, with more than 500 titles covering 25 different categories:

Business	History	Reference
Careers	Home Improvement	Religion
Children's Storybooks	Everything Kids	Self-Help
Computers	Languages	Sports & Fitness
Cooking	Music	Travel
Crafts and Hobbies	New Age	Wedding
Education/Schools	Parenting	Writing
Games and Puzzles	Personal Finance	
Health	Pets	